MERMAID COMIC BOOK

FOR GIRLS AGES 9-12

Awesome Mermaid Comic Book For Writing And Drawing

Nooo

BOOM!

This Mermaid Comic Book Belongs To:

____

LOL

AARGH!

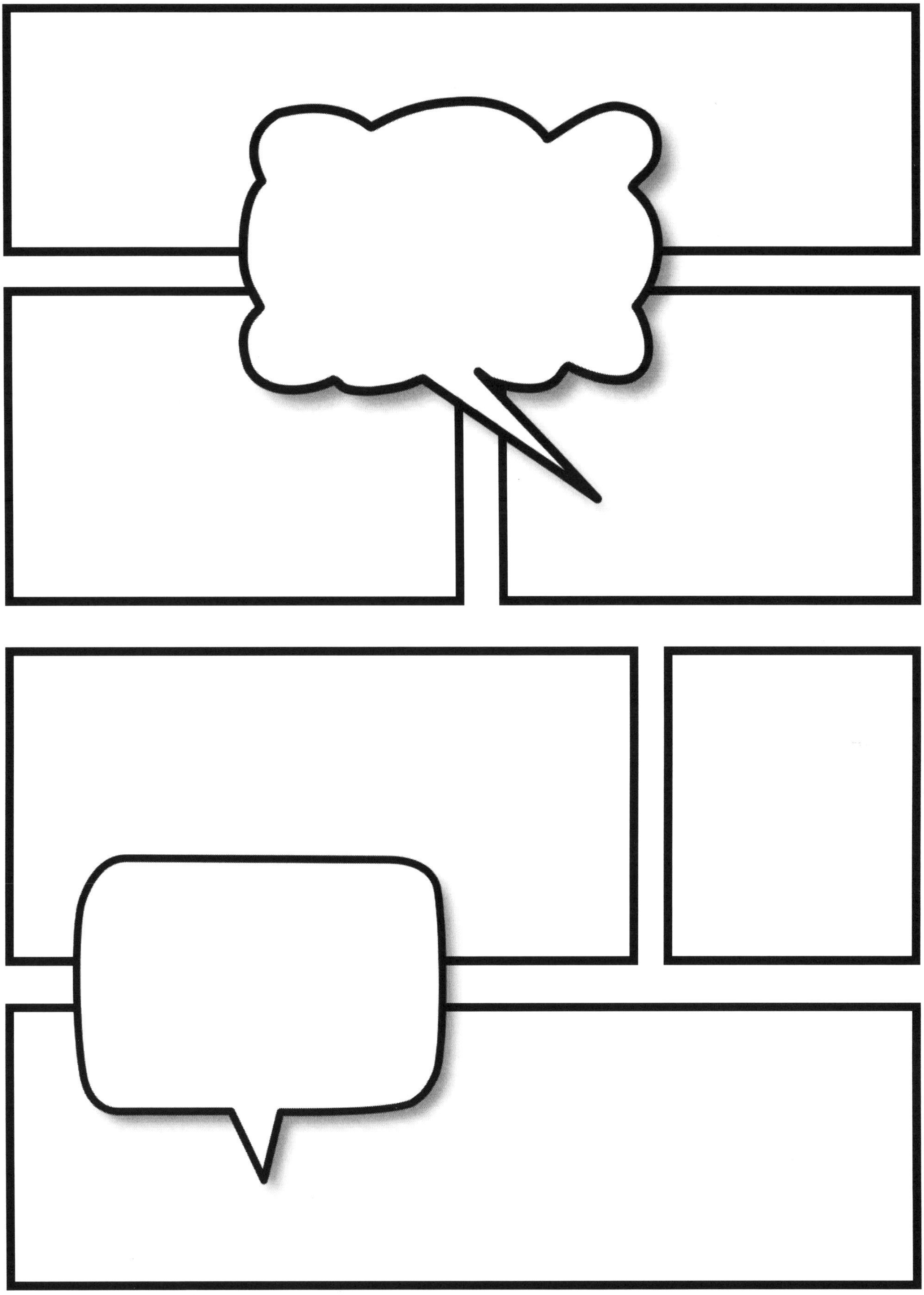

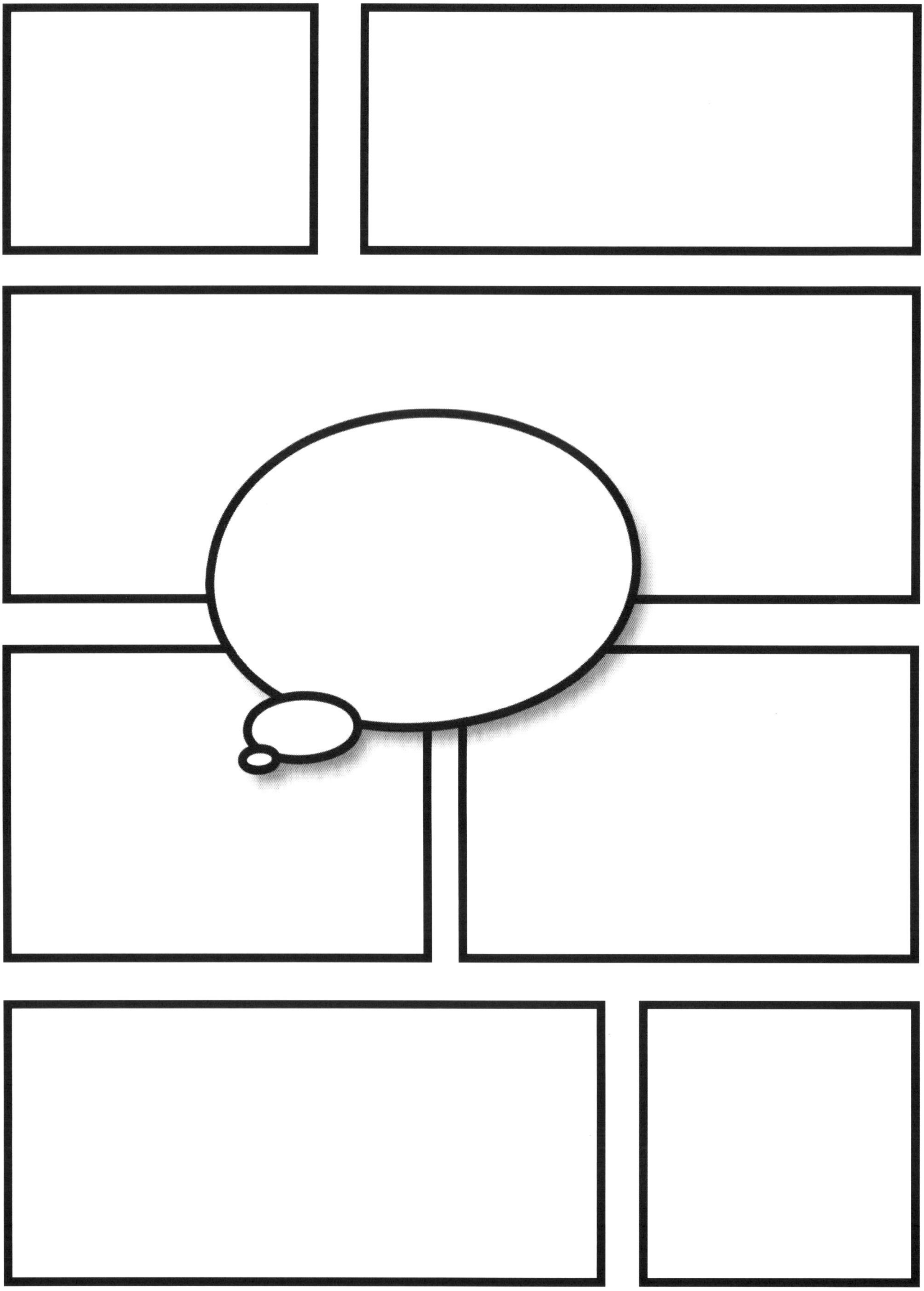

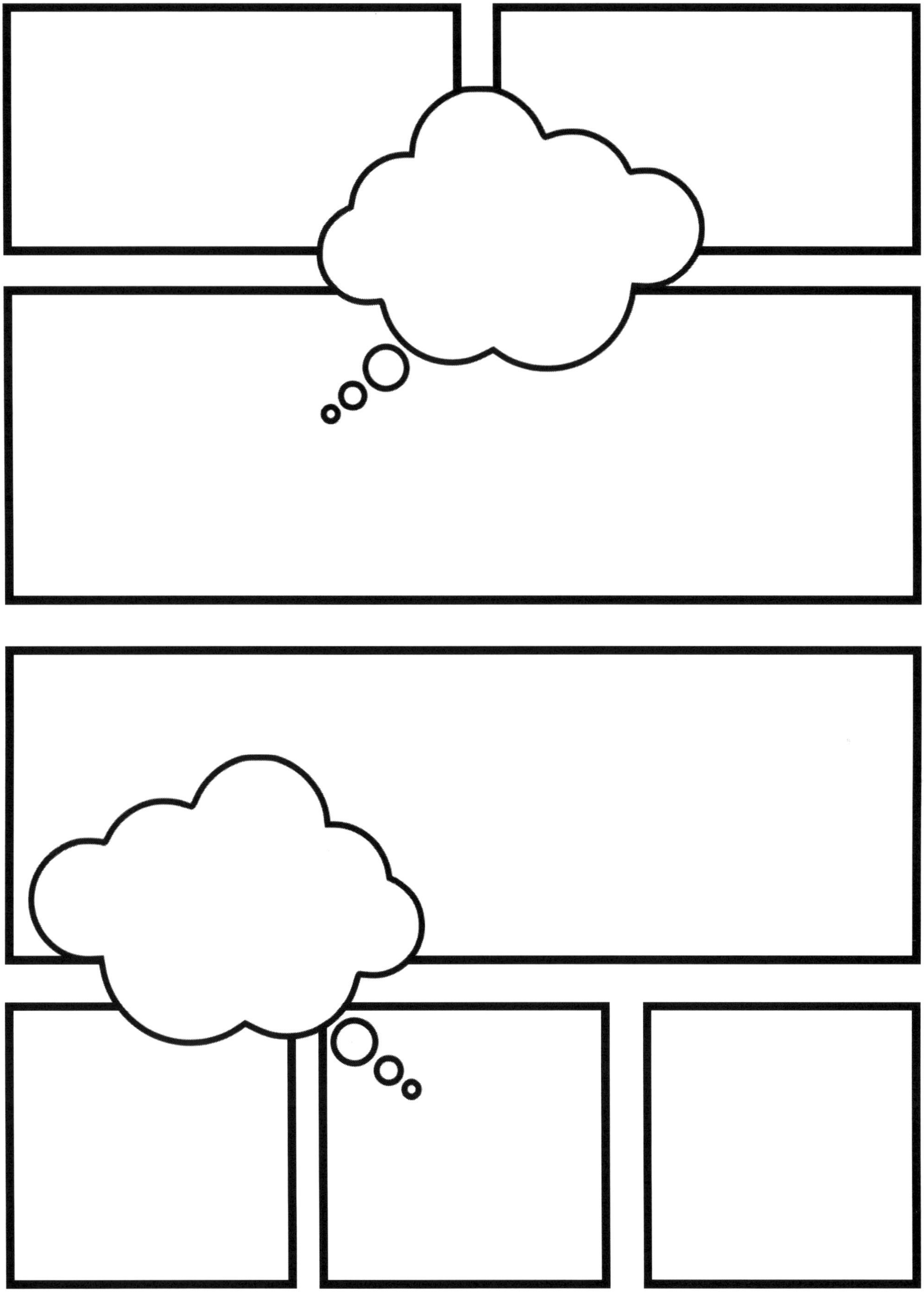

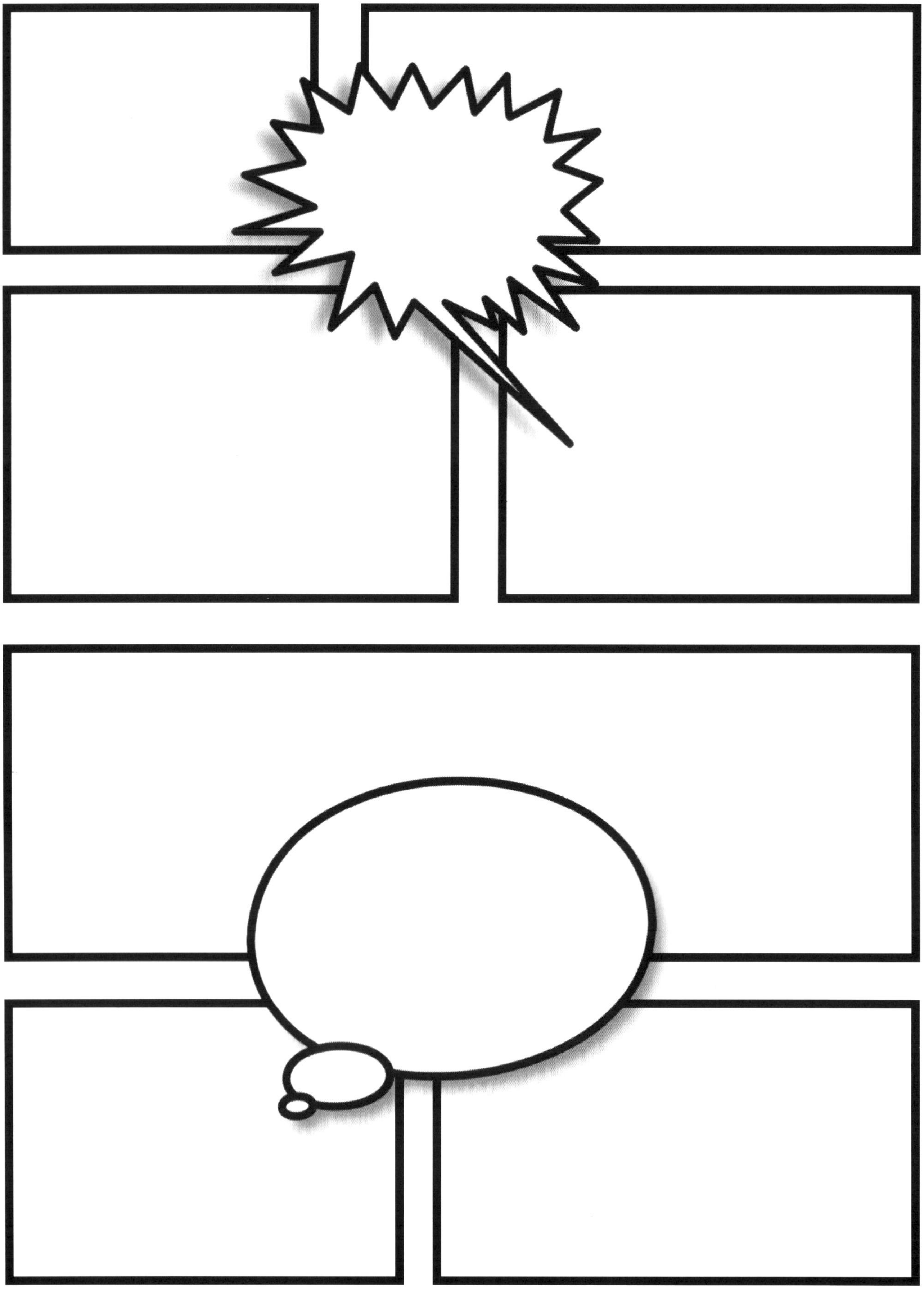

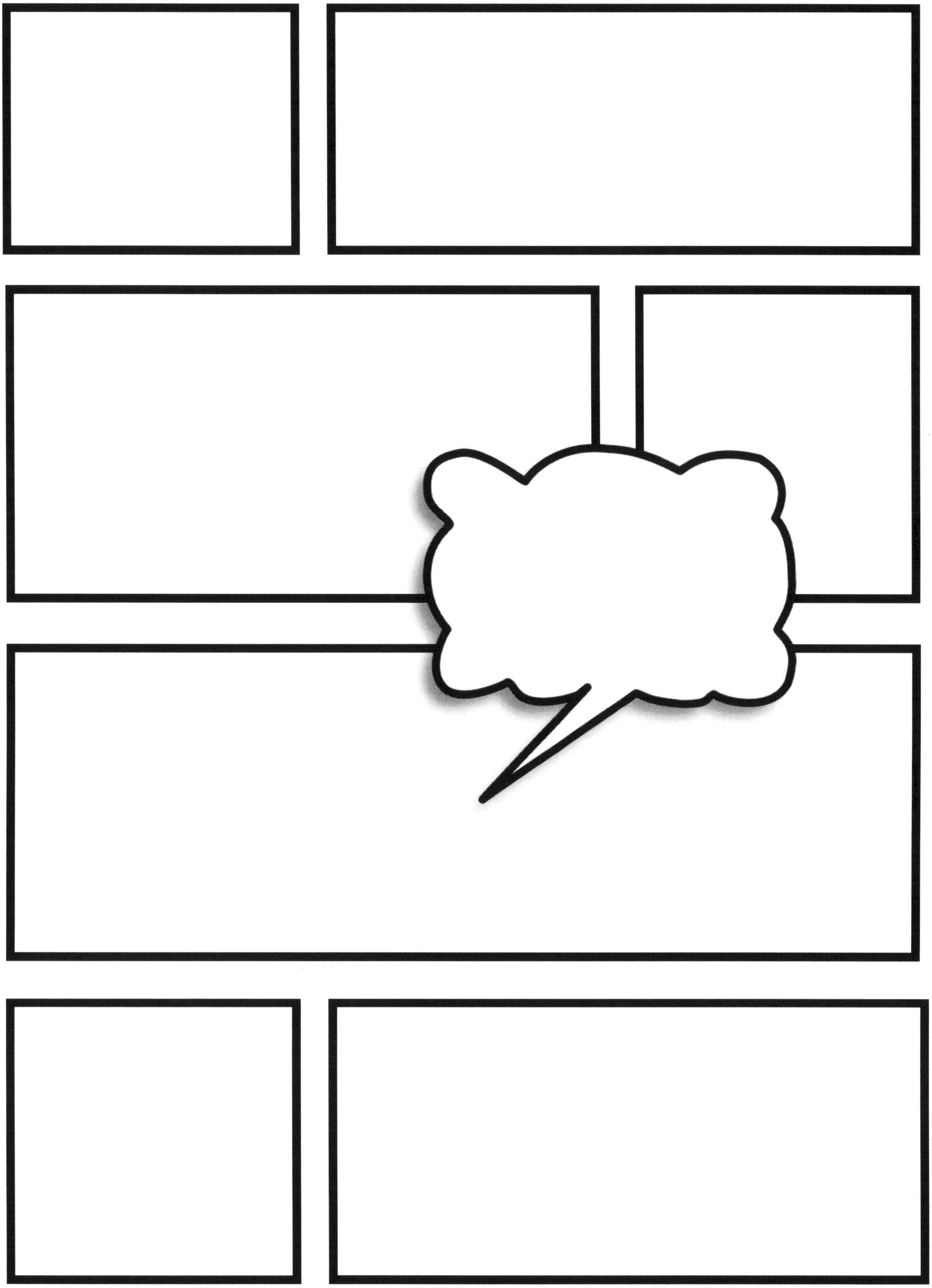

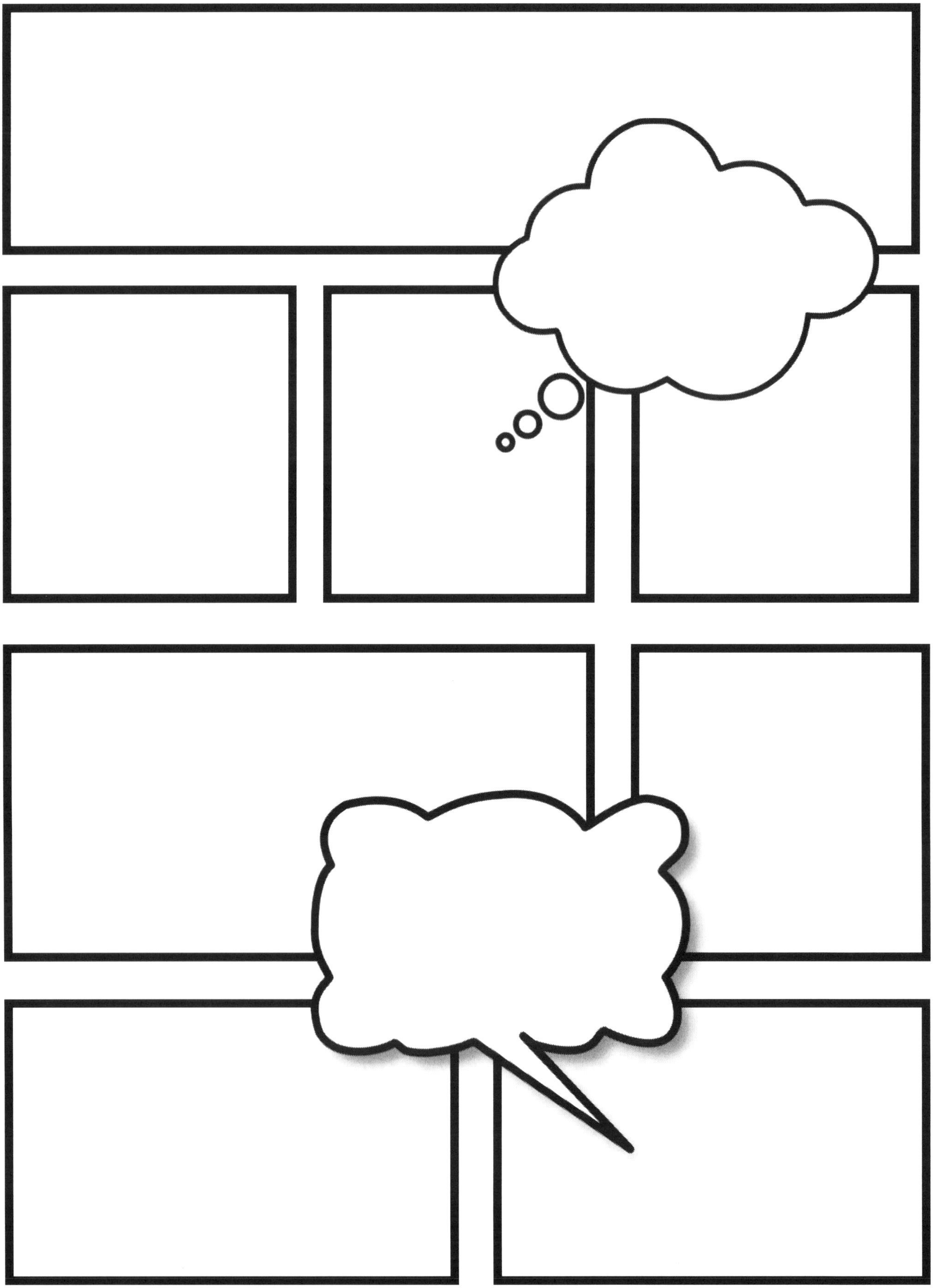

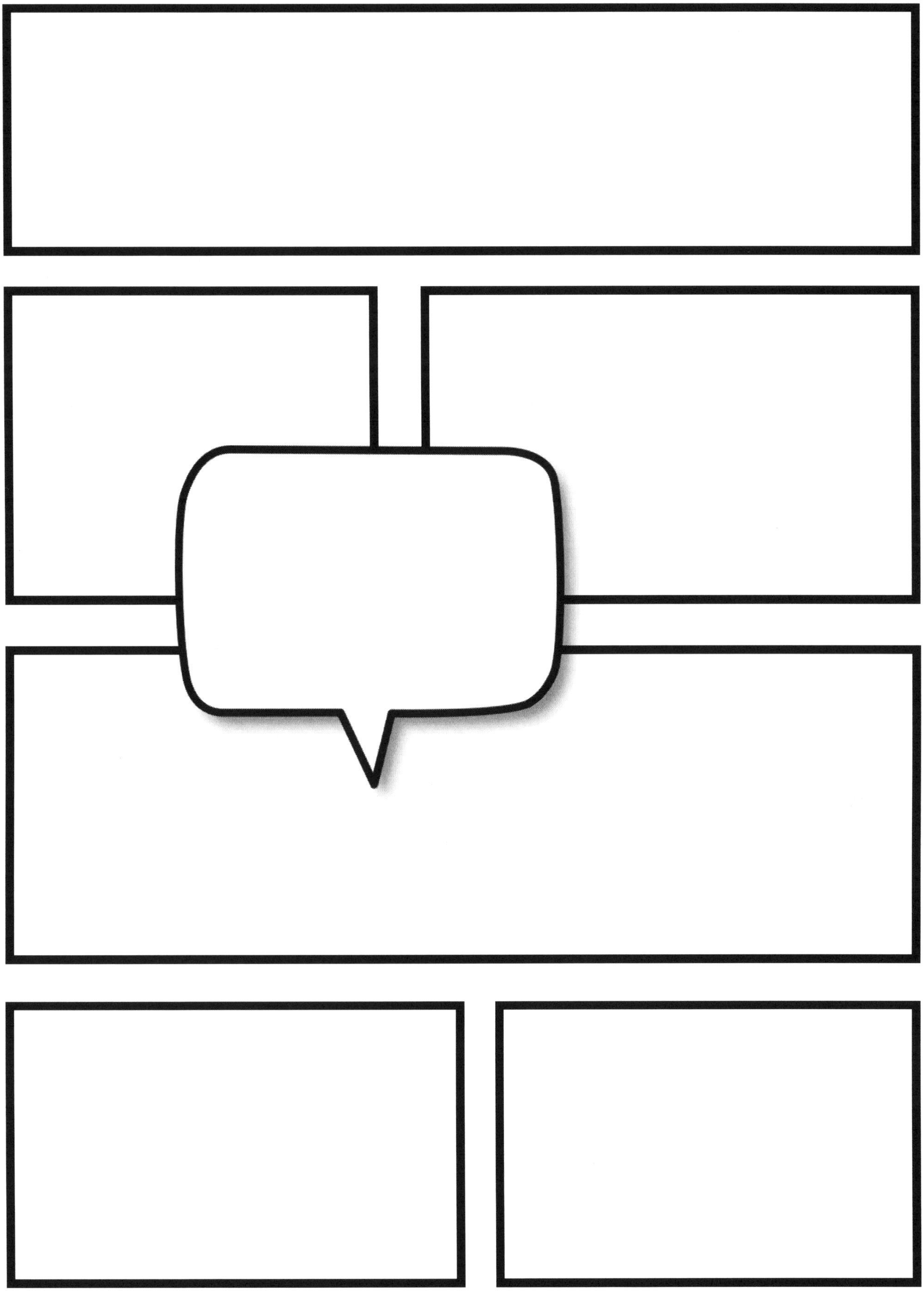

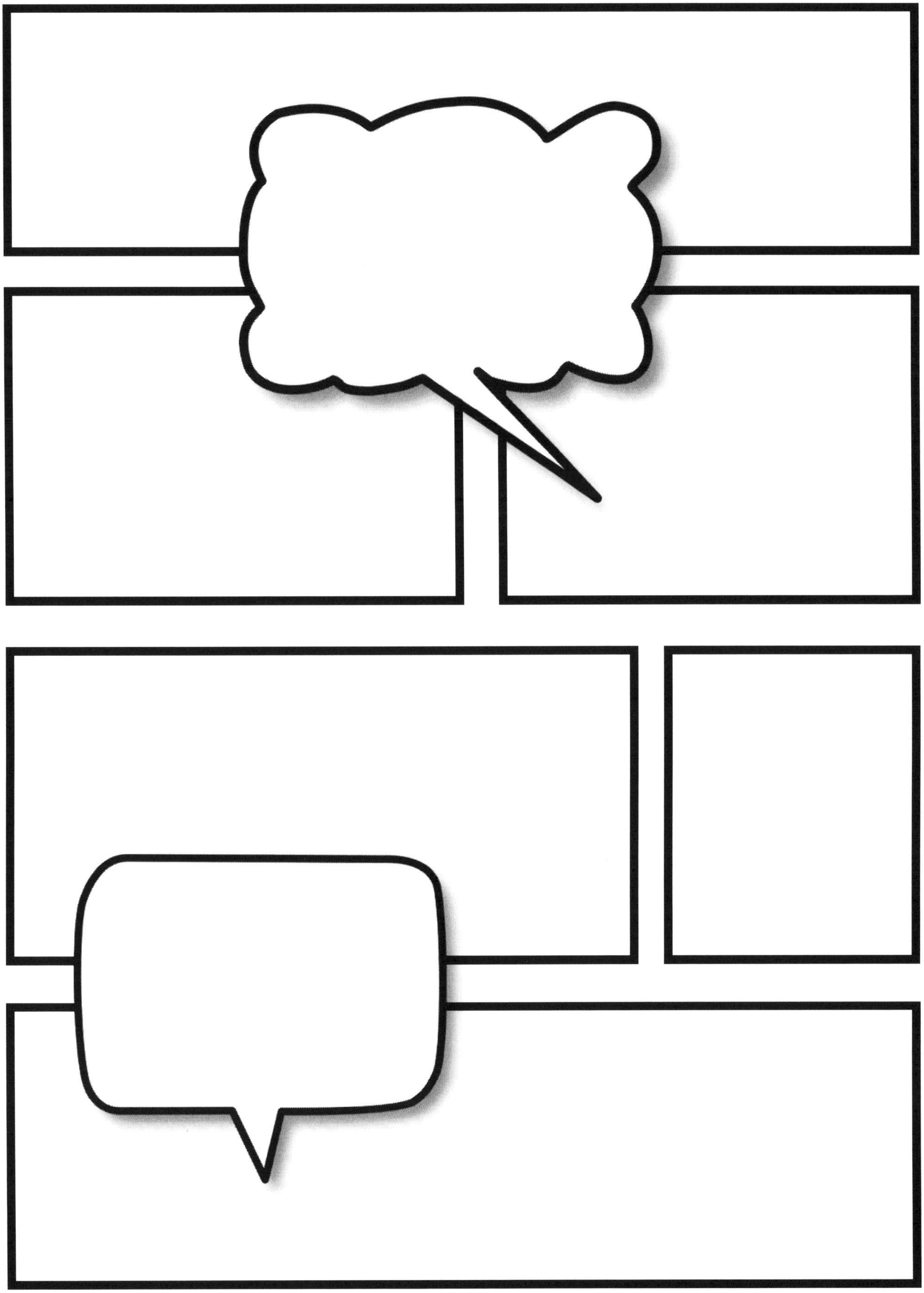

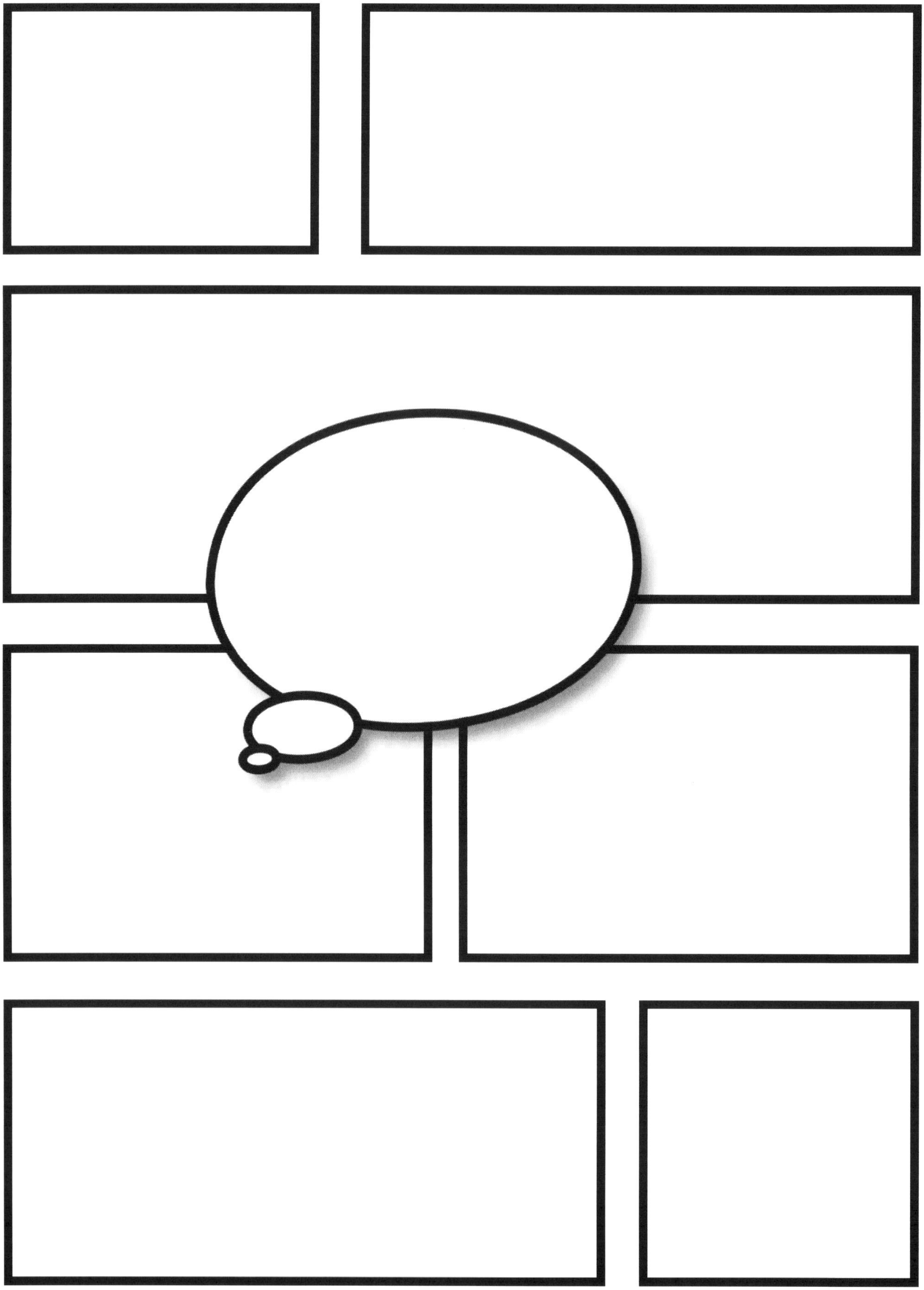

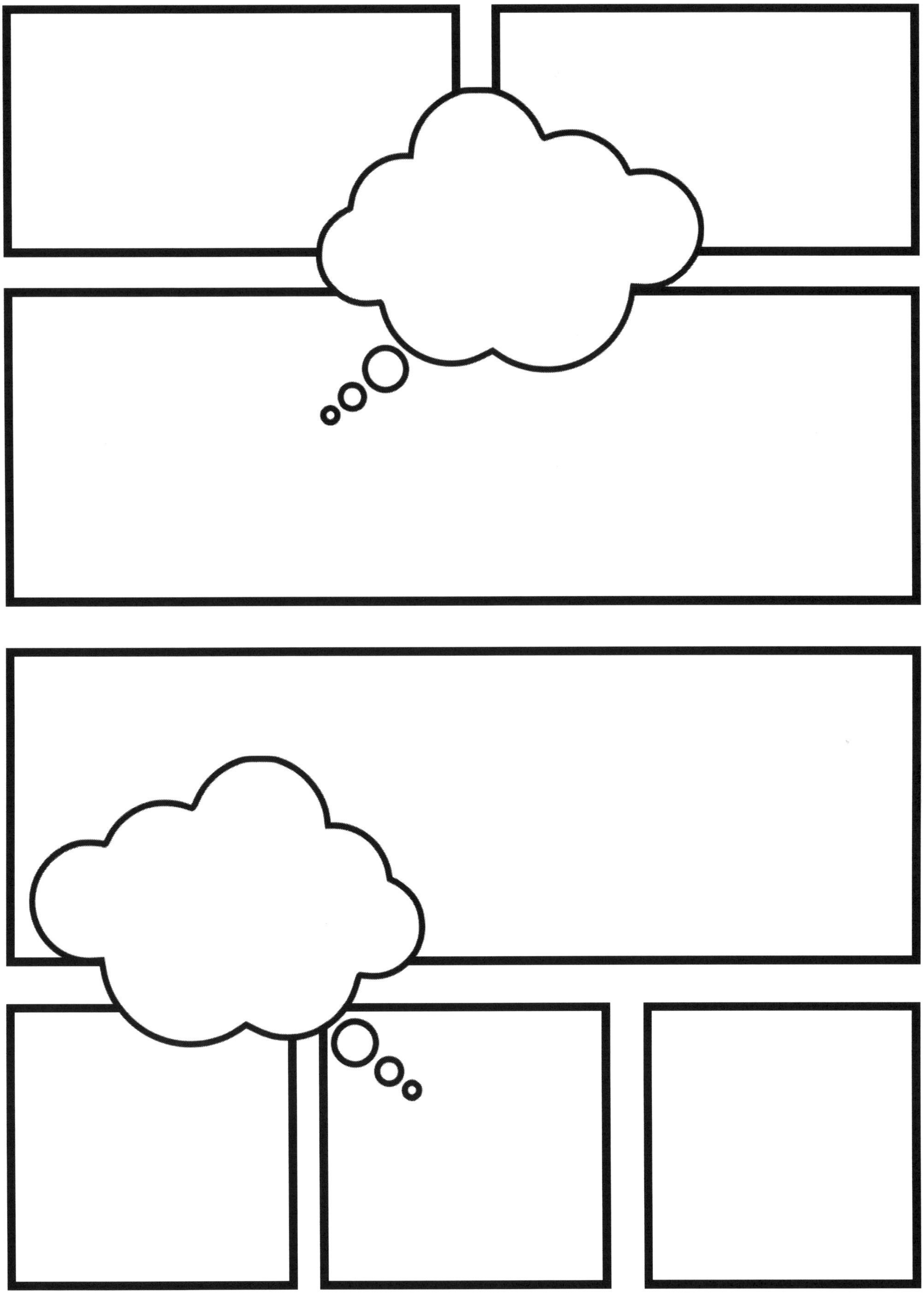

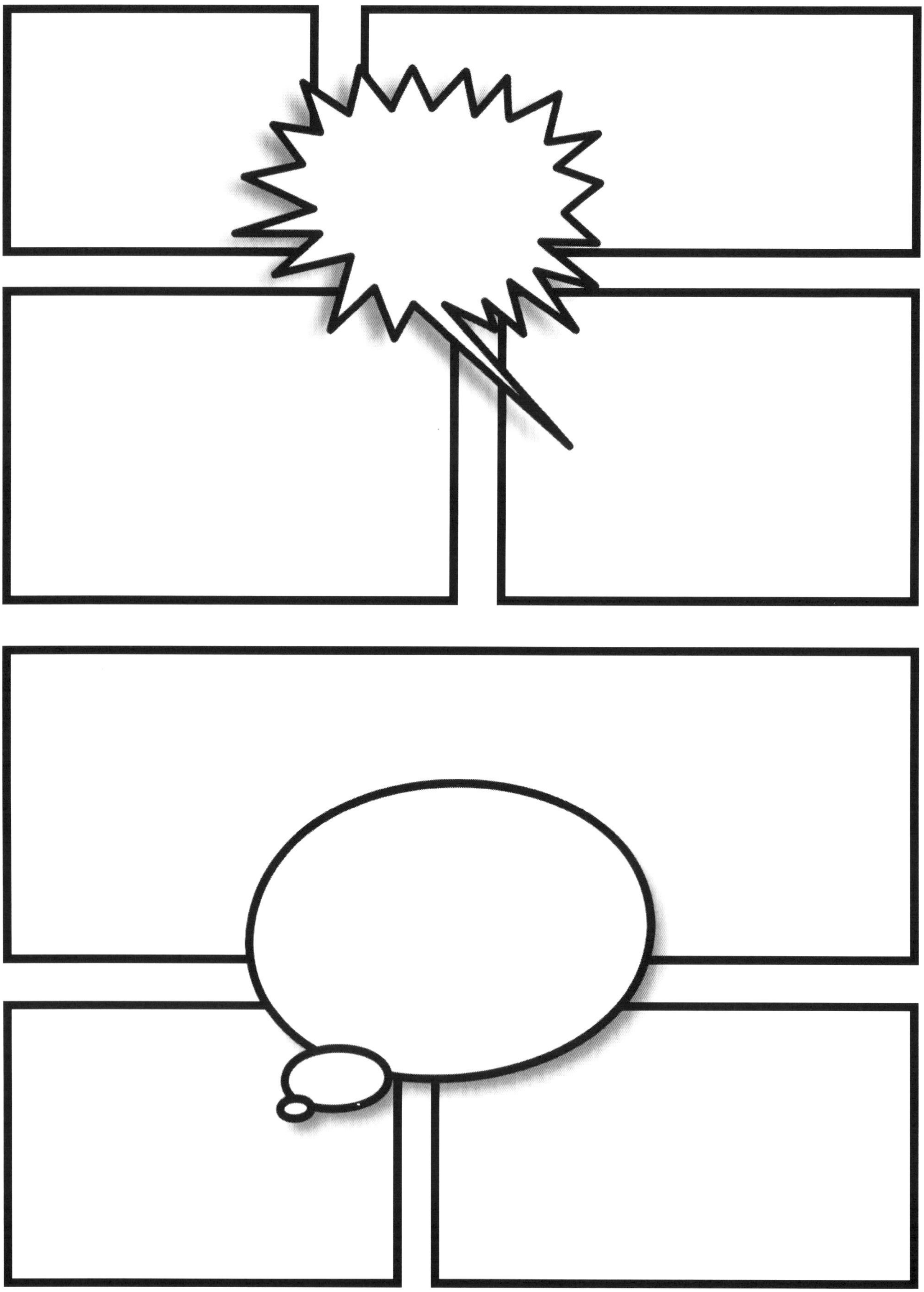

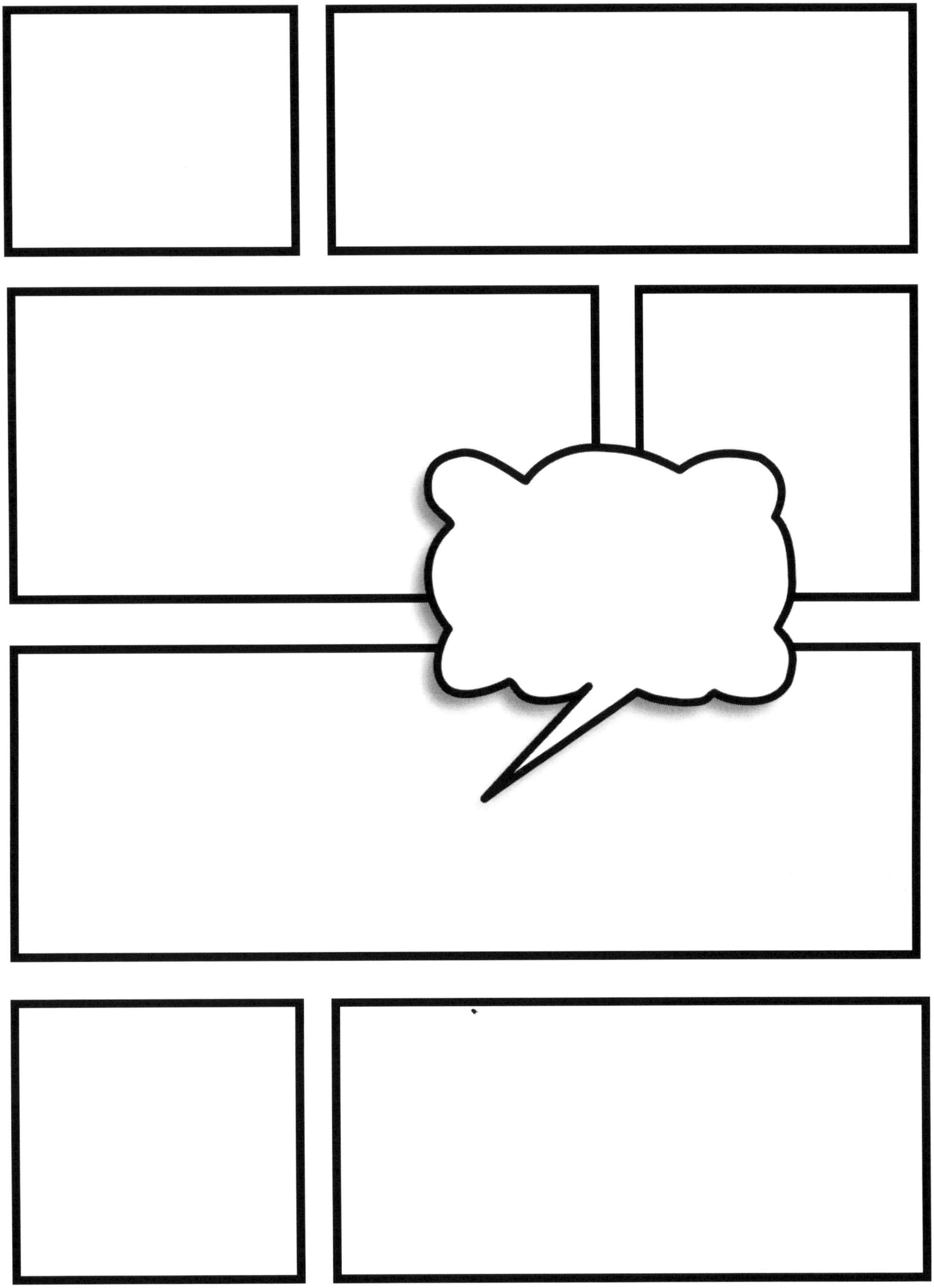

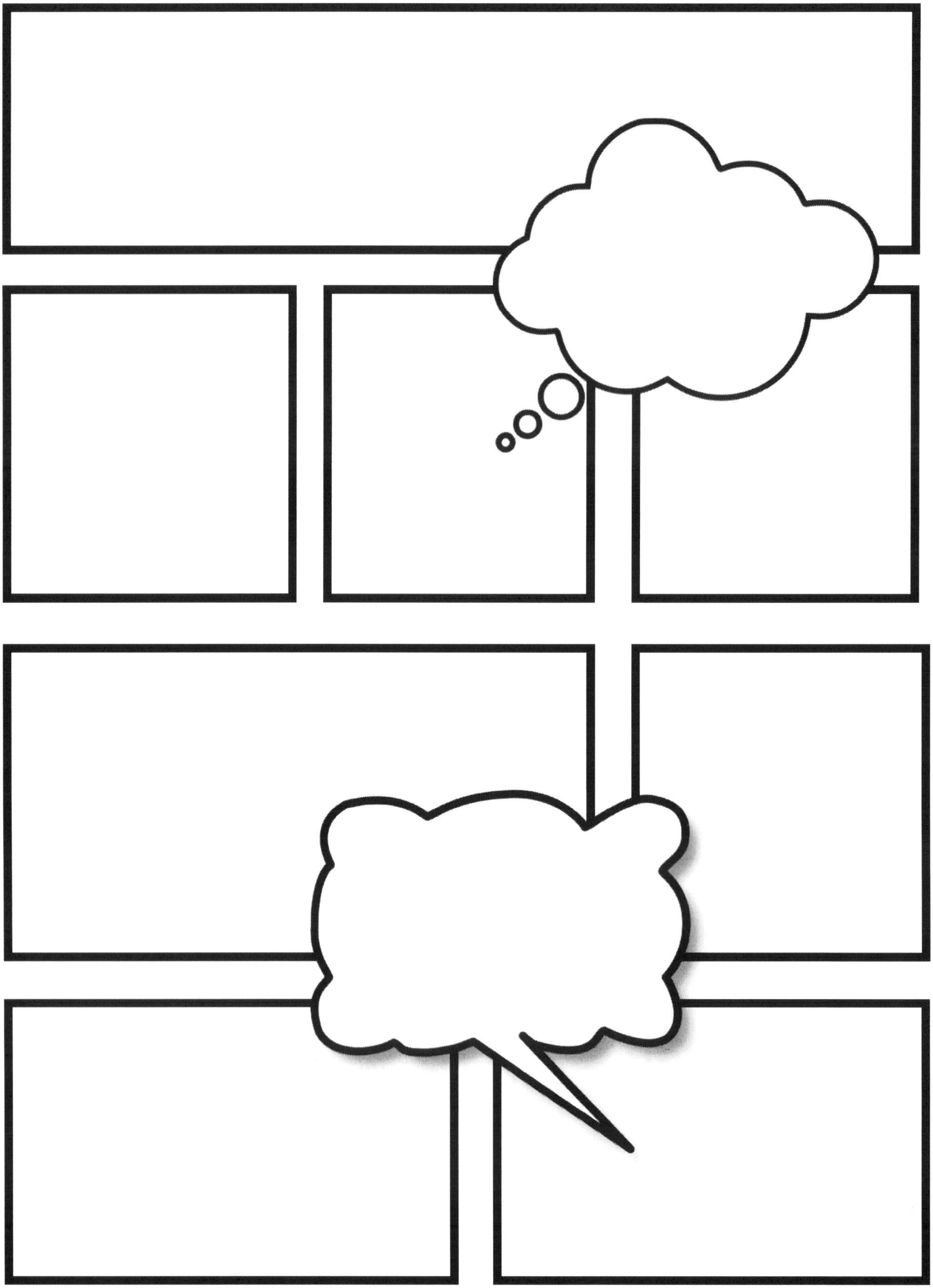

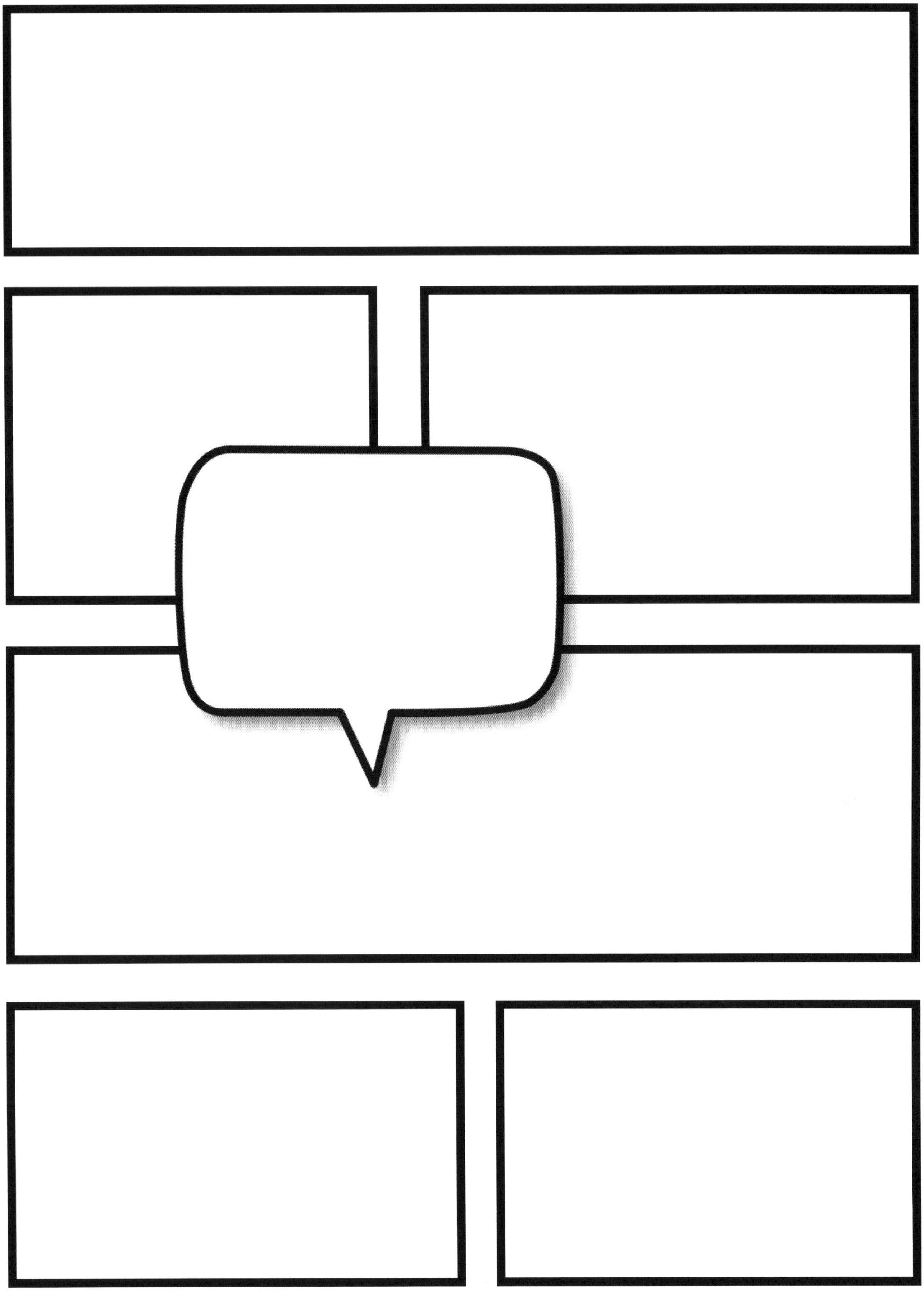

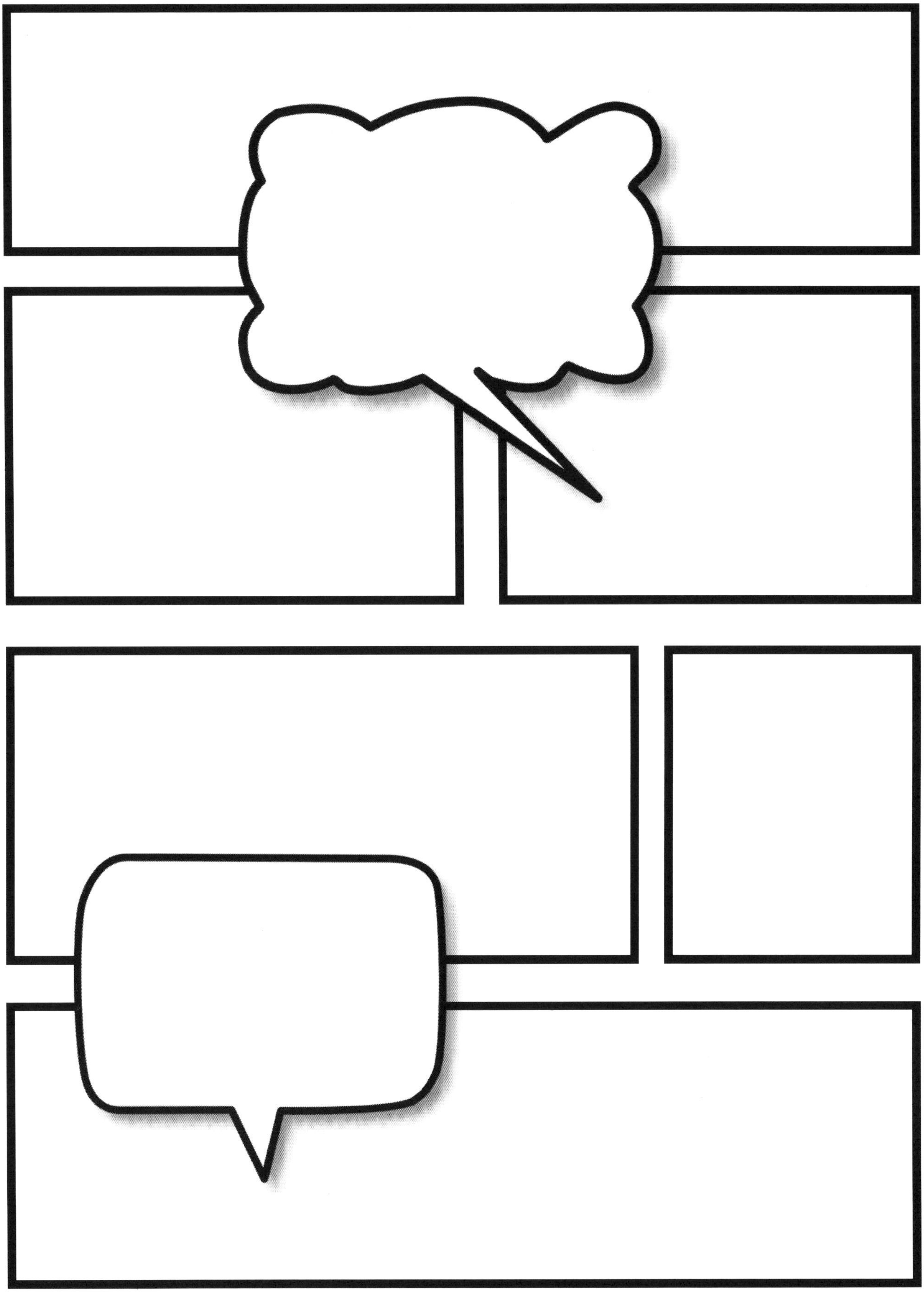

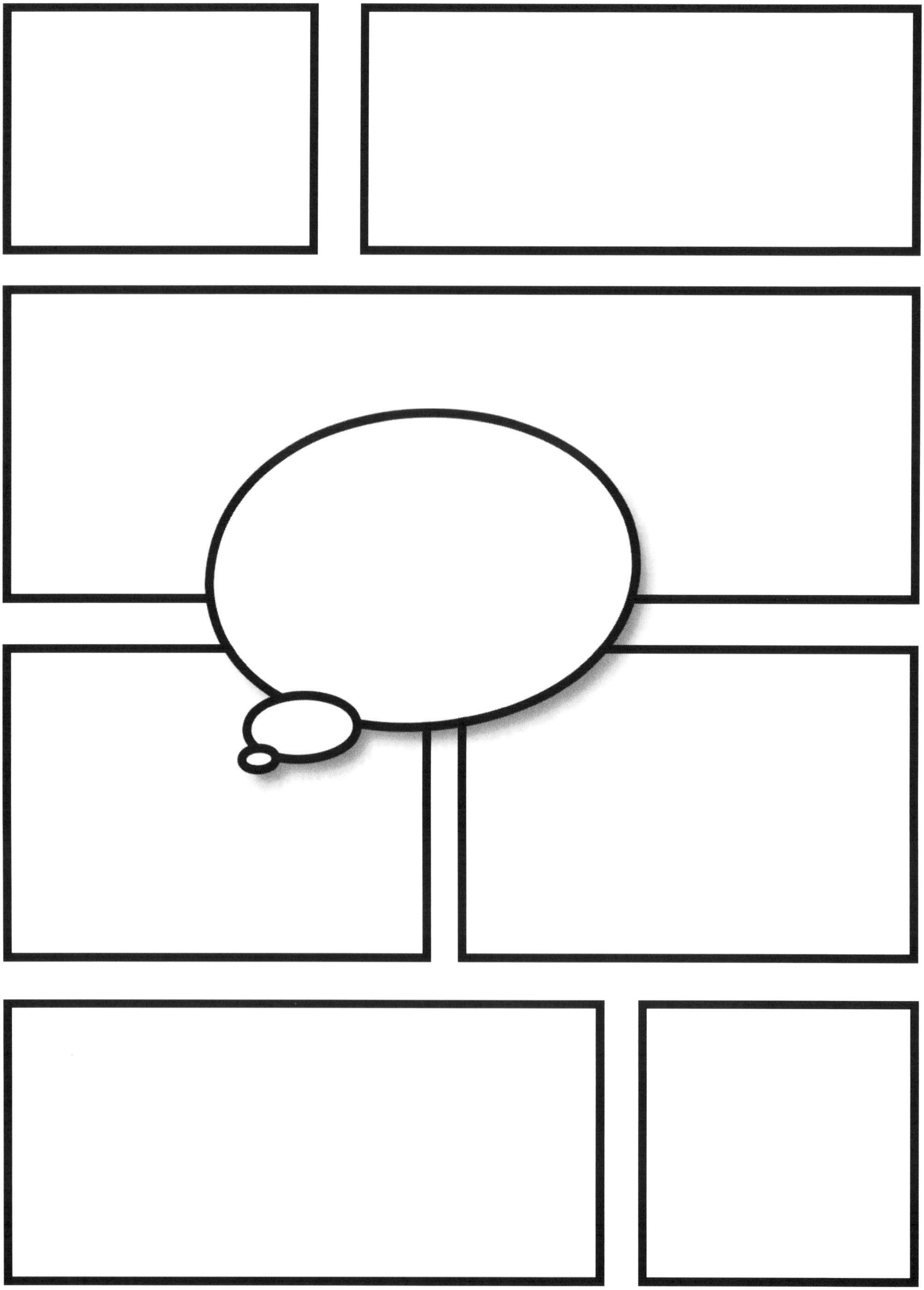

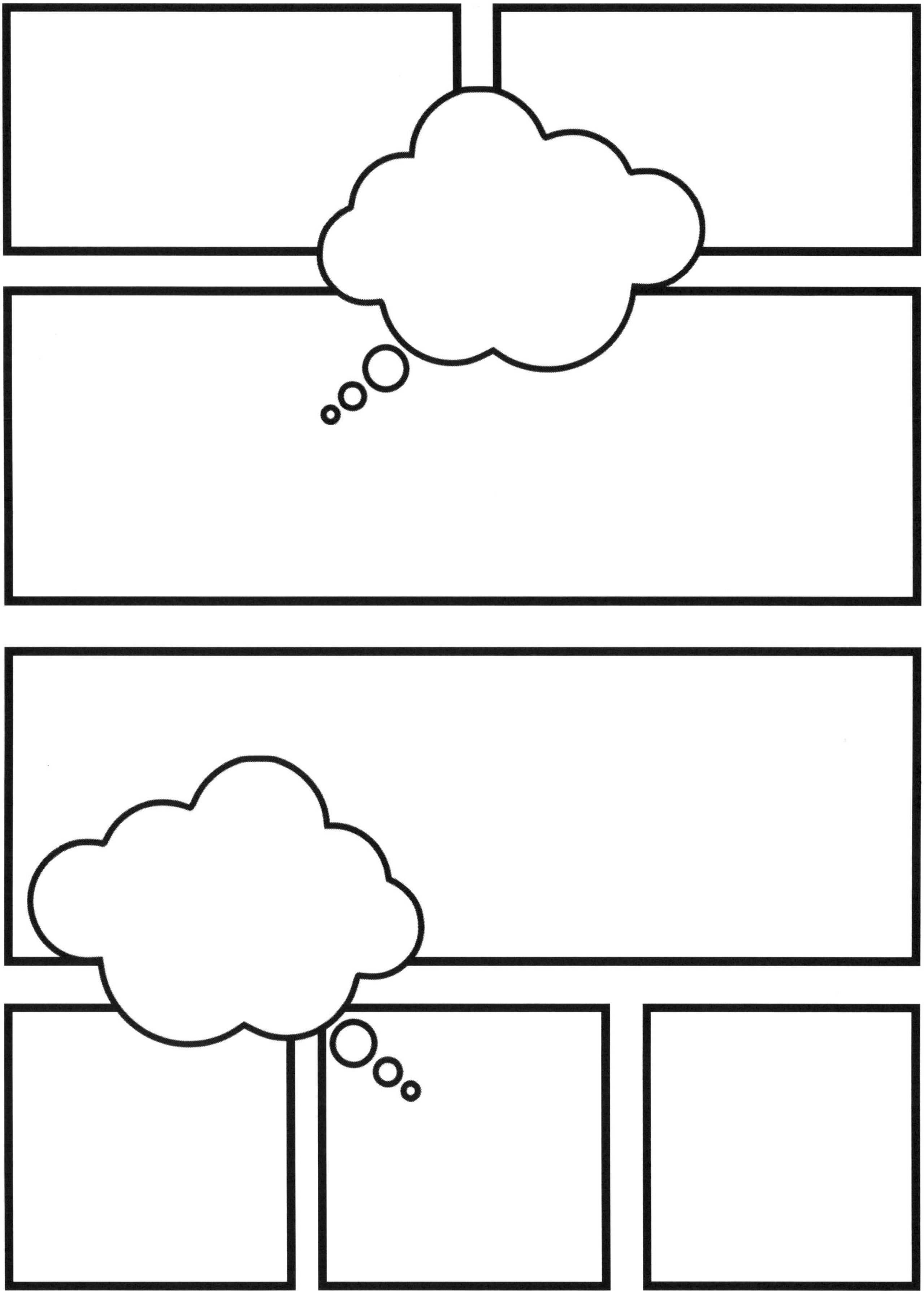

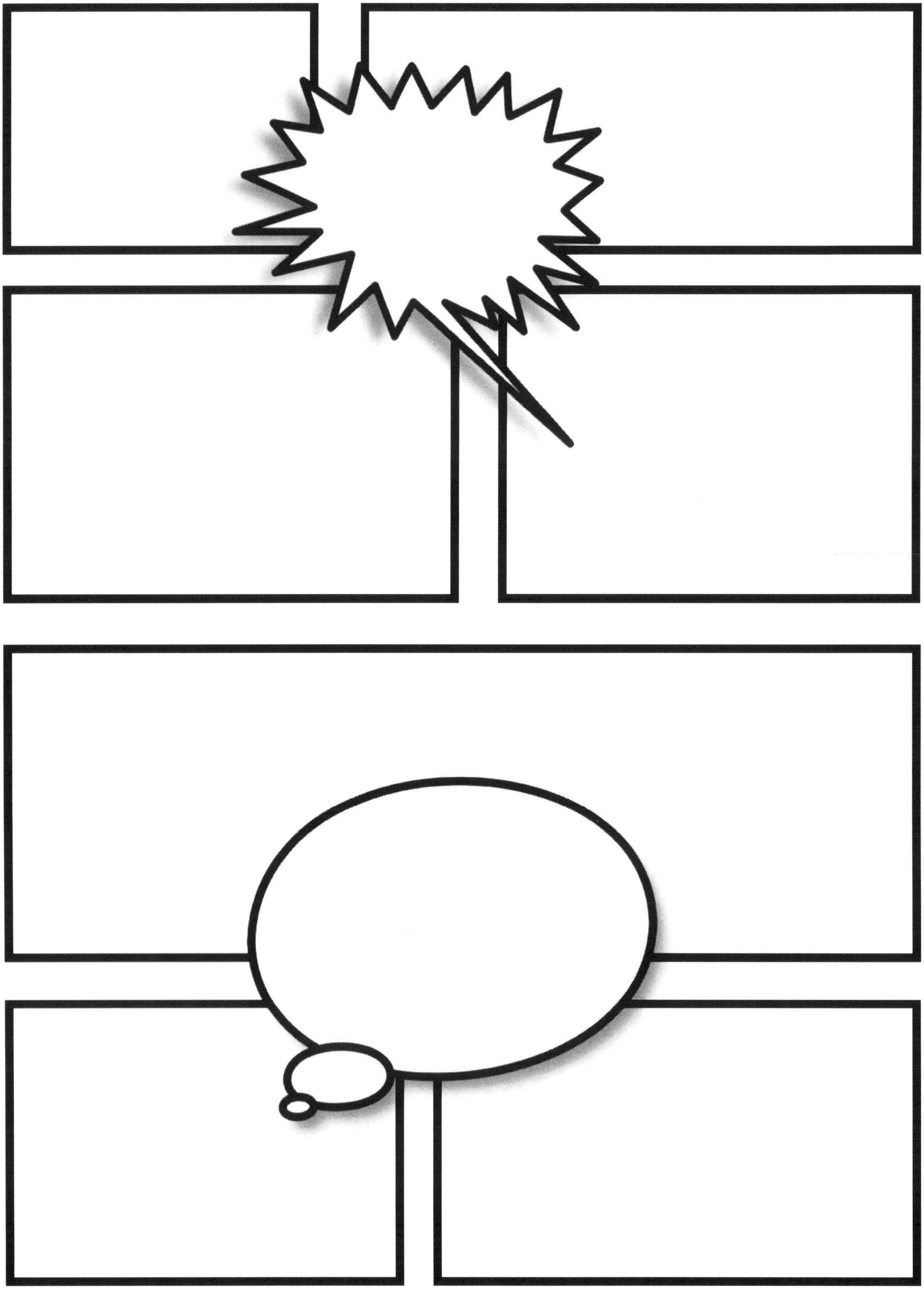

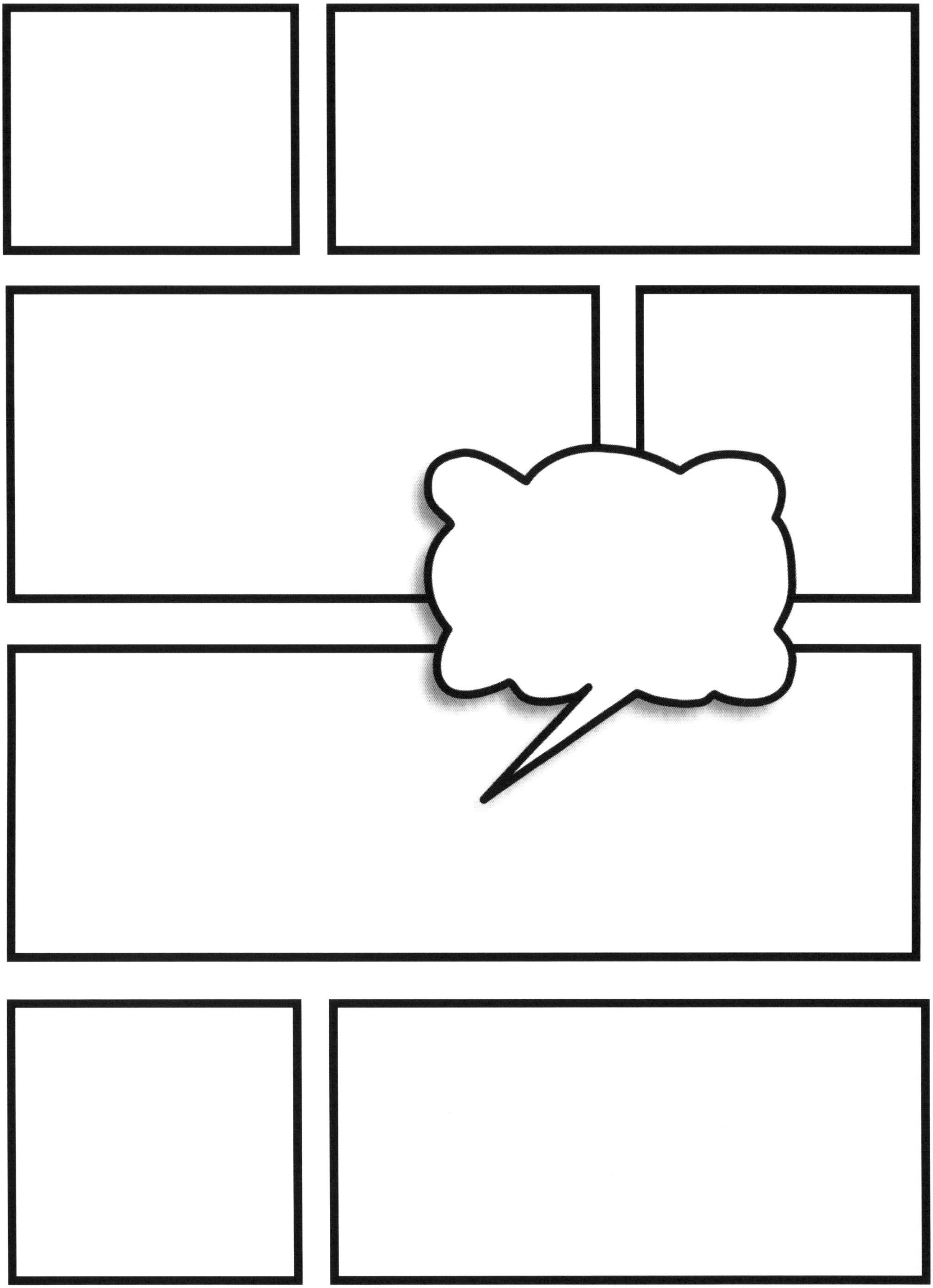

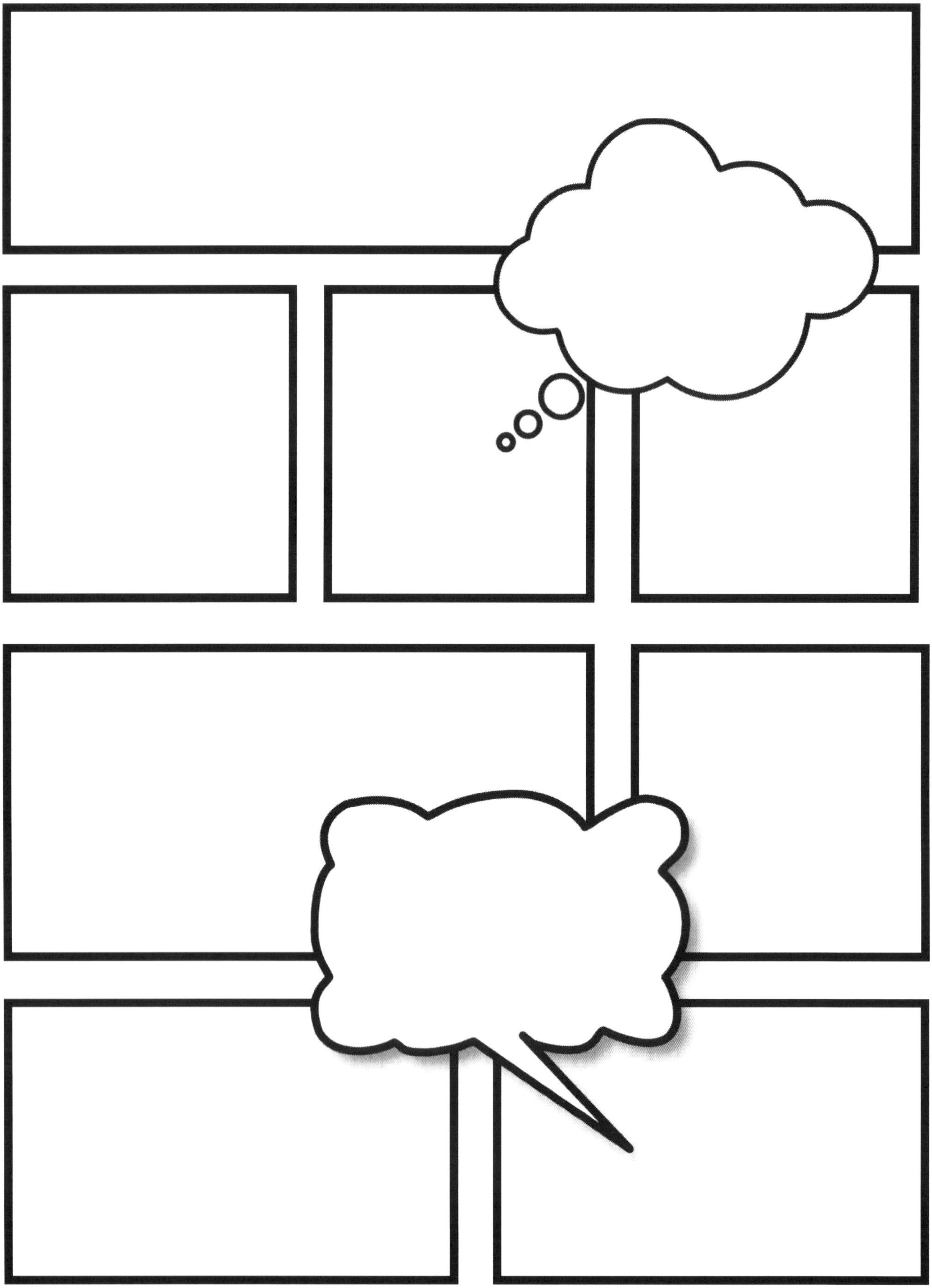

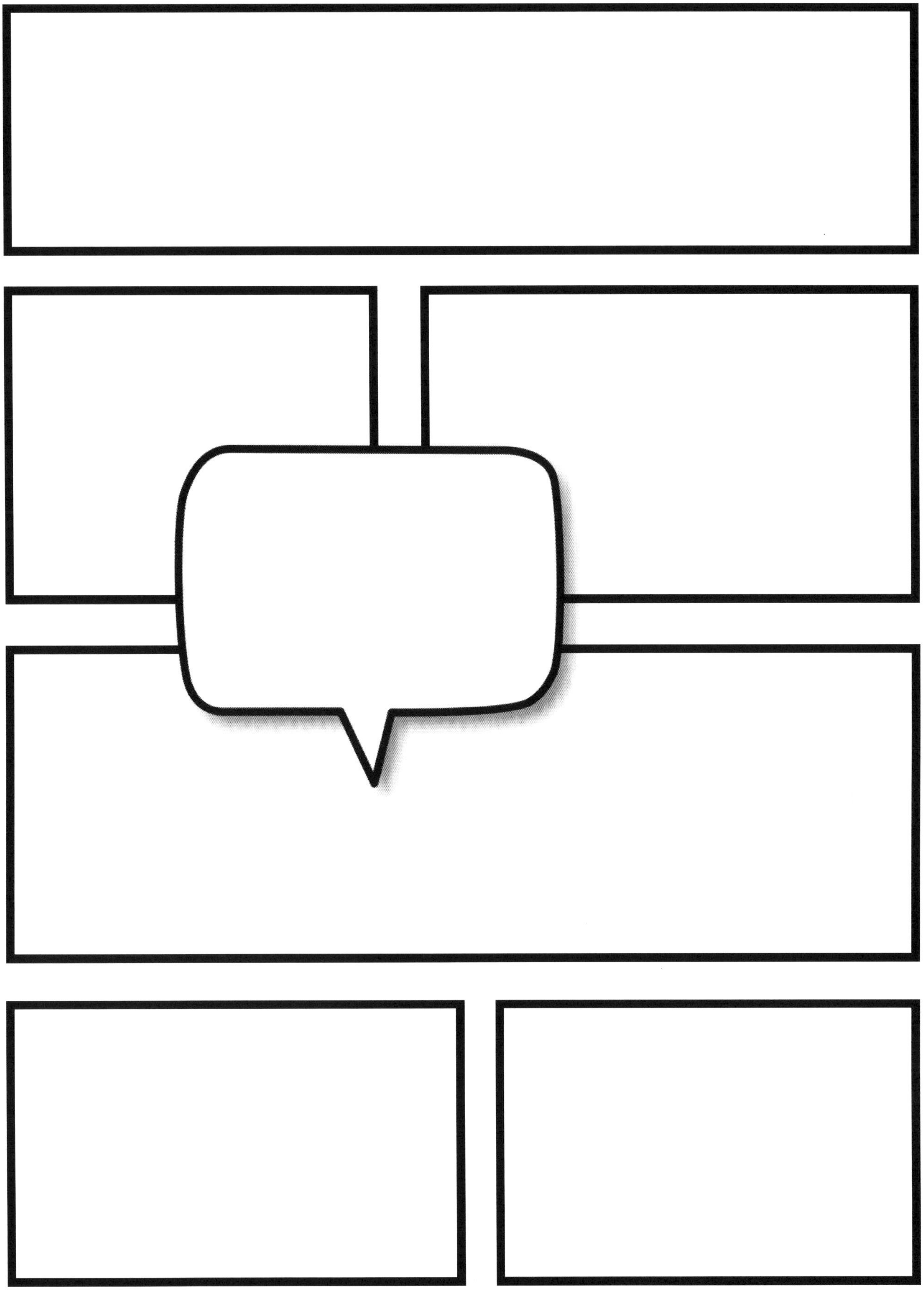

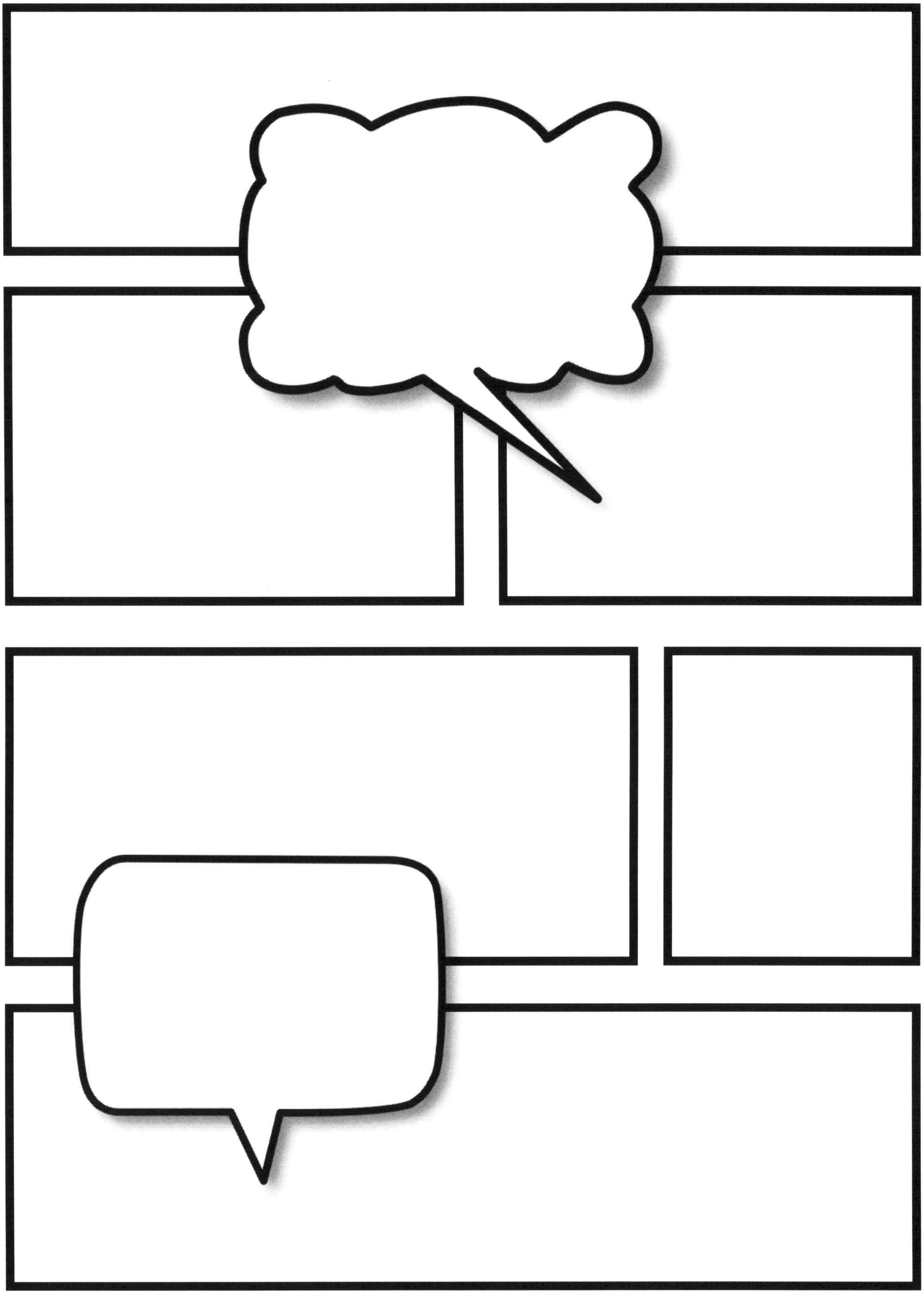

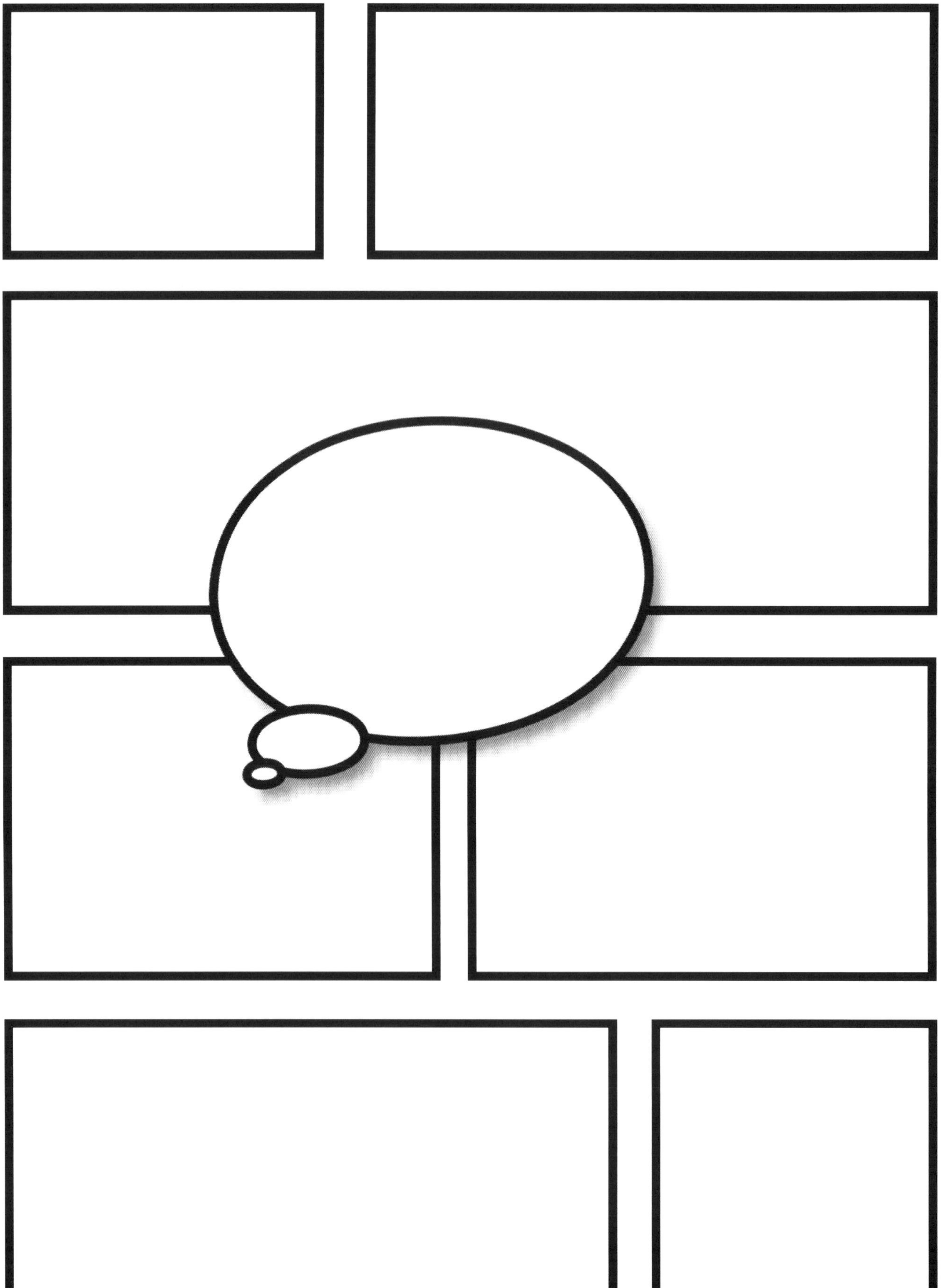

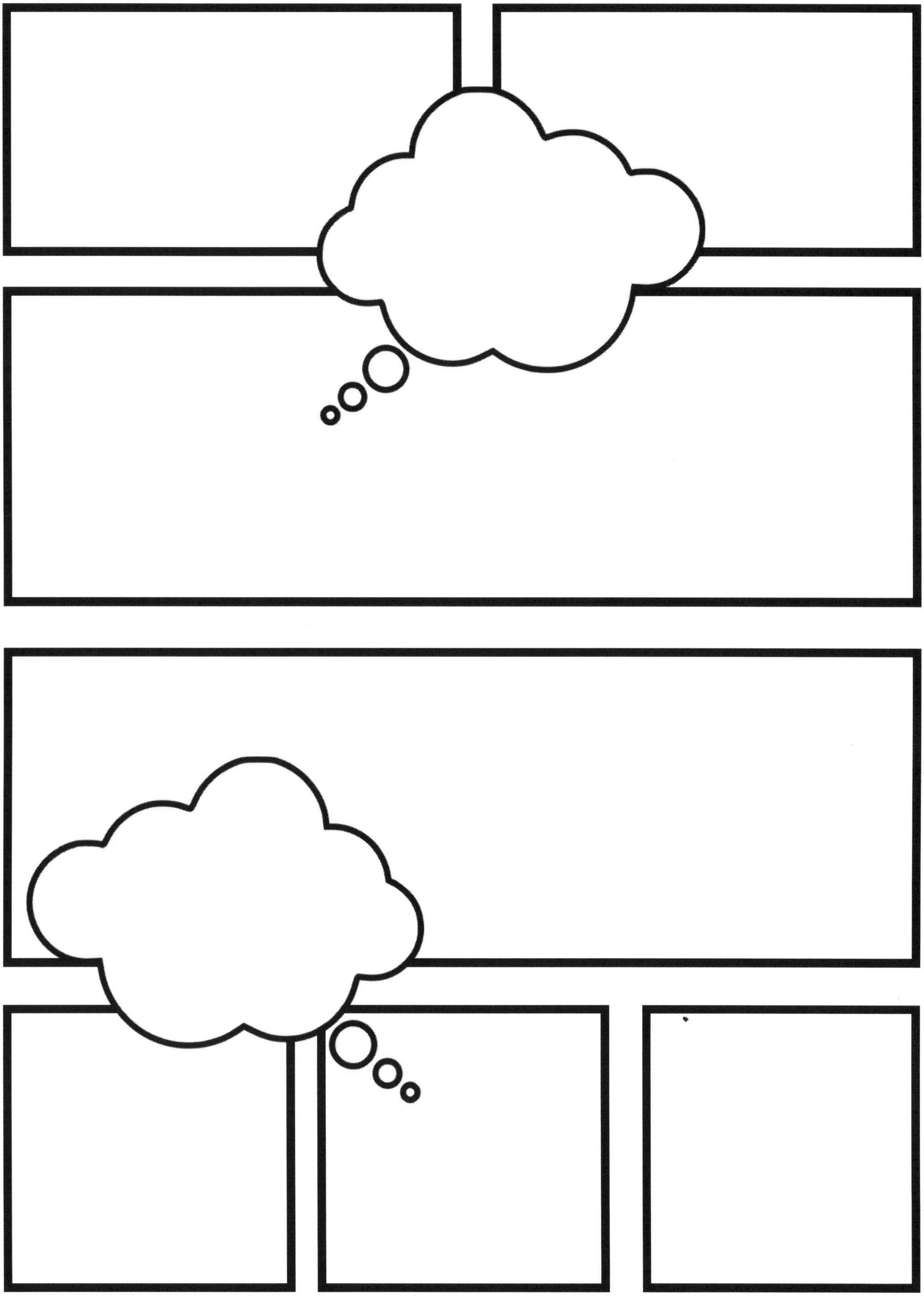

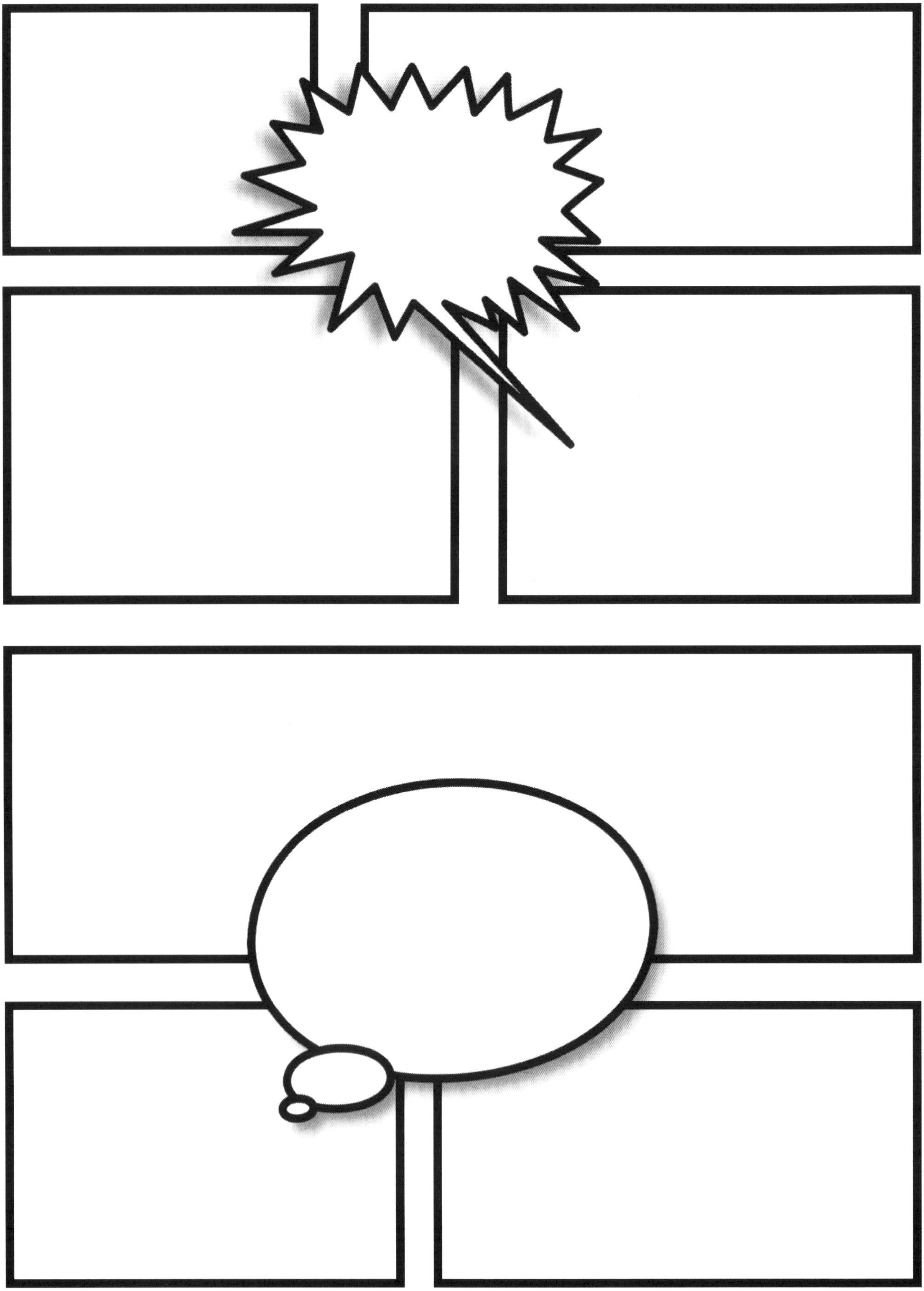

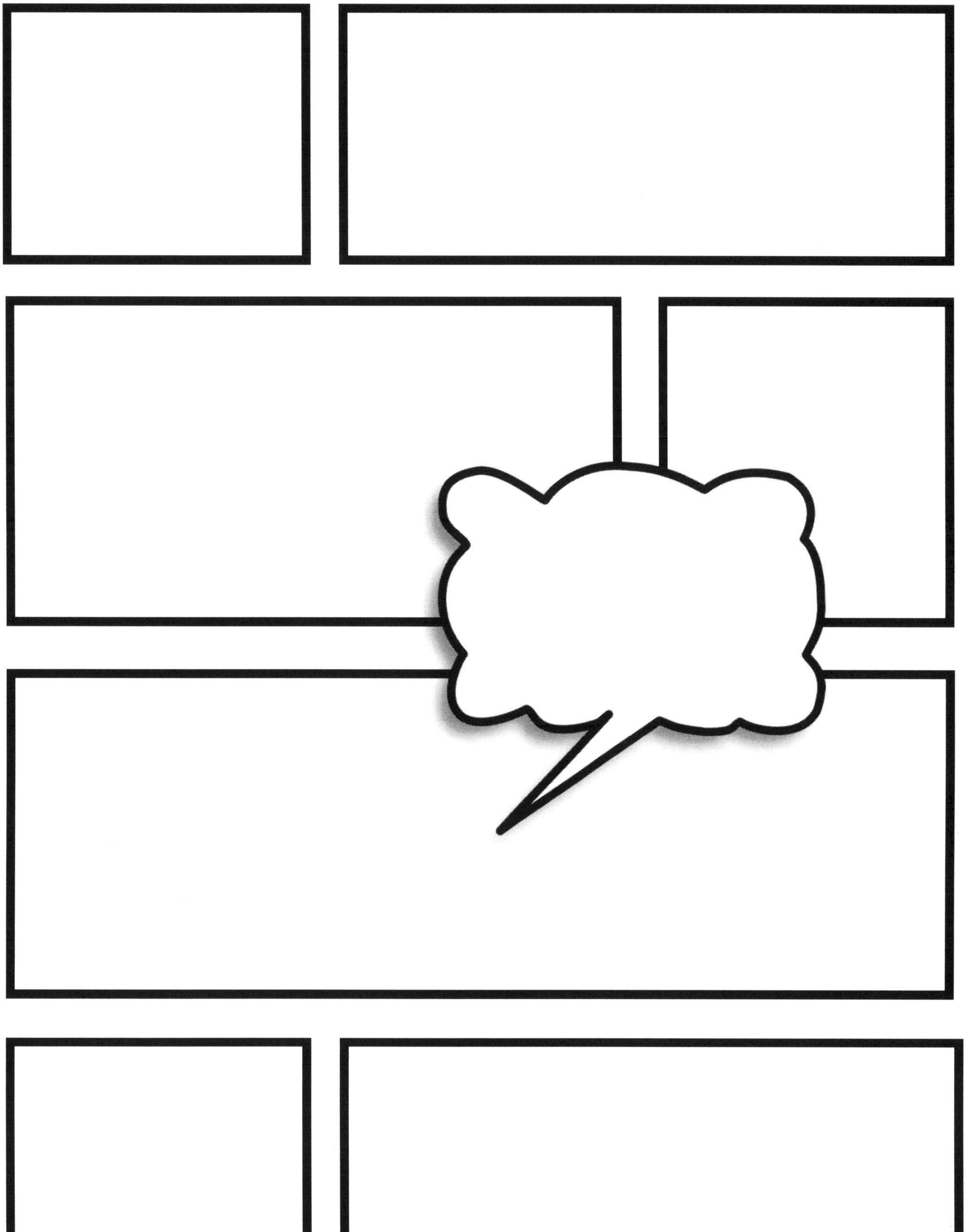

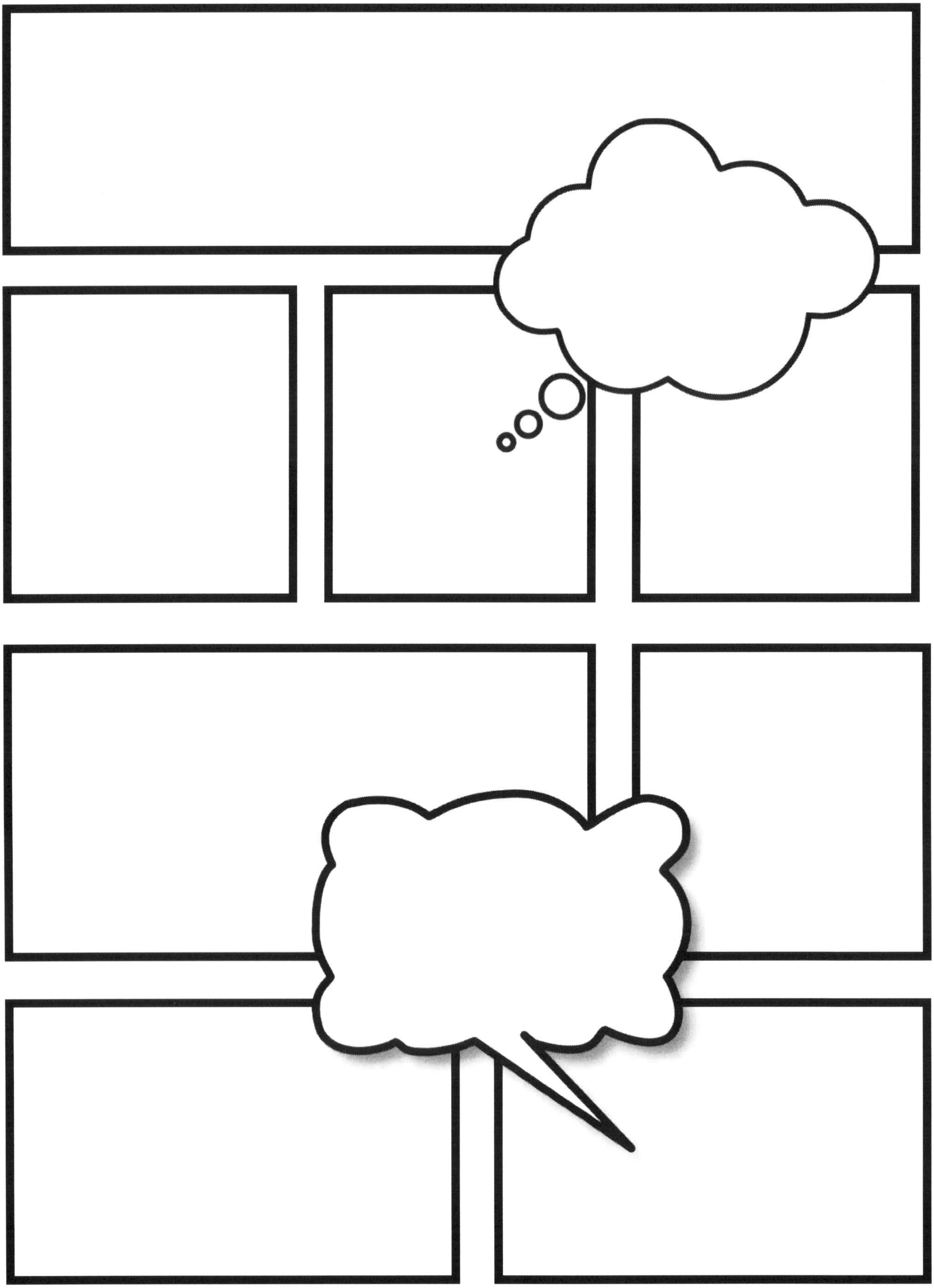

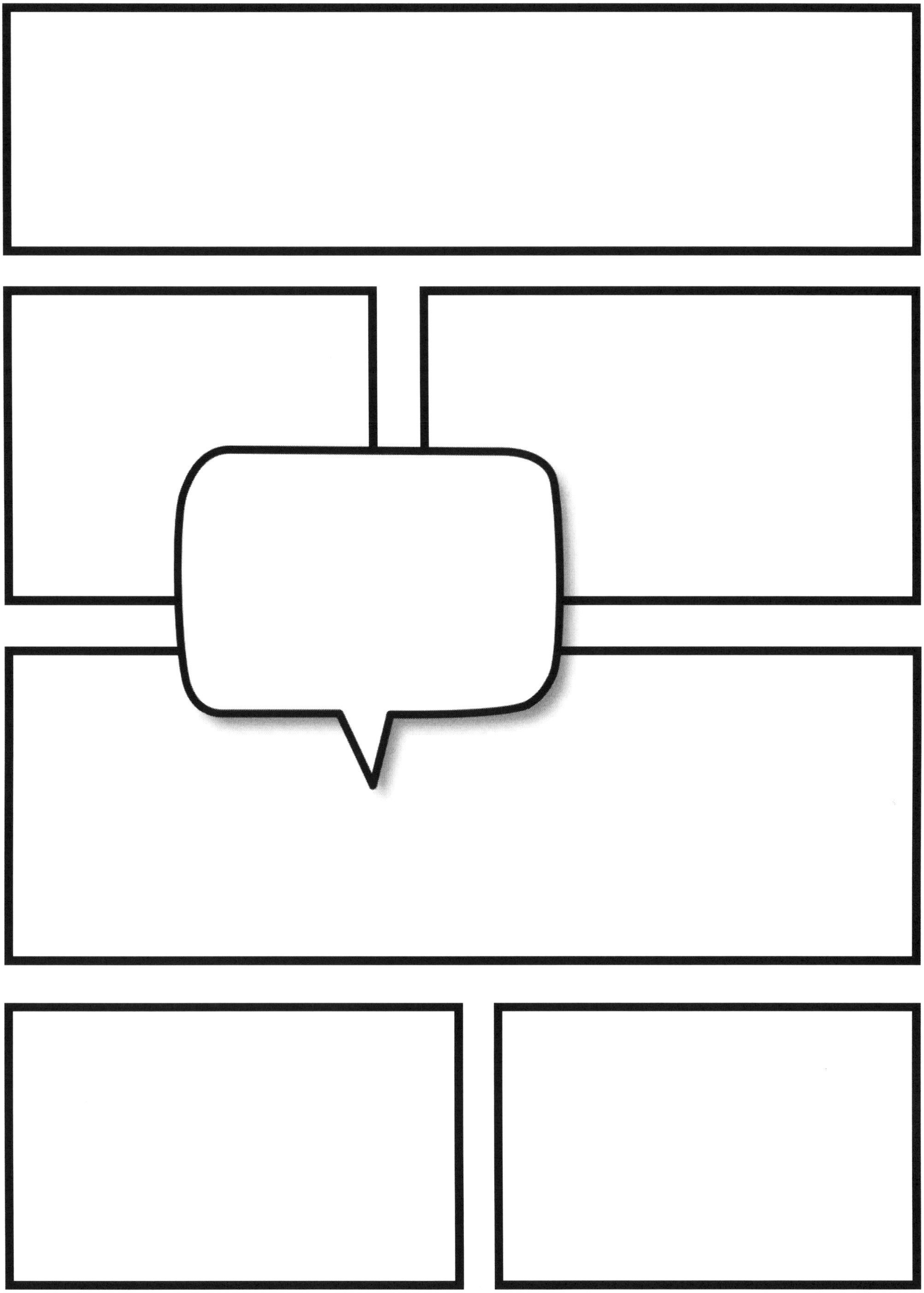

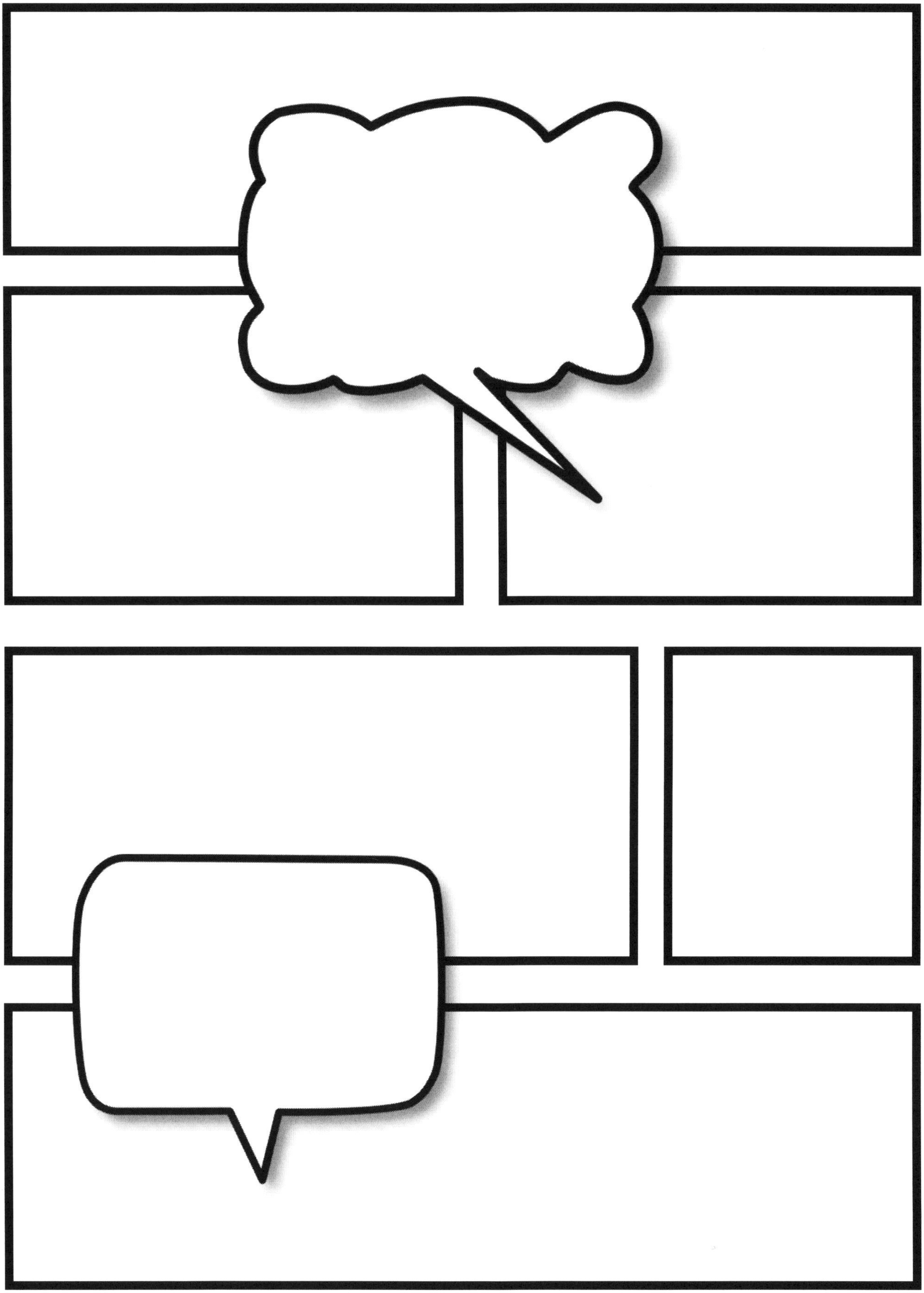

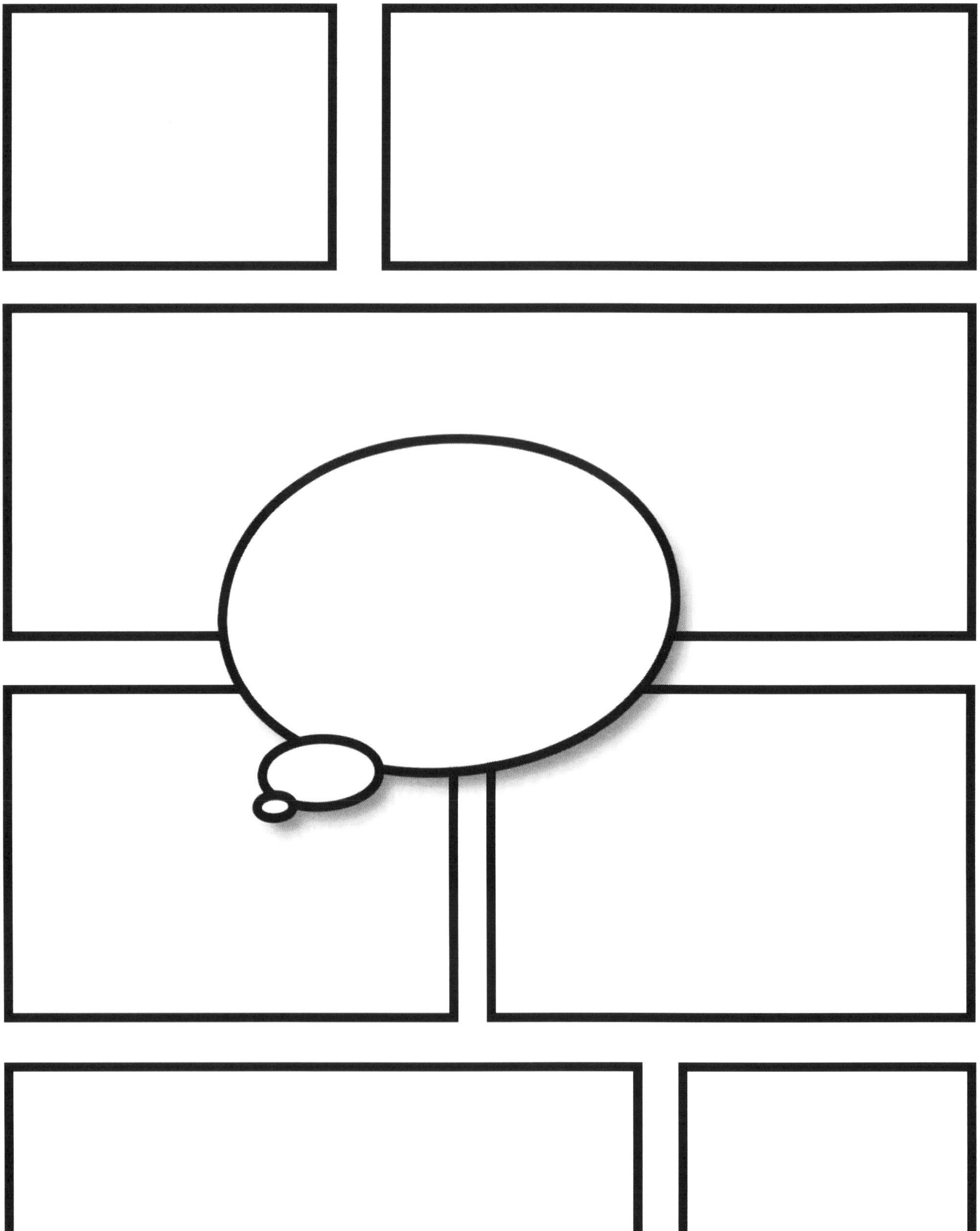

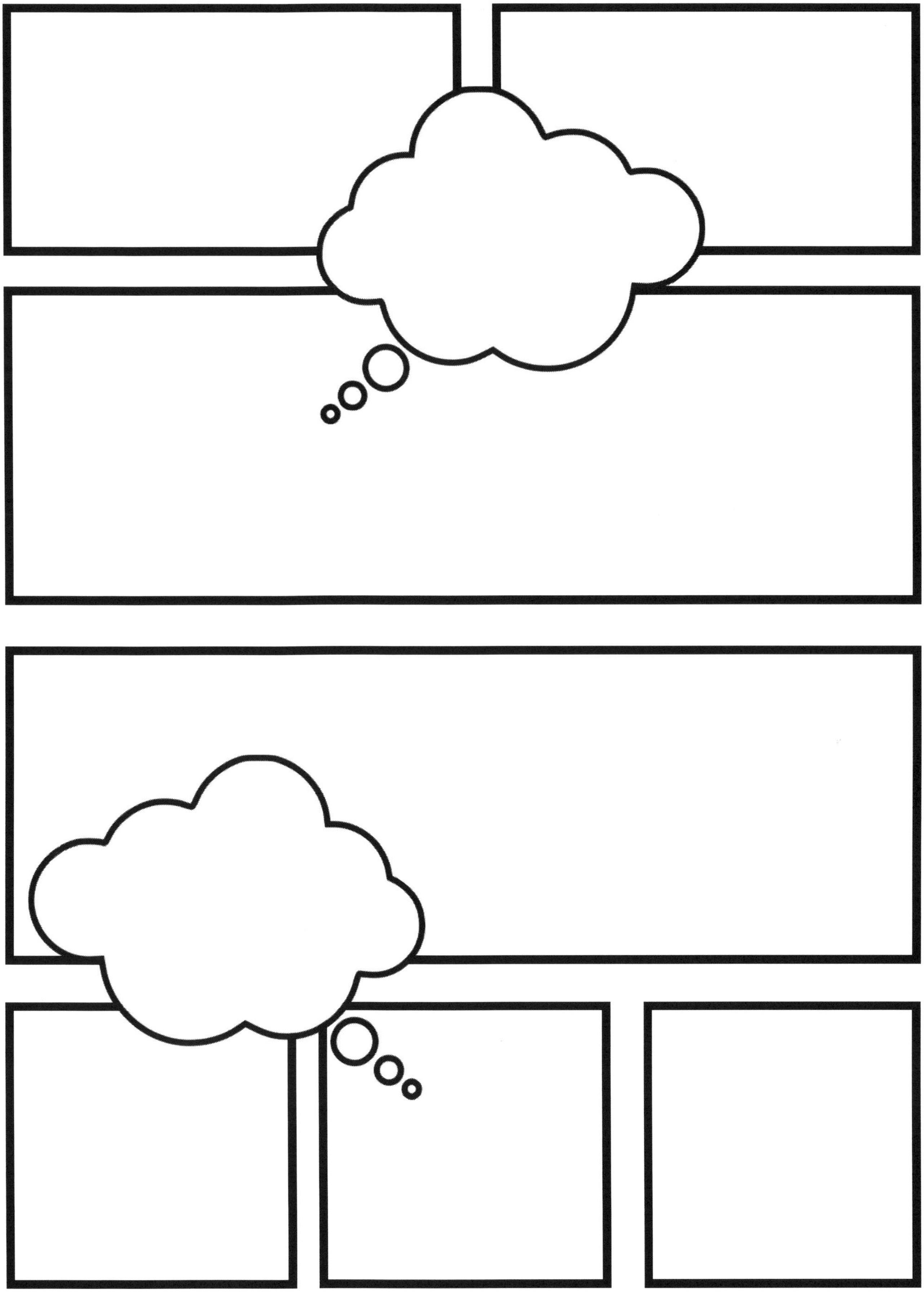

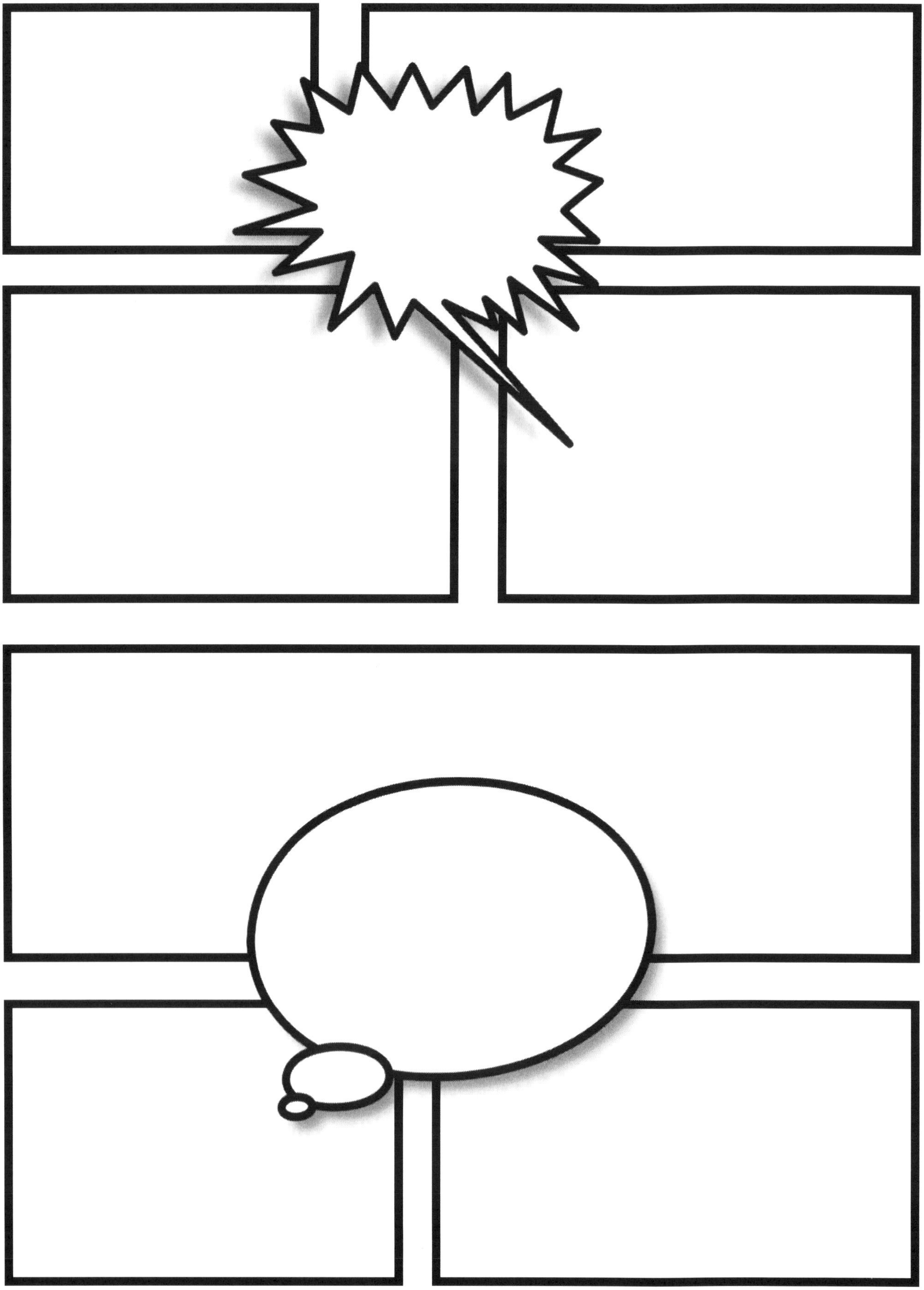

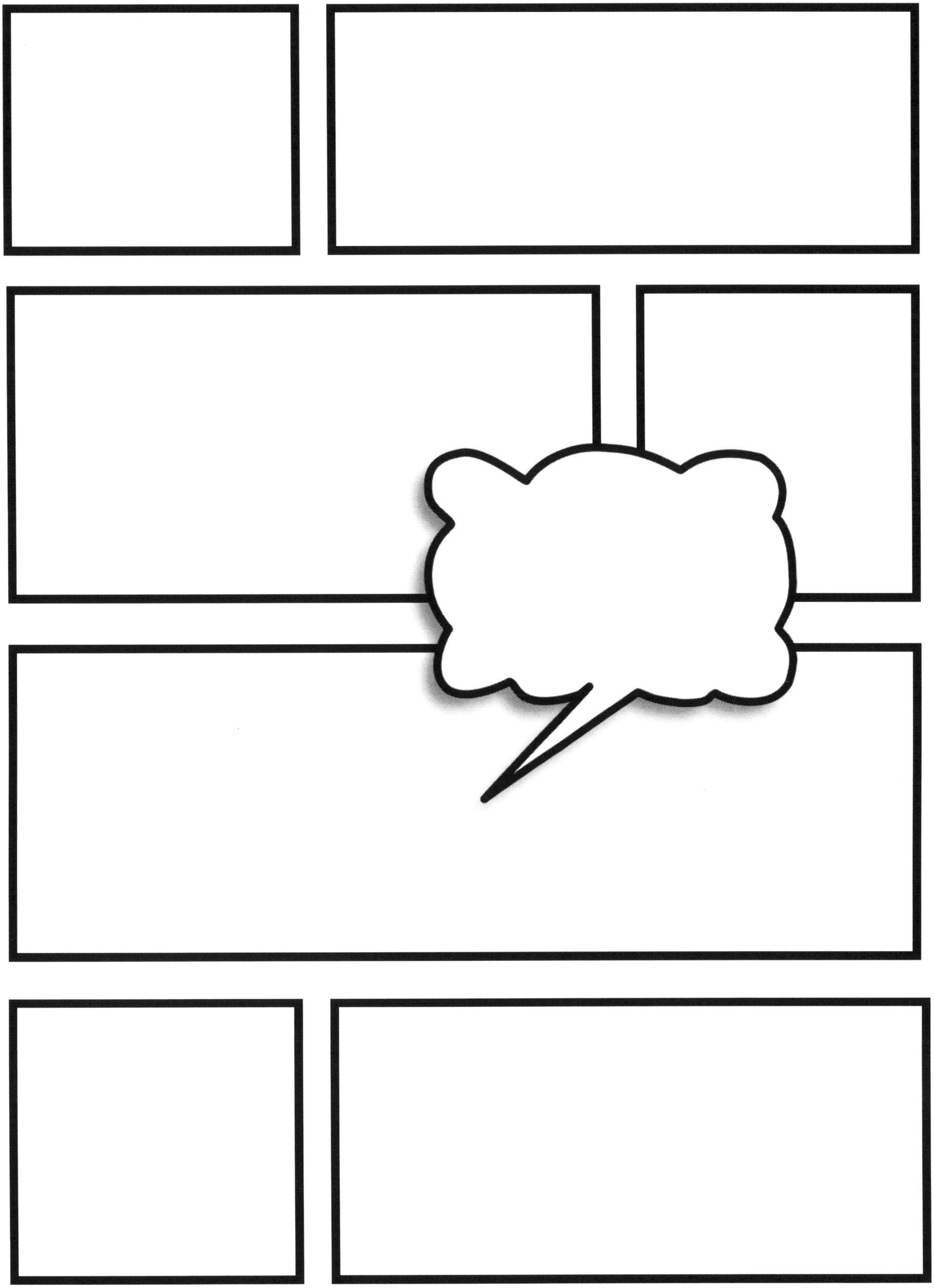

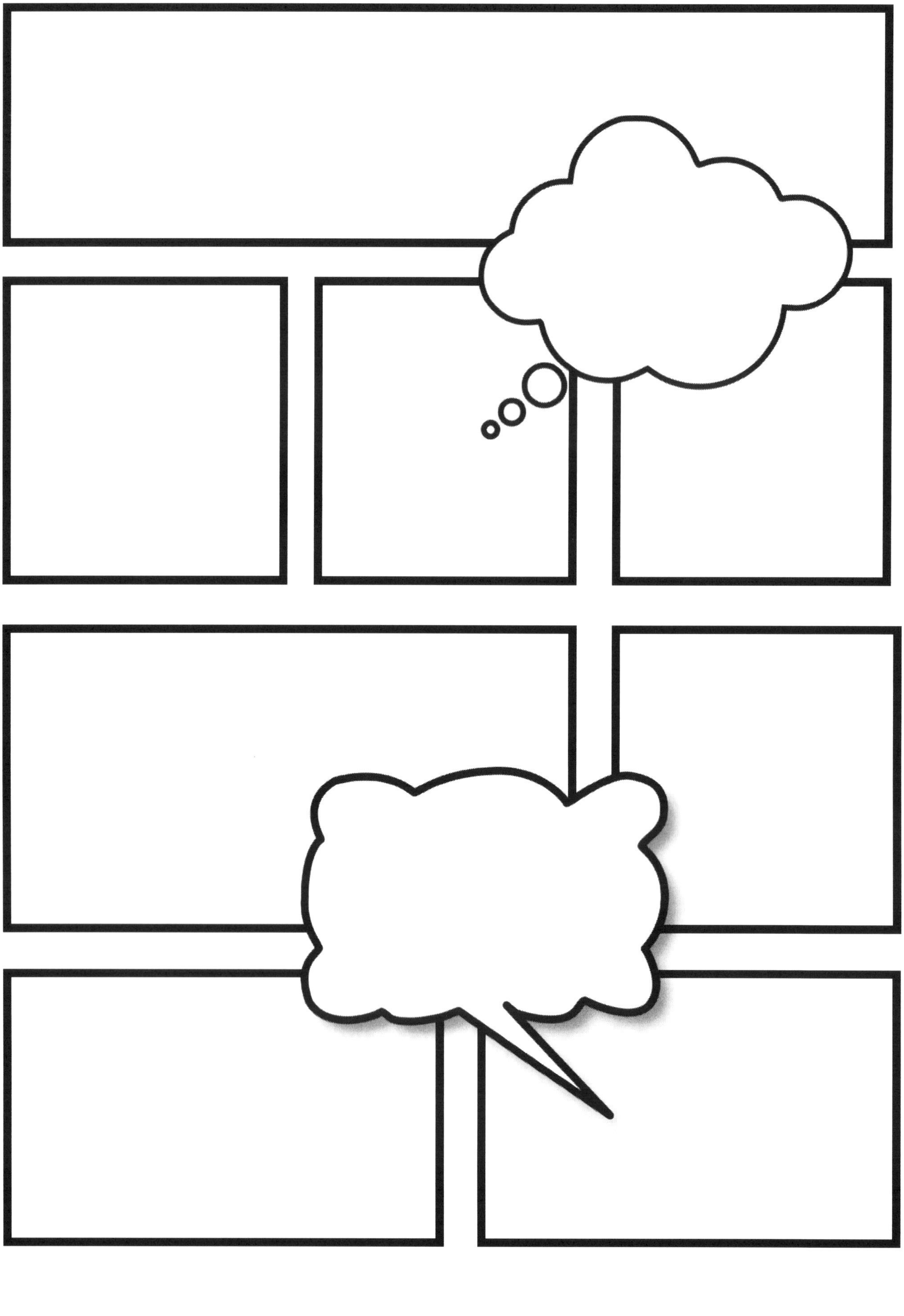

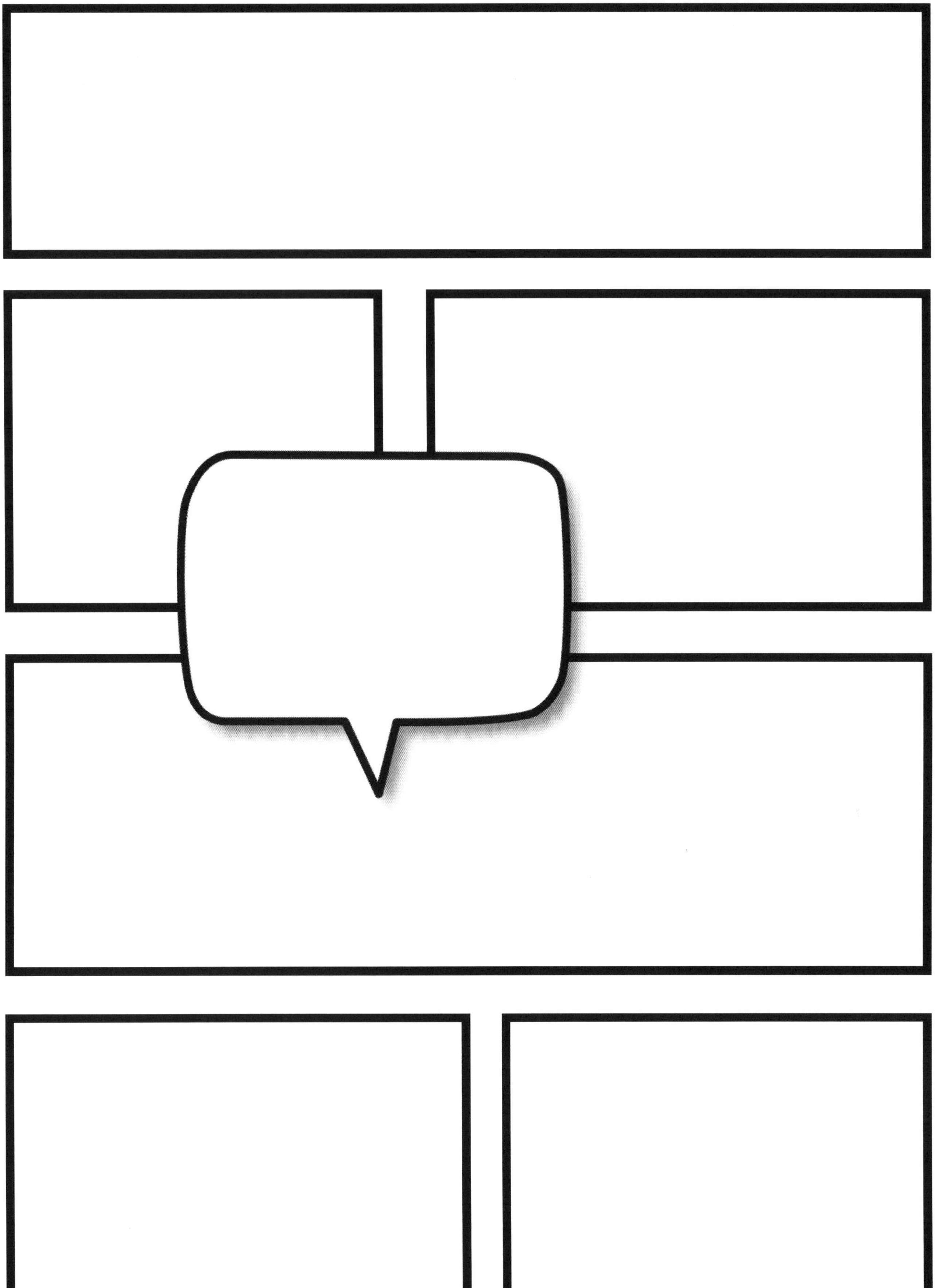

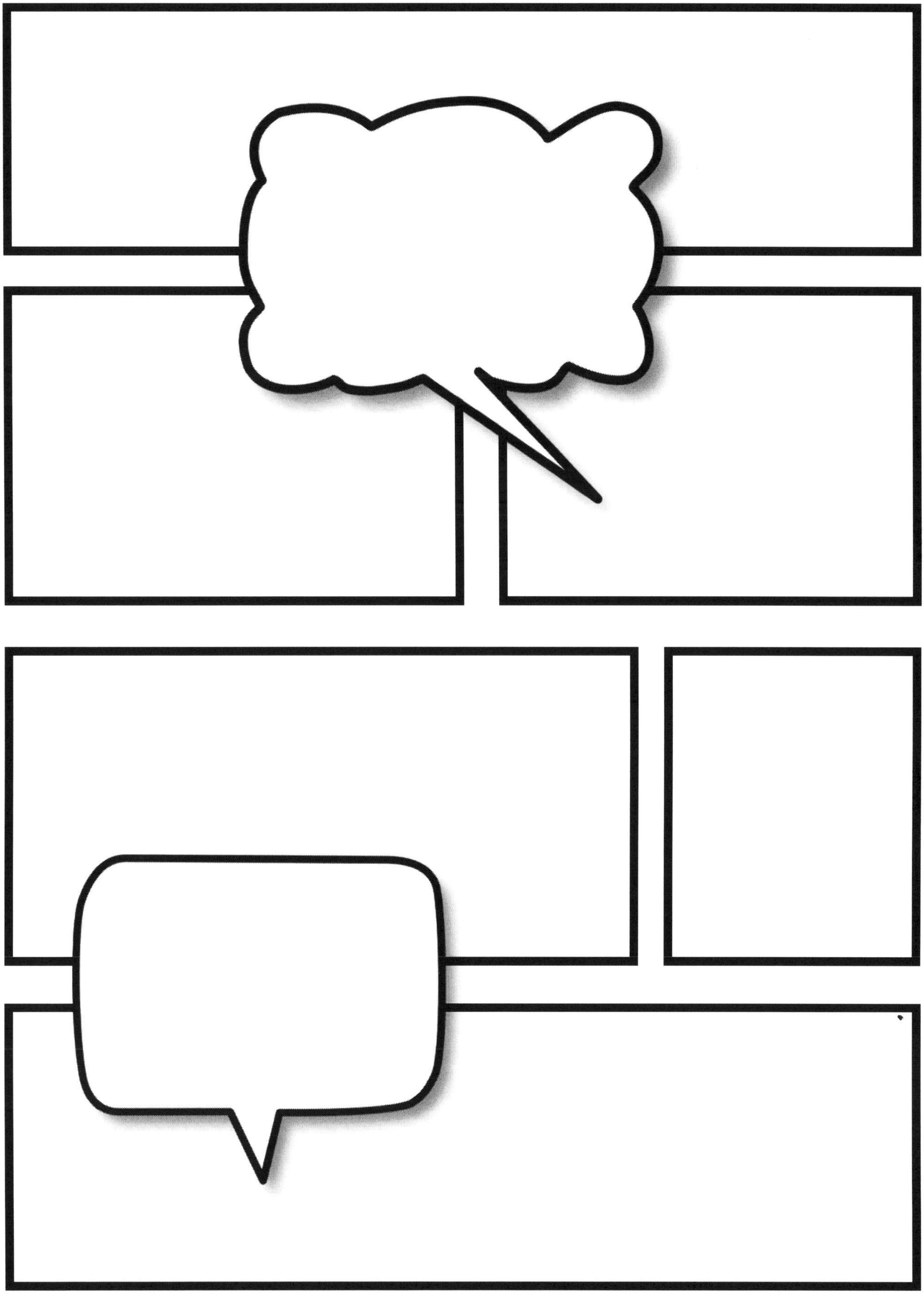

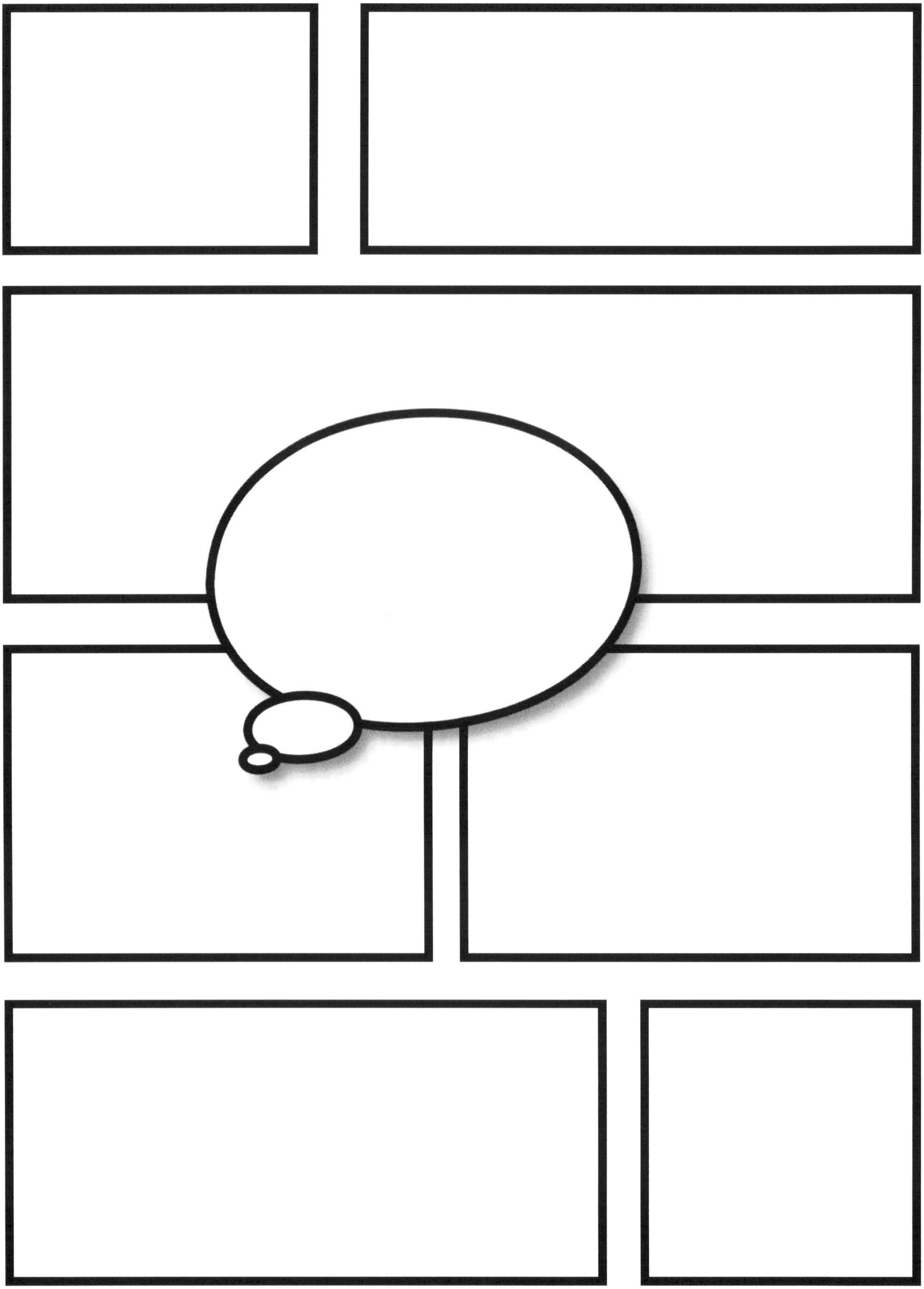

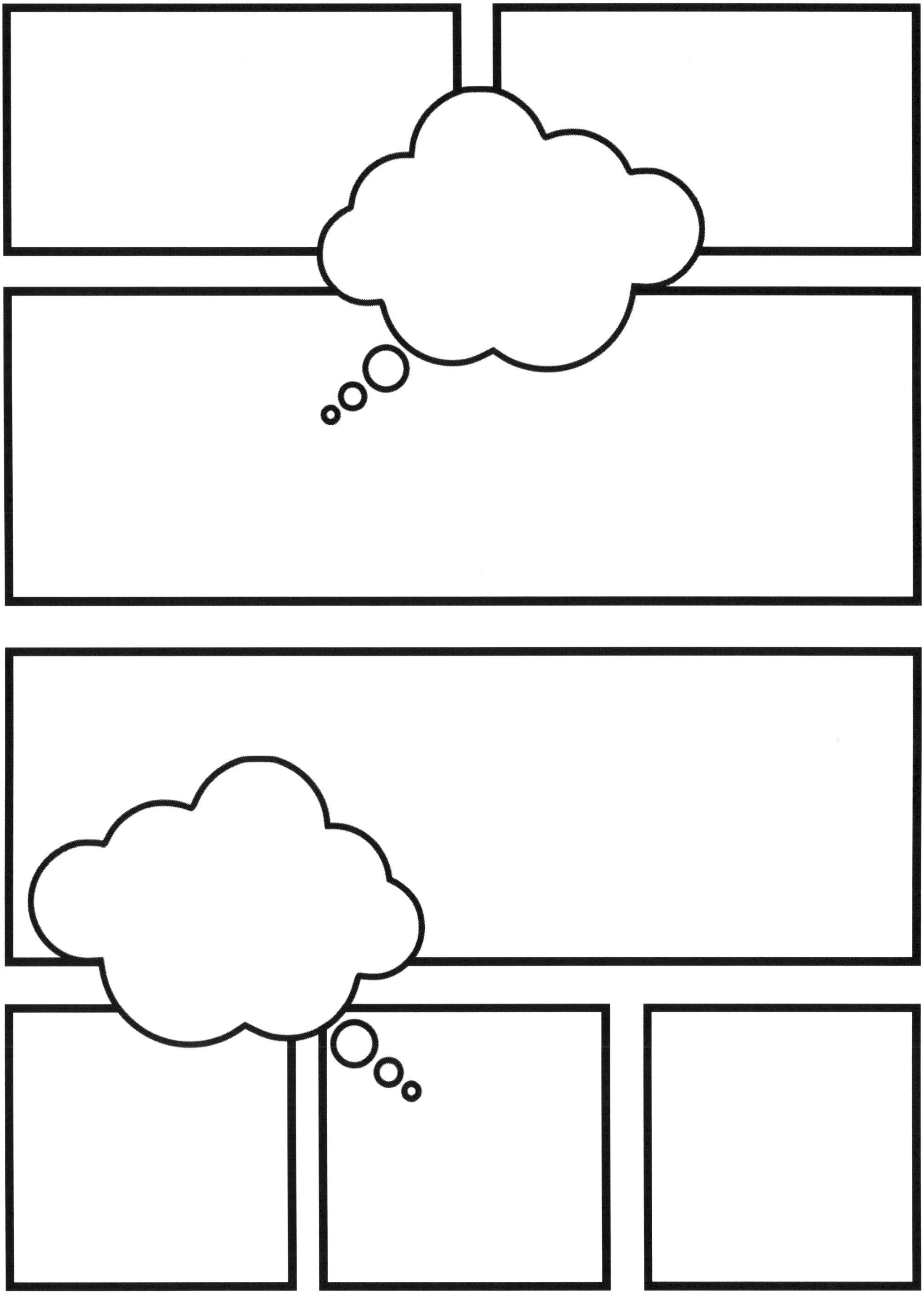

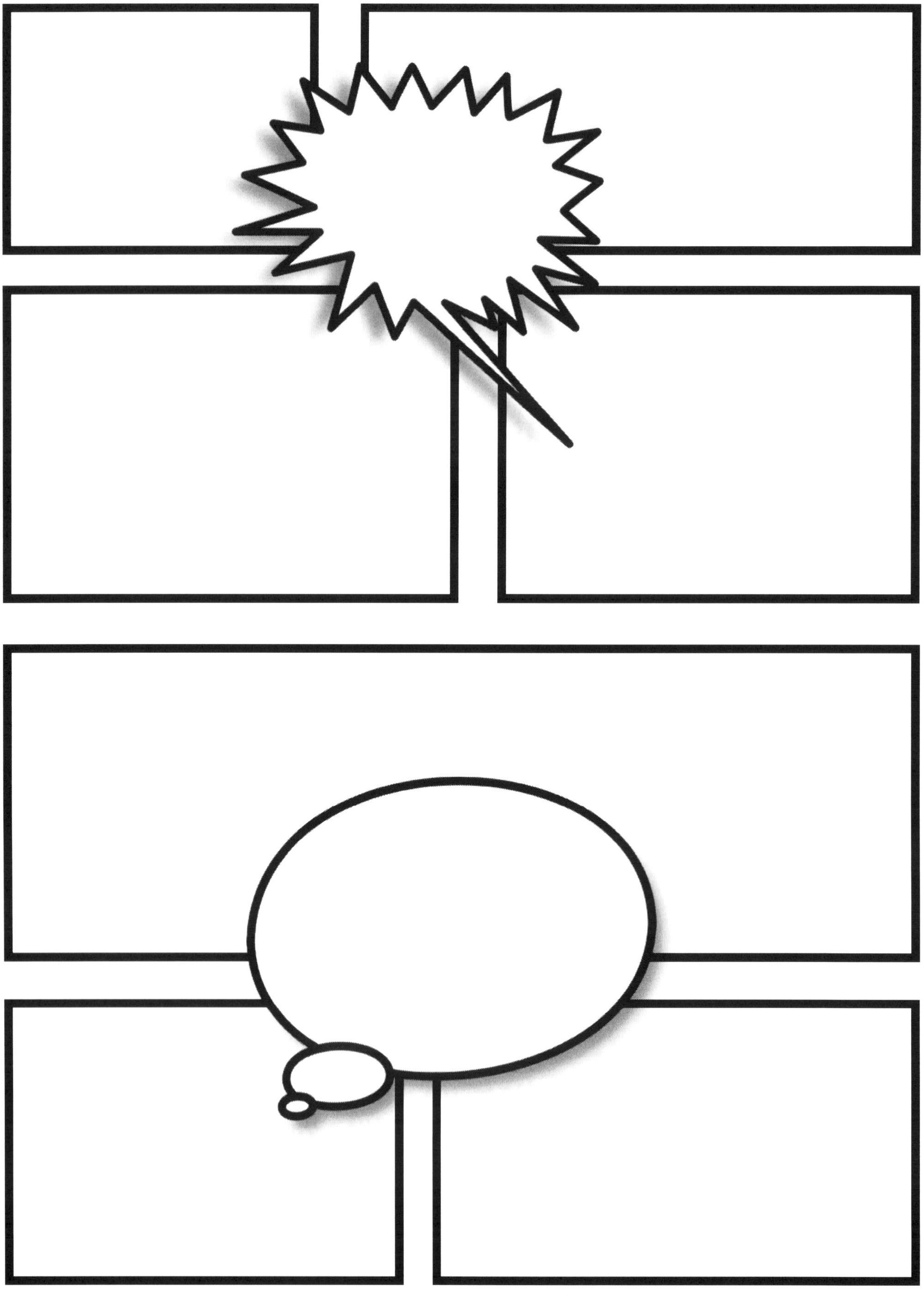

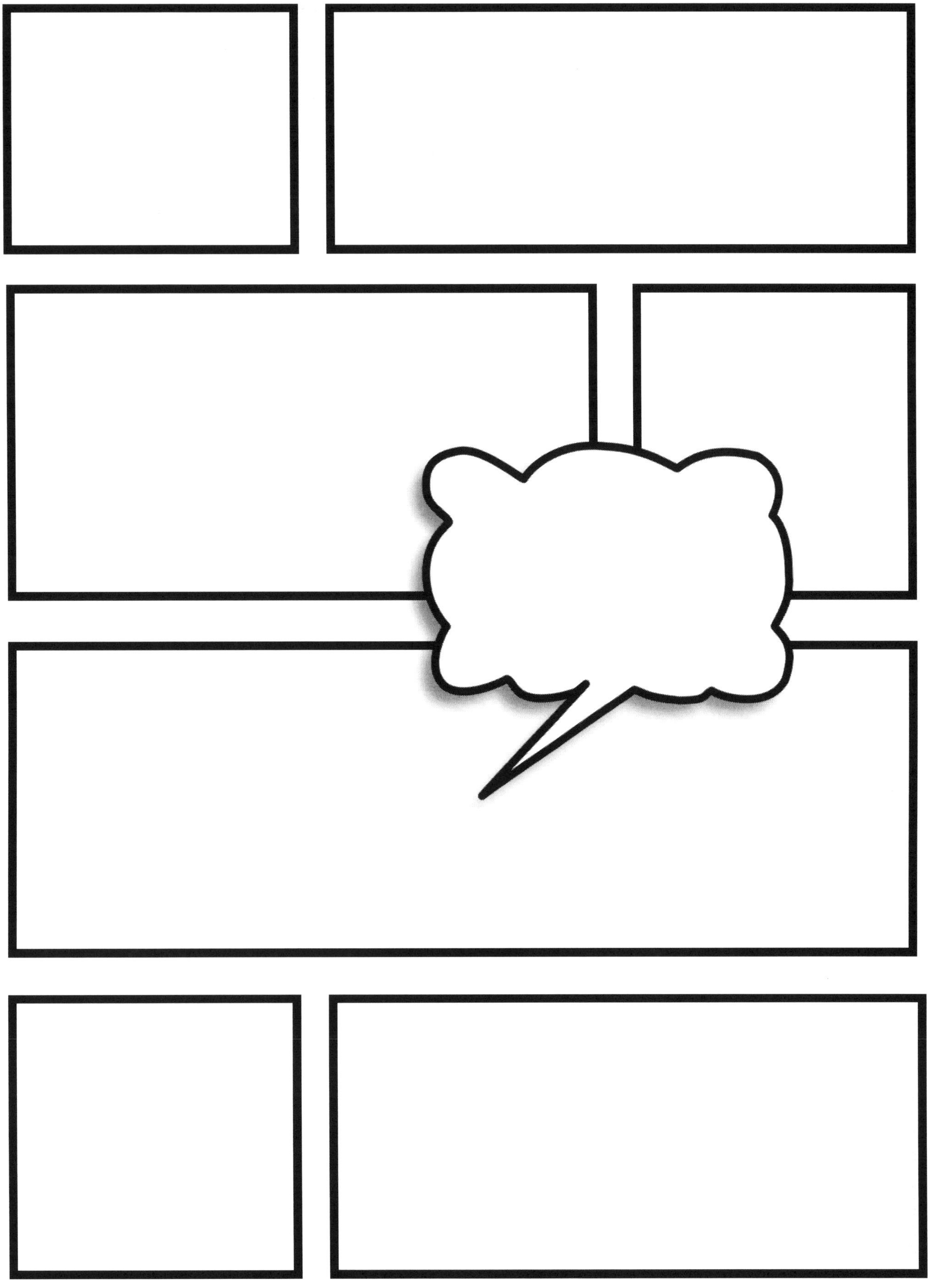

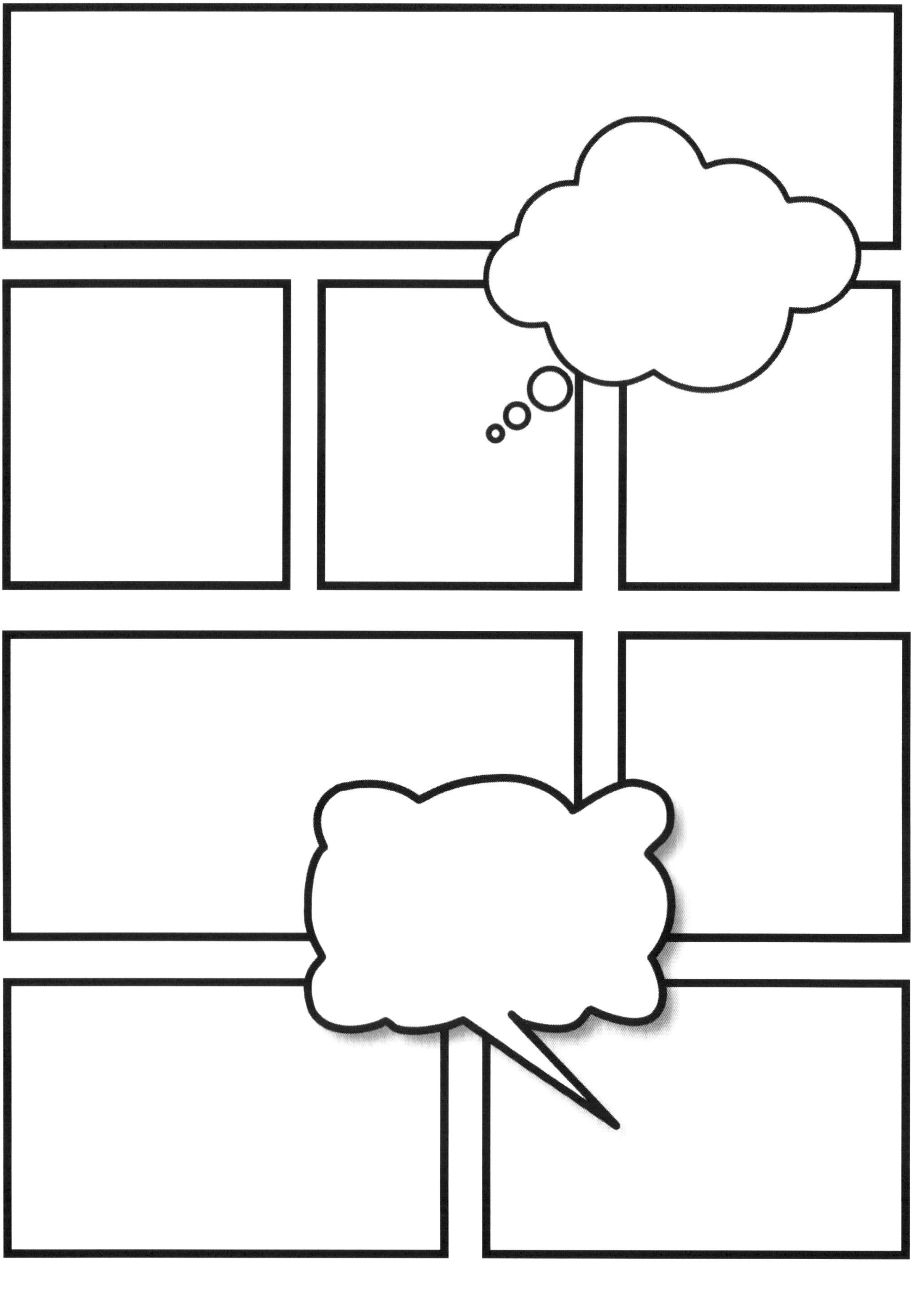

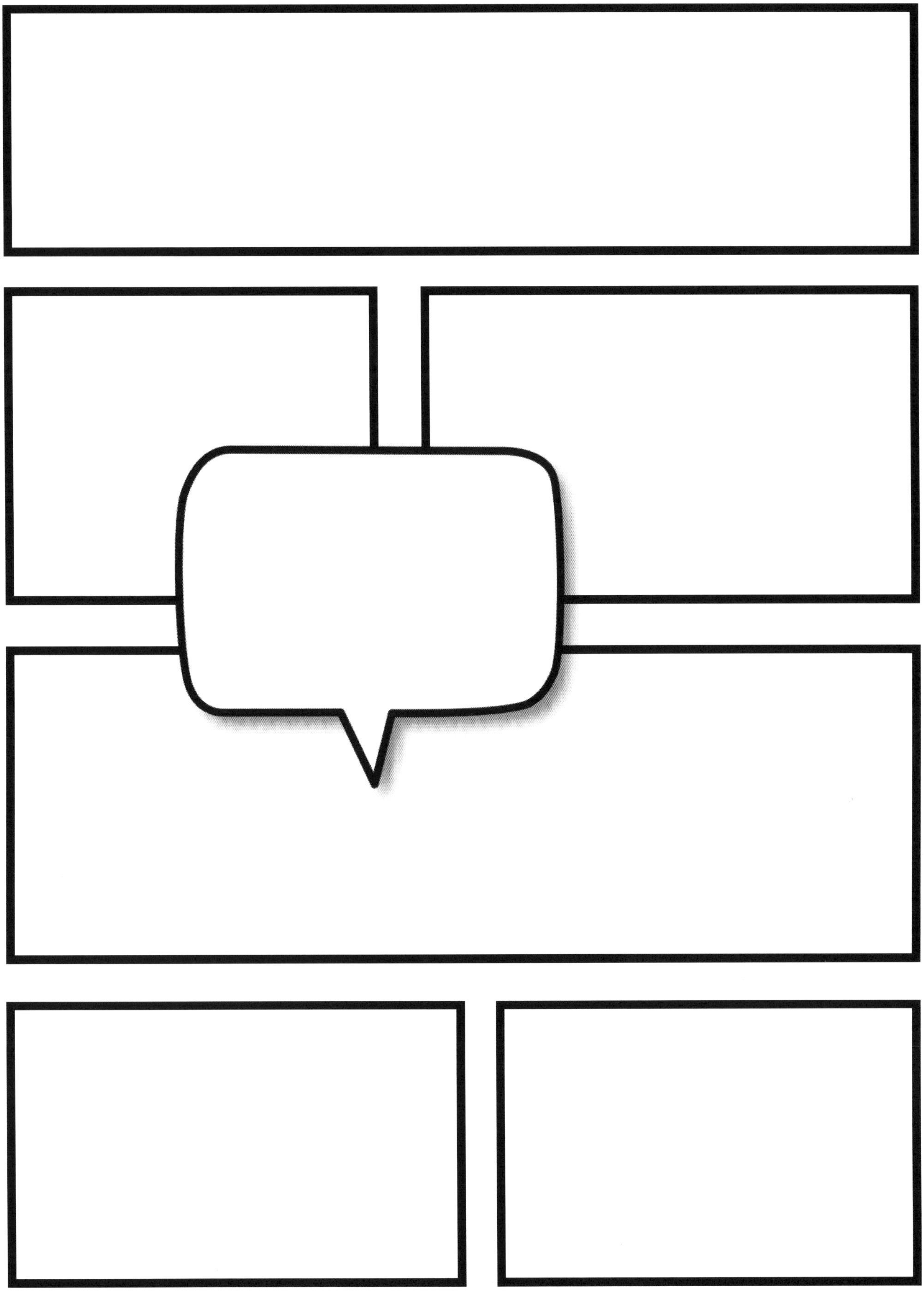

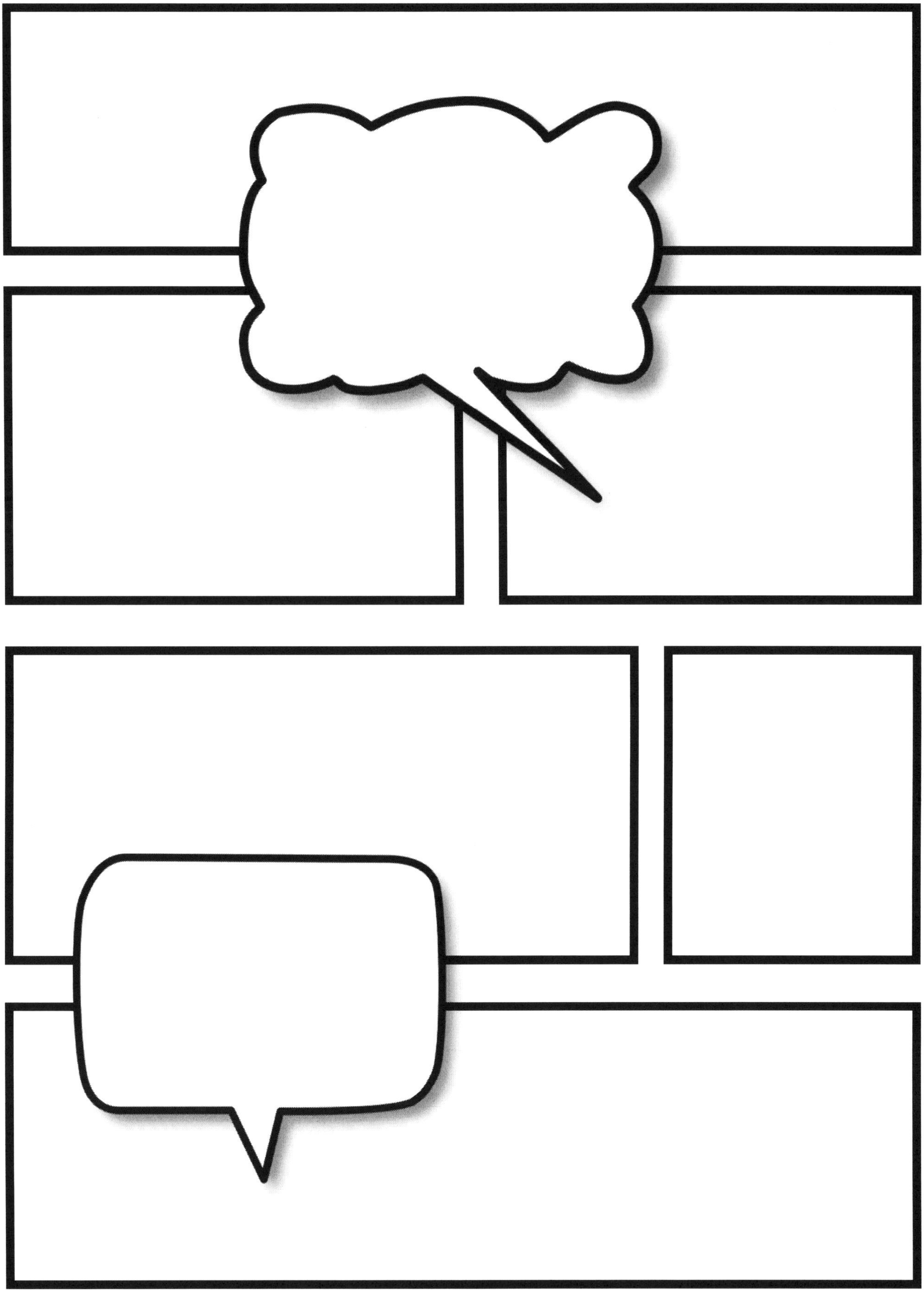

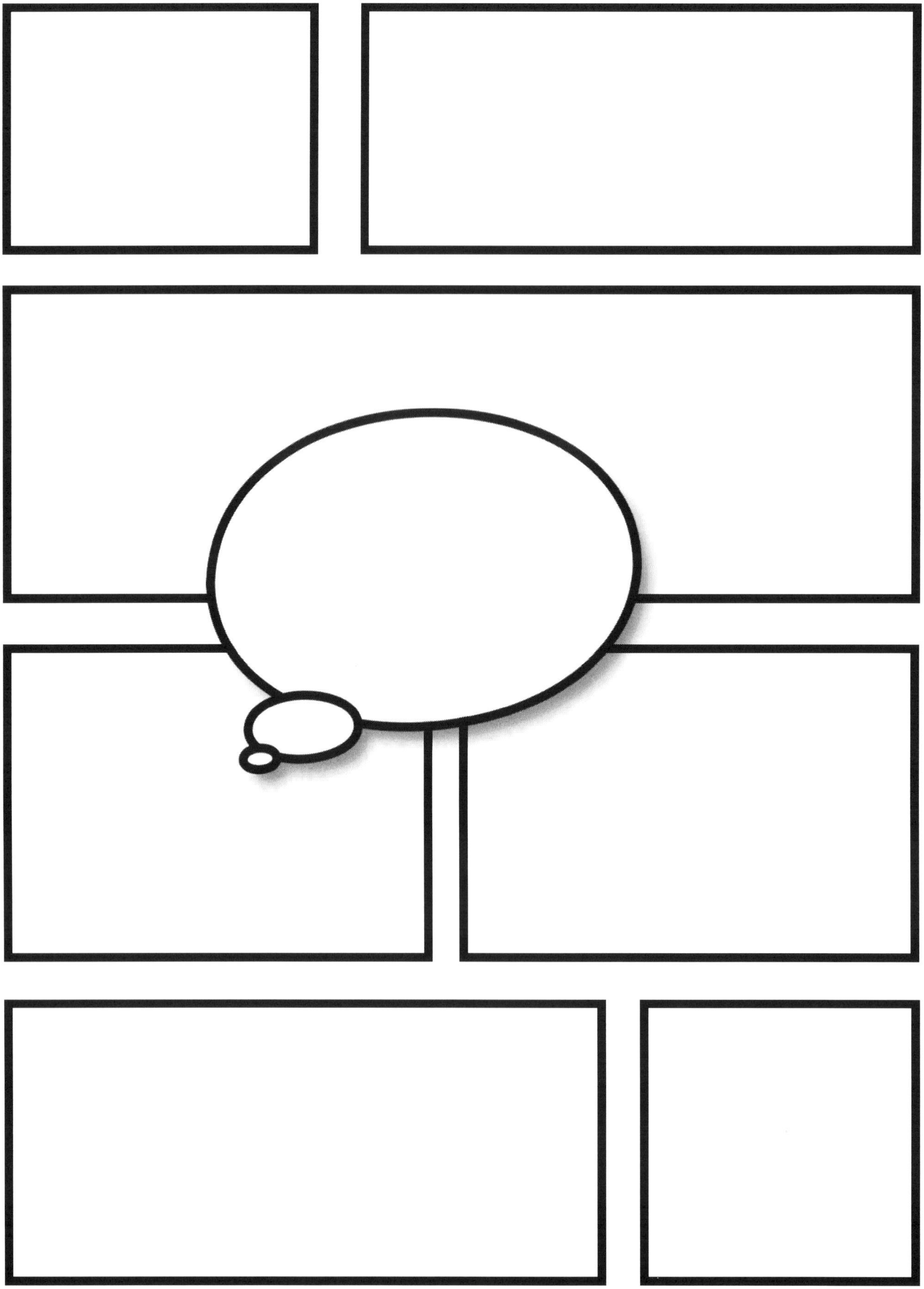

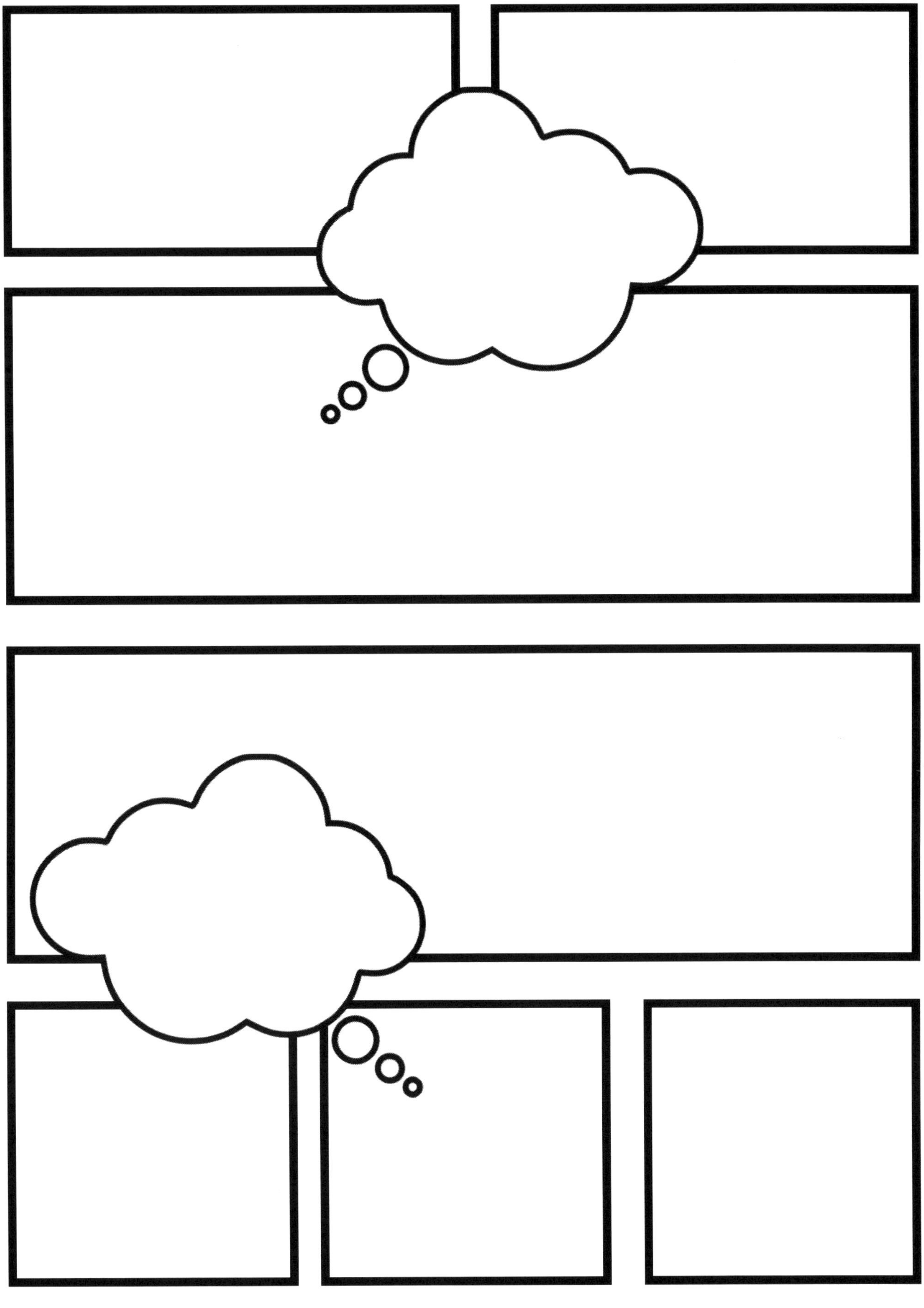

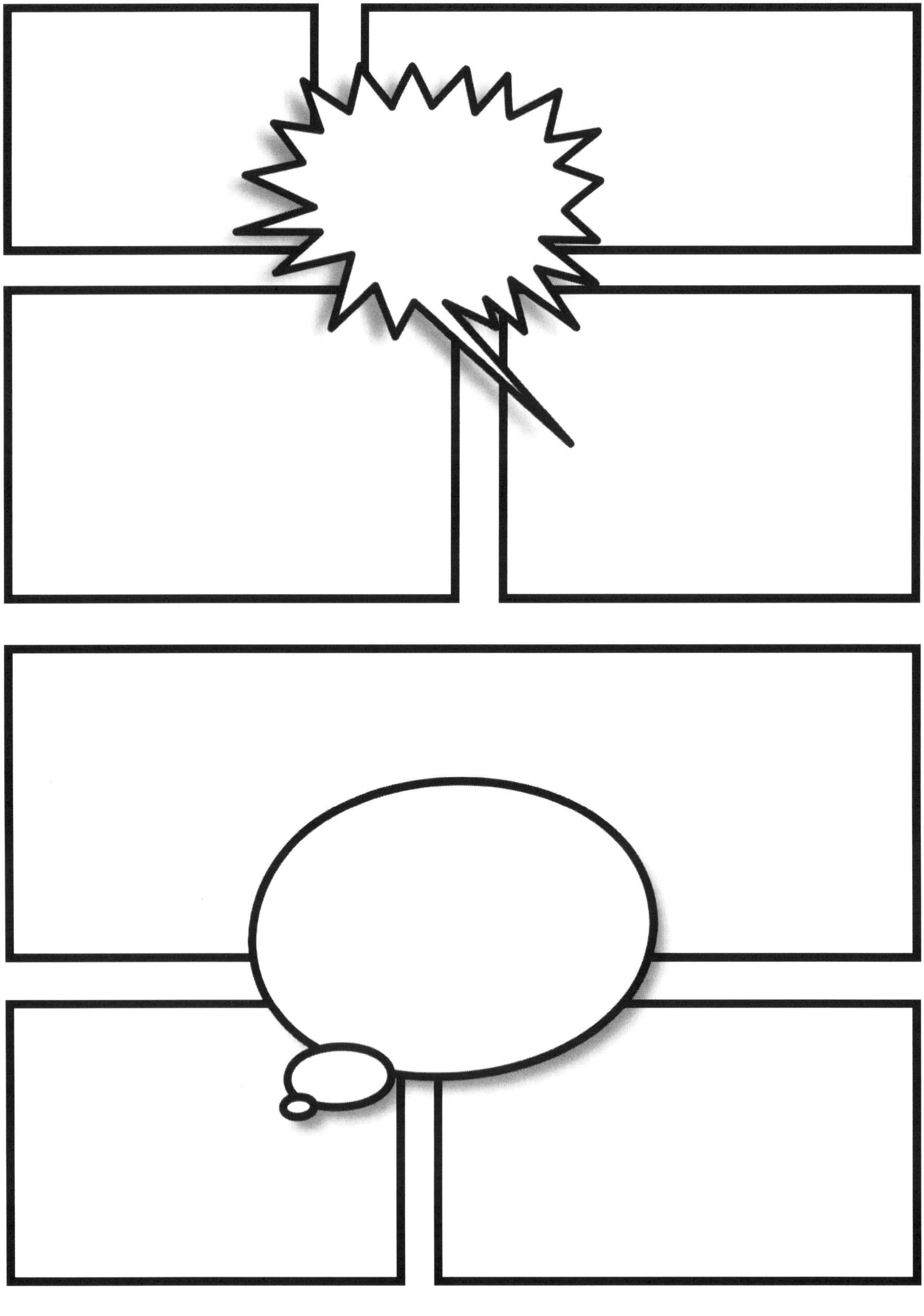

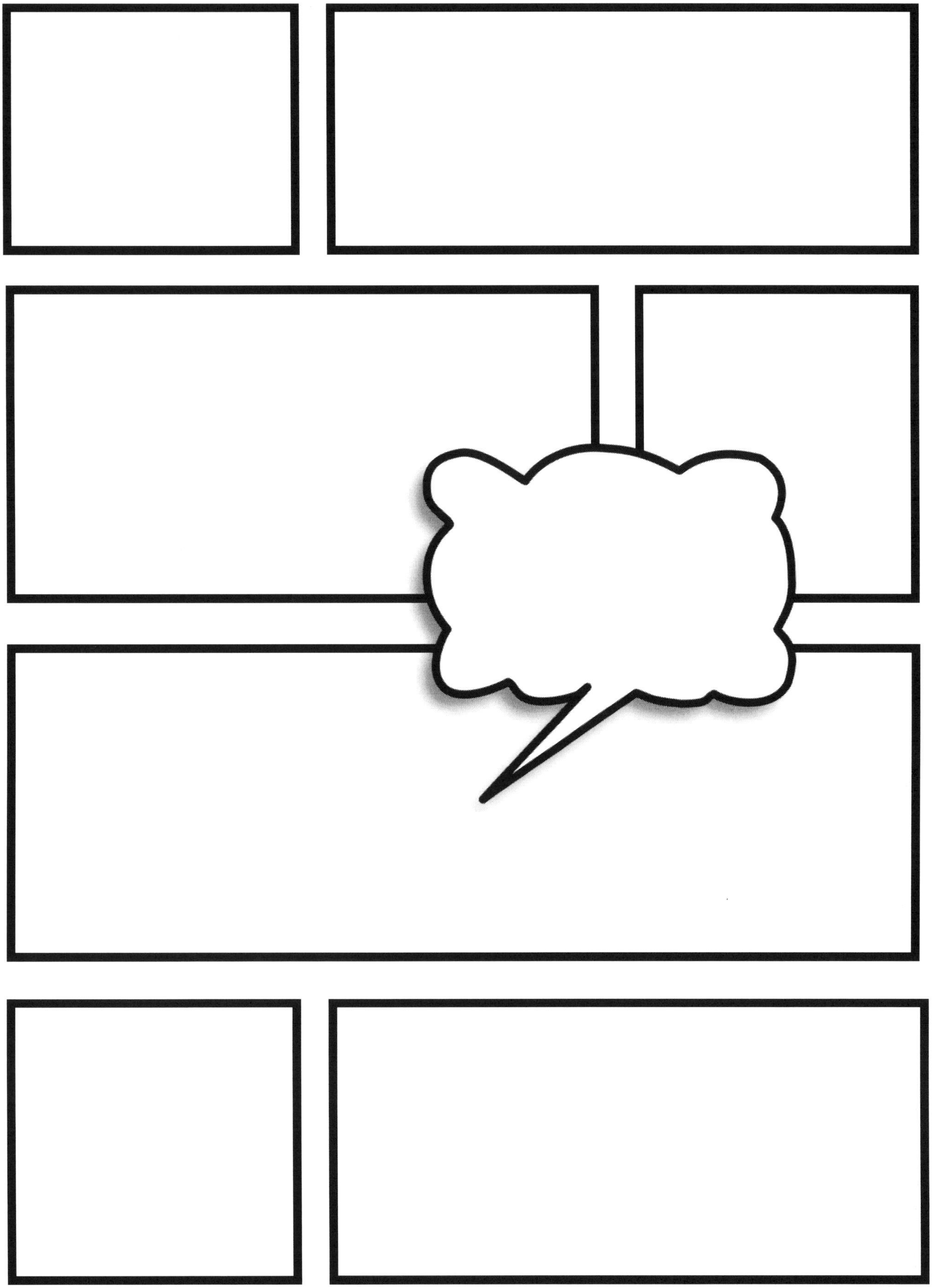

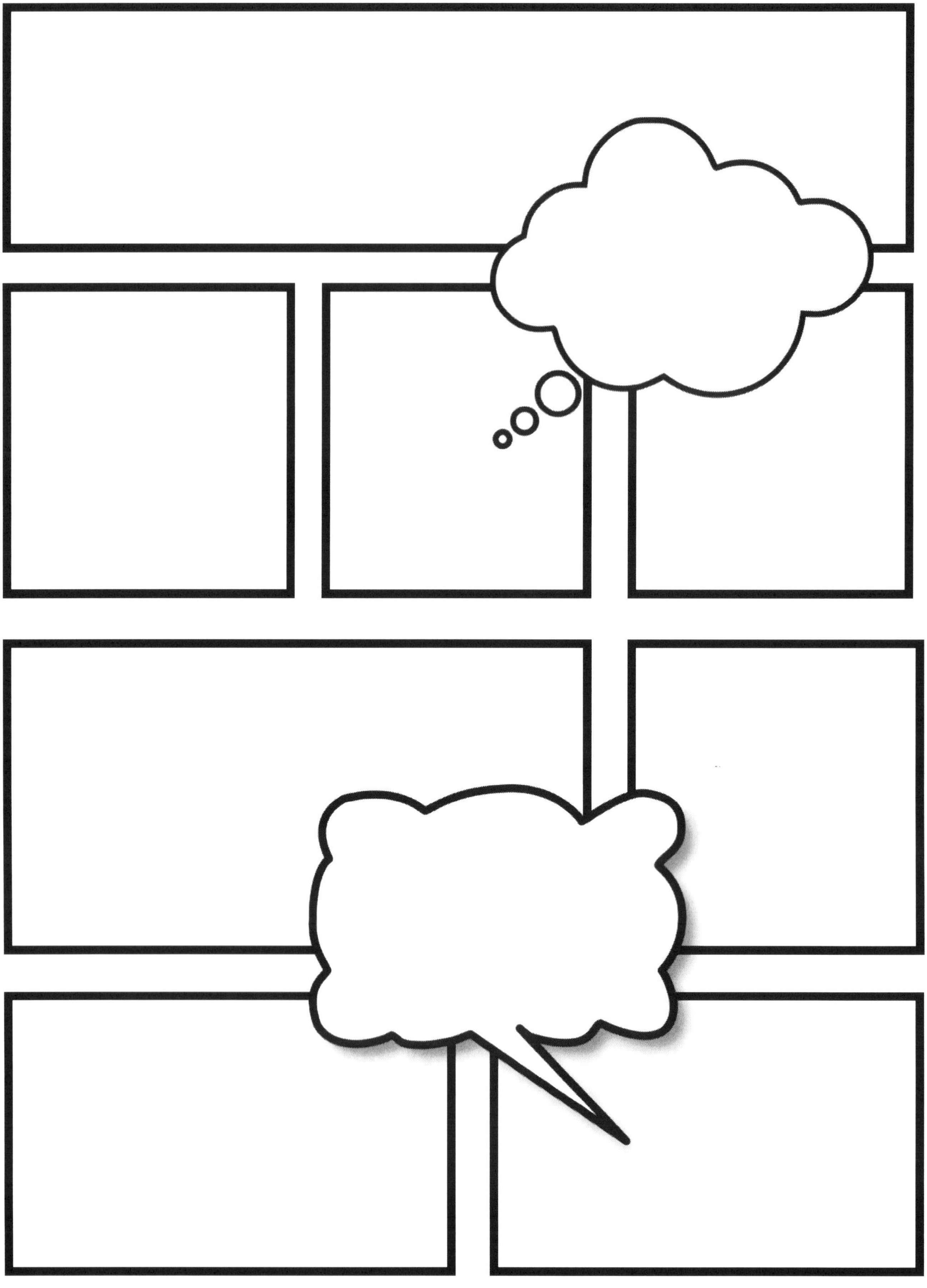

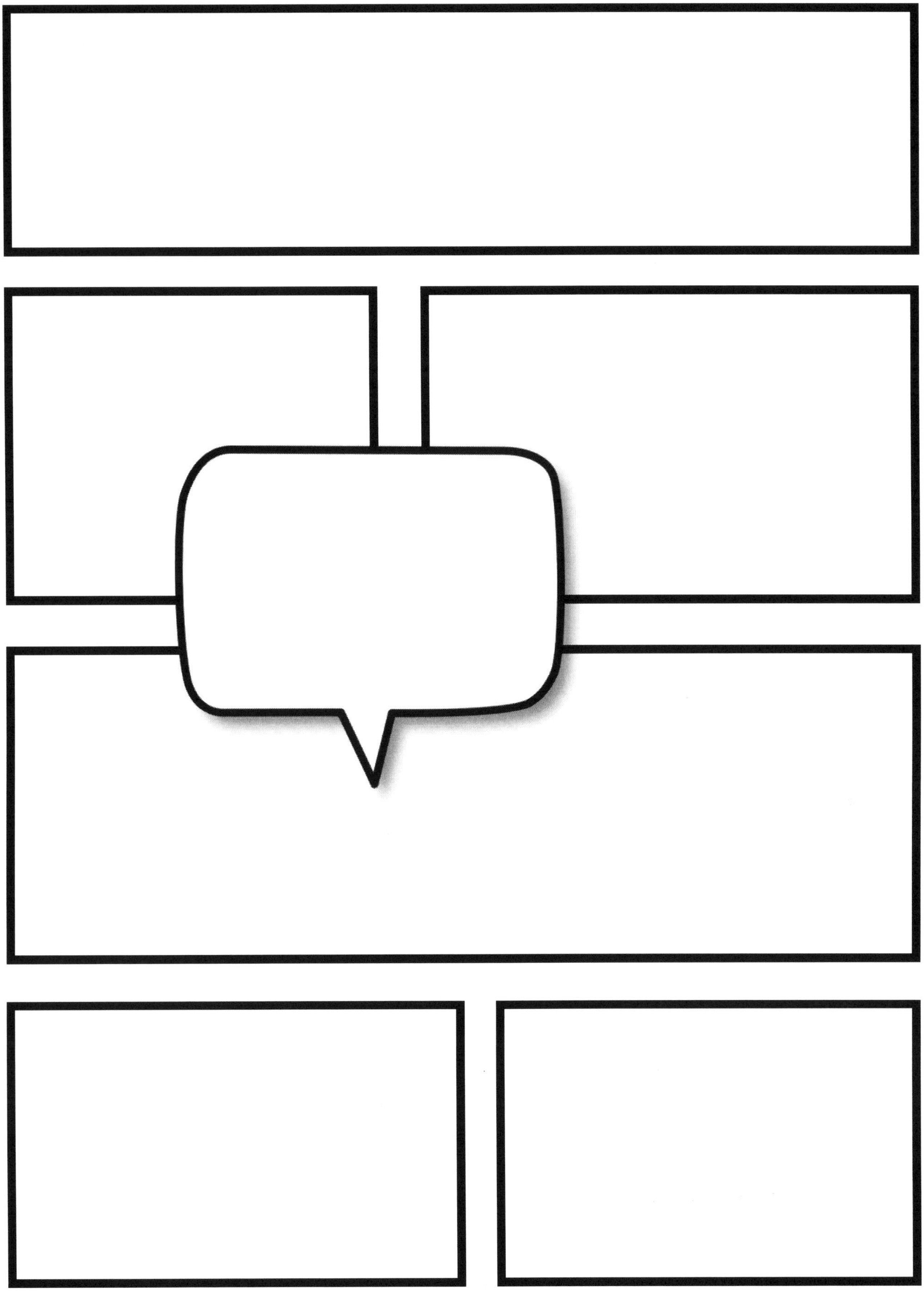

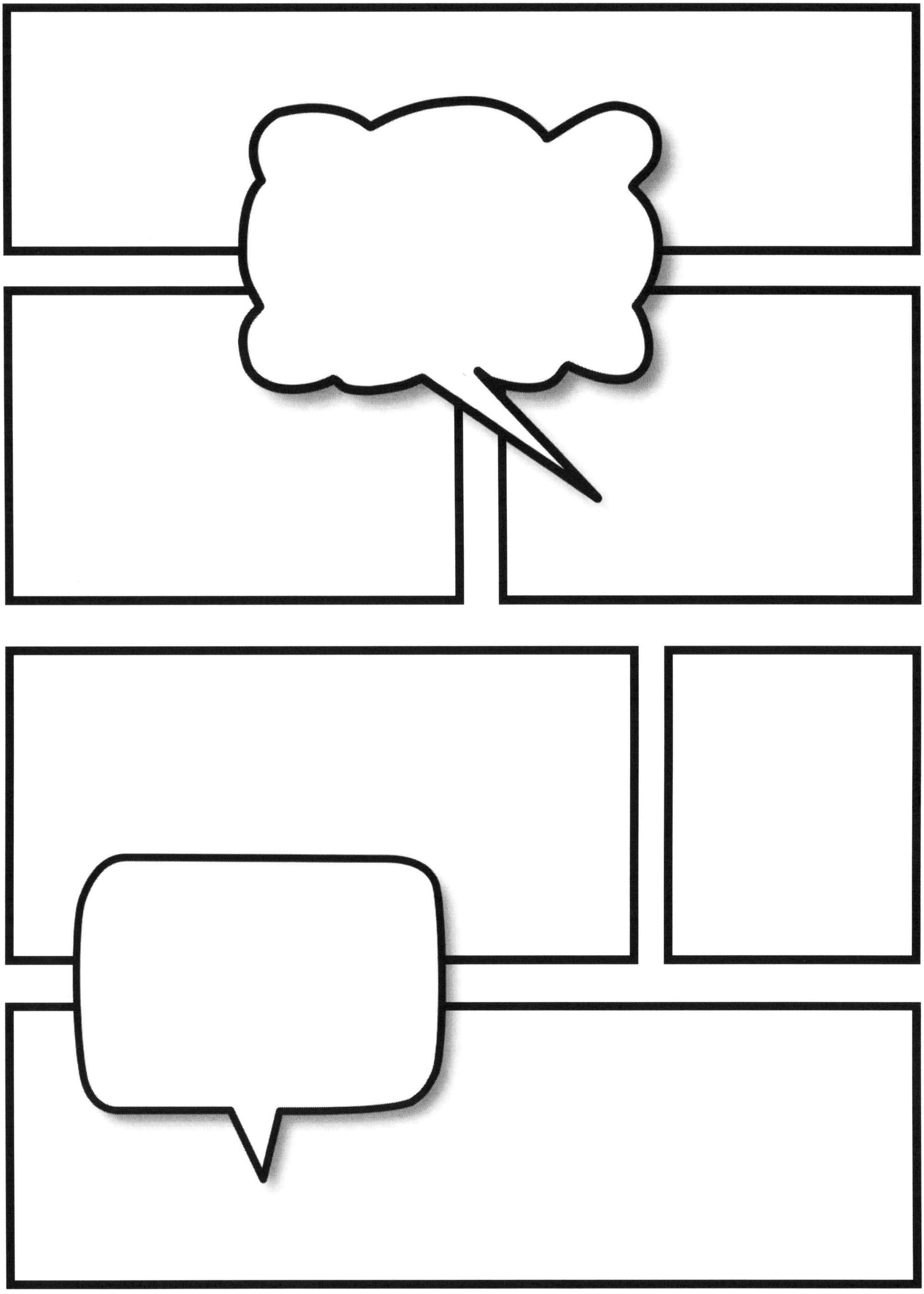

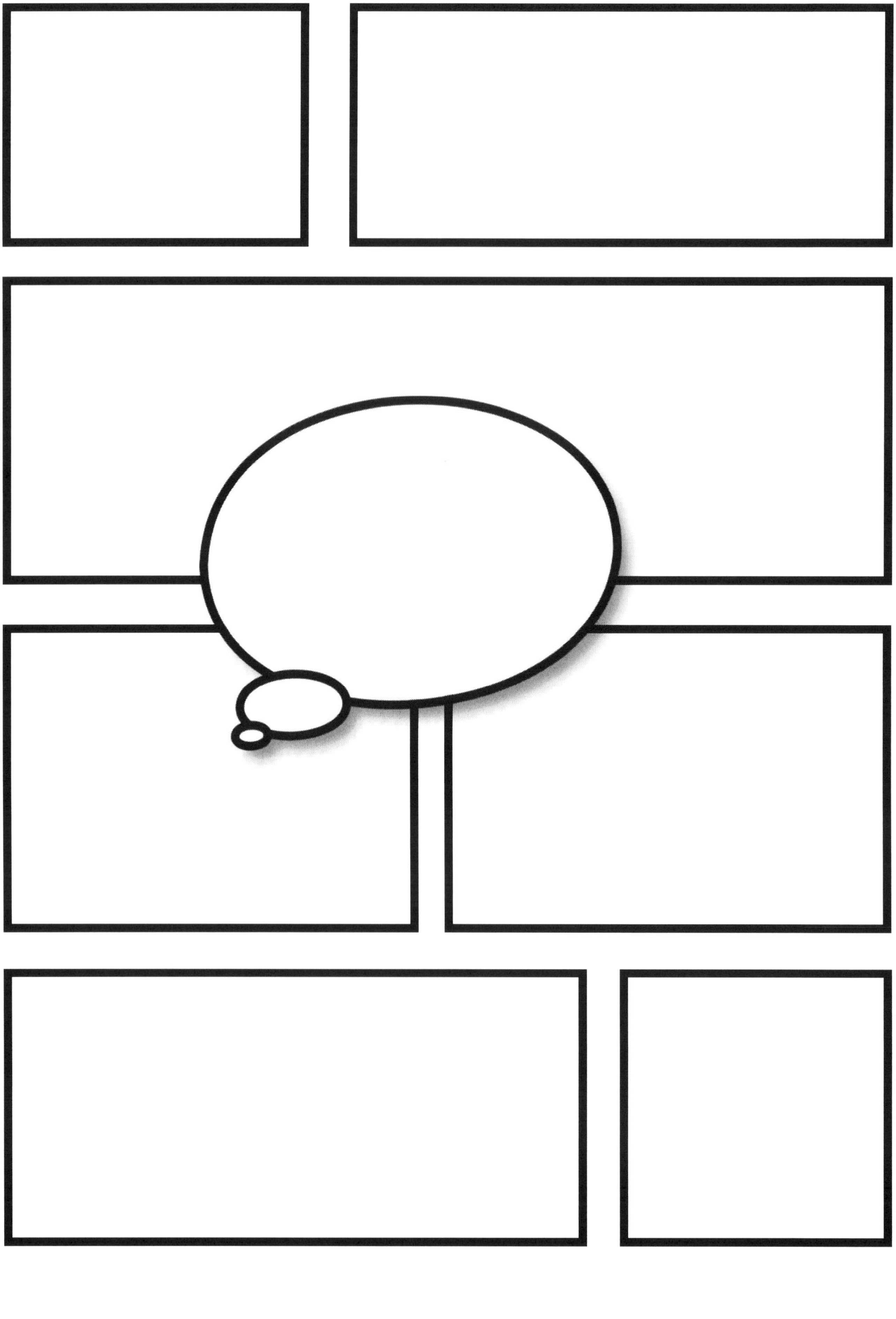

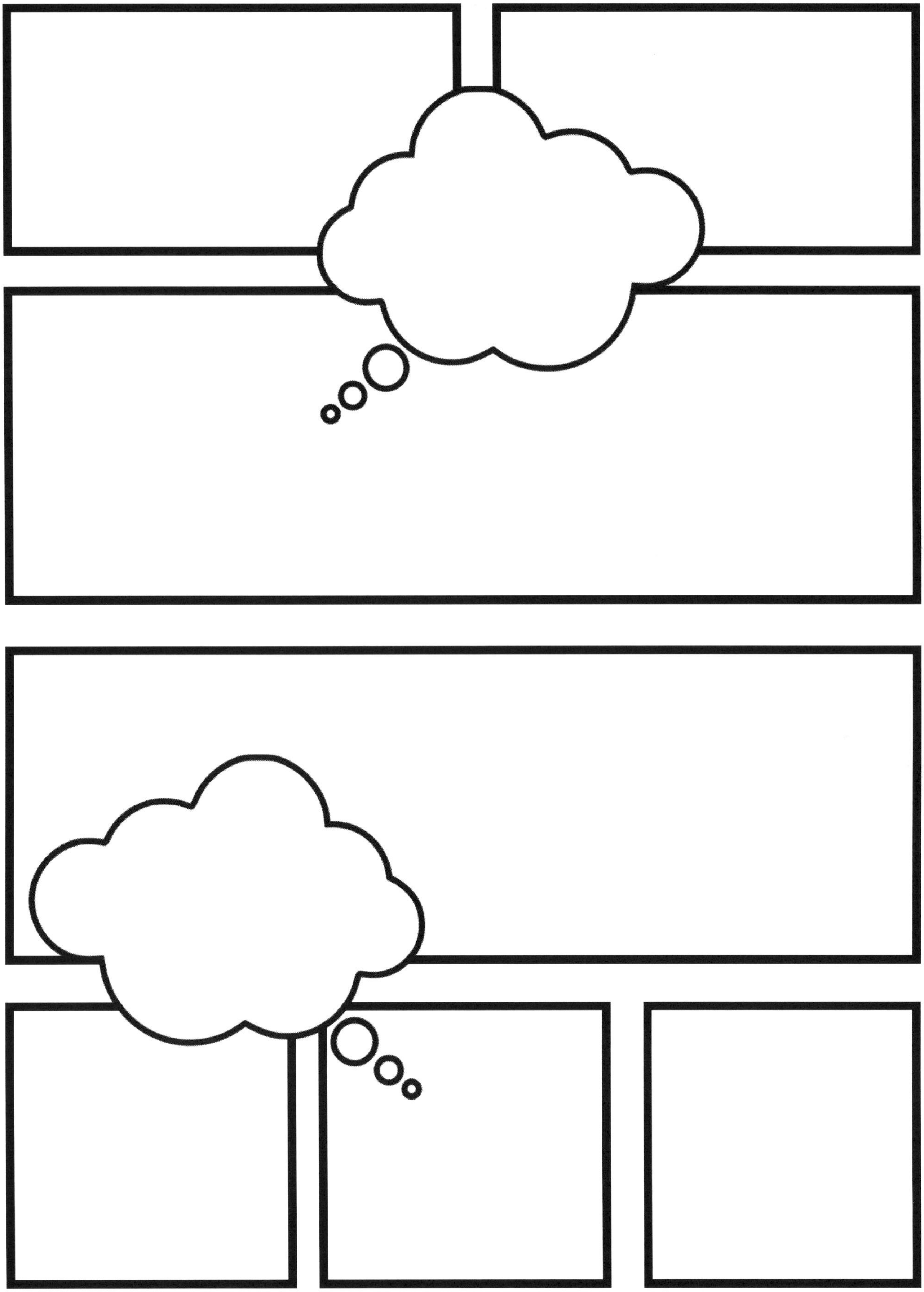

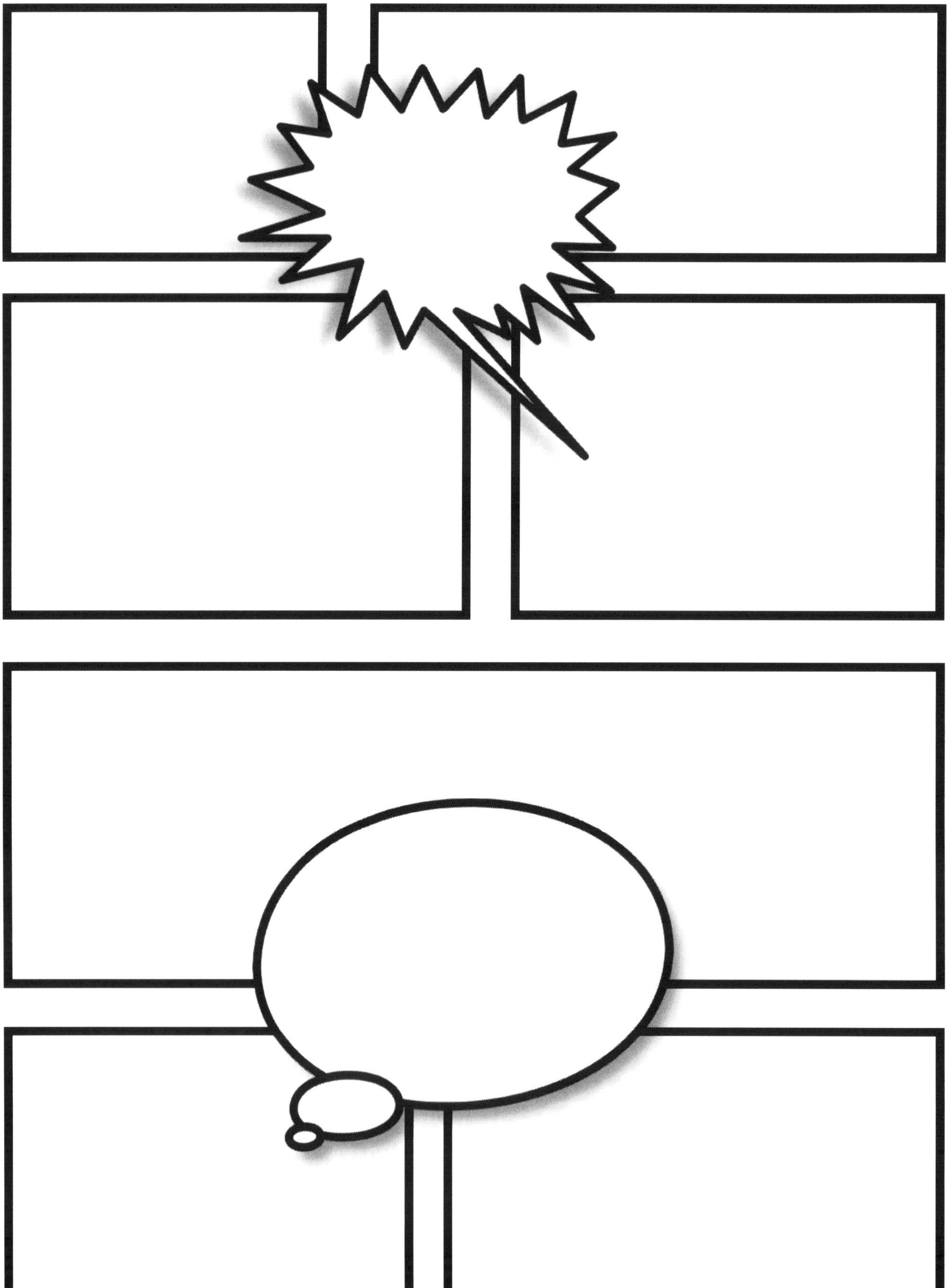

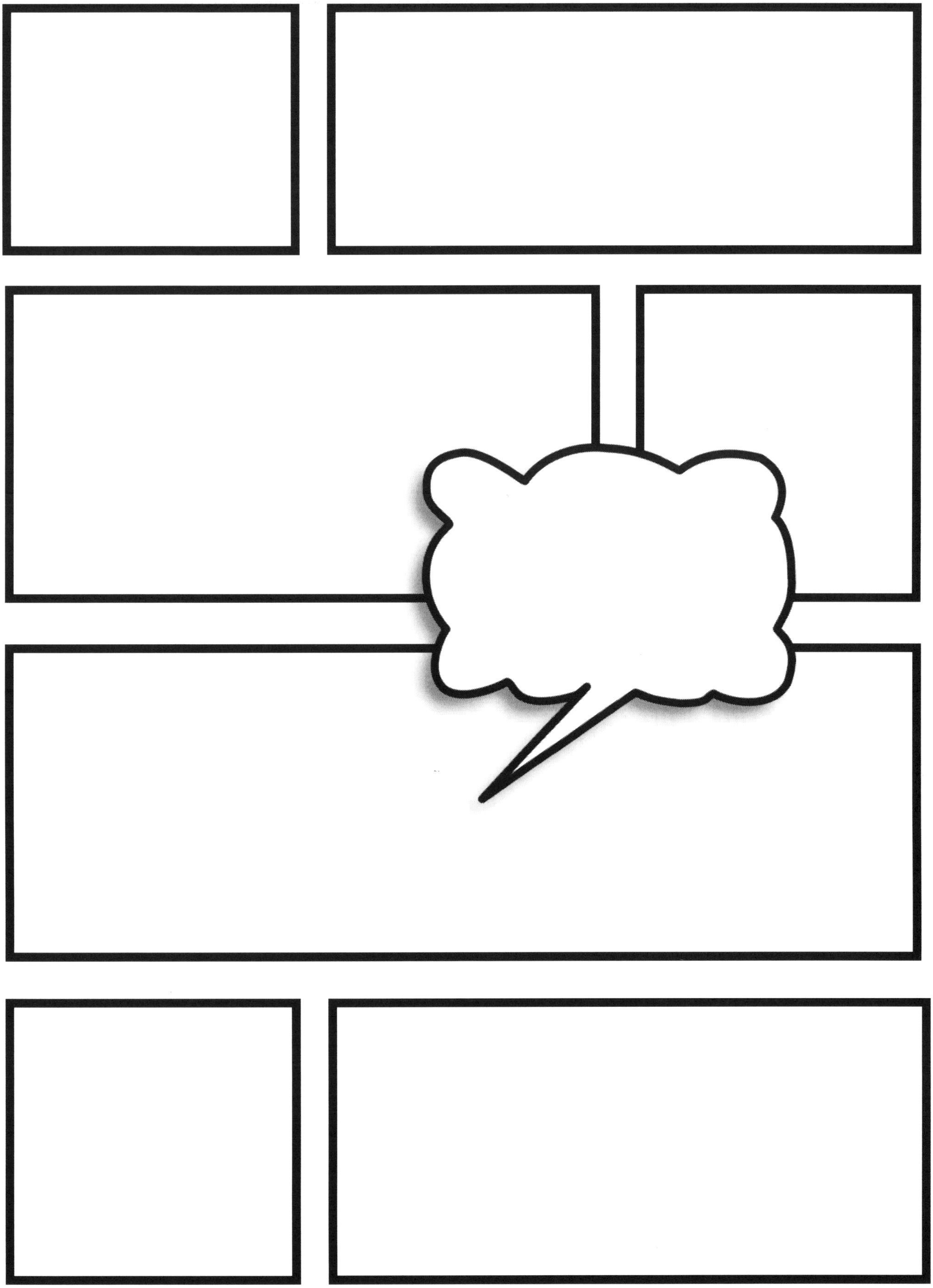

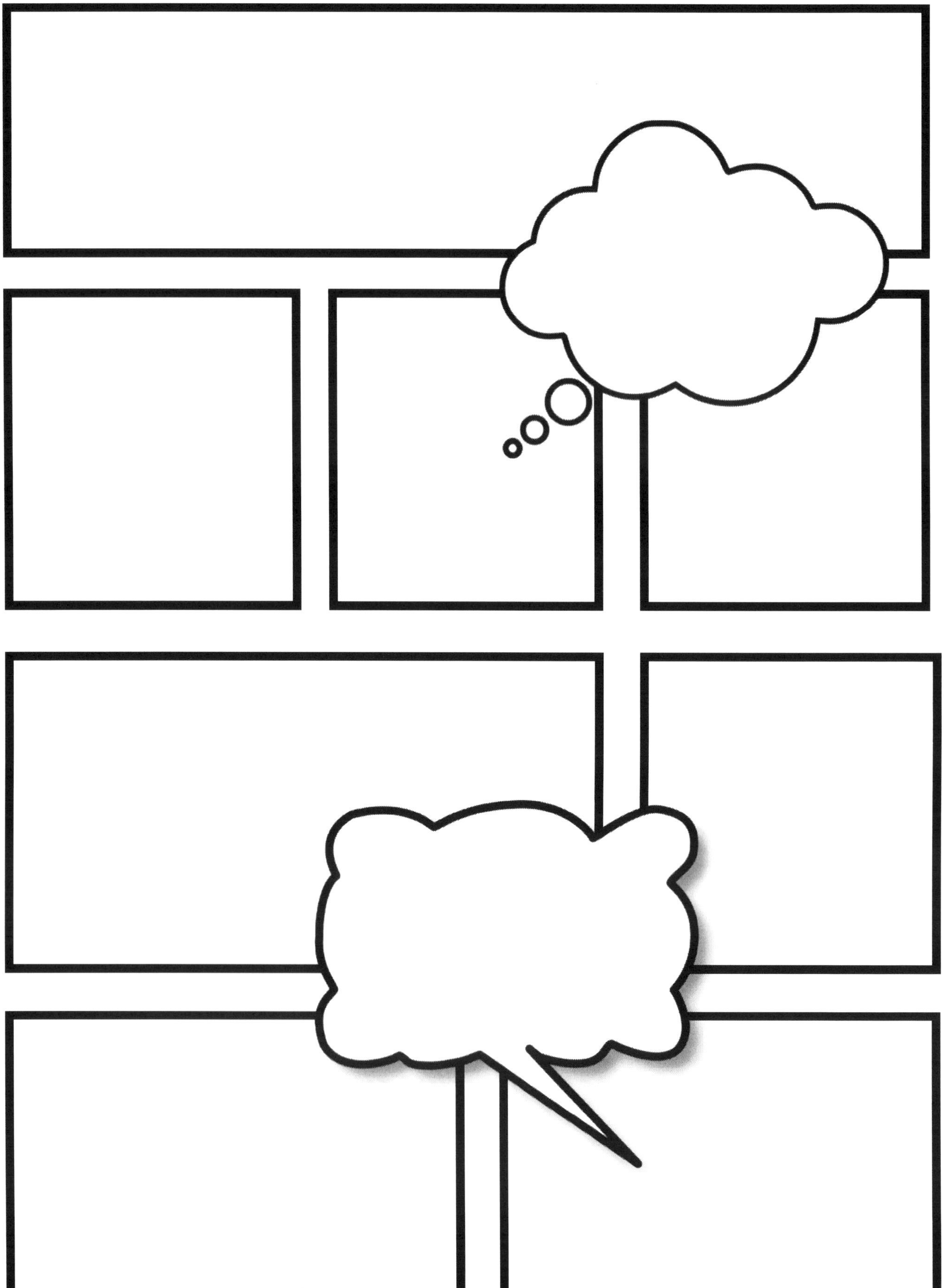

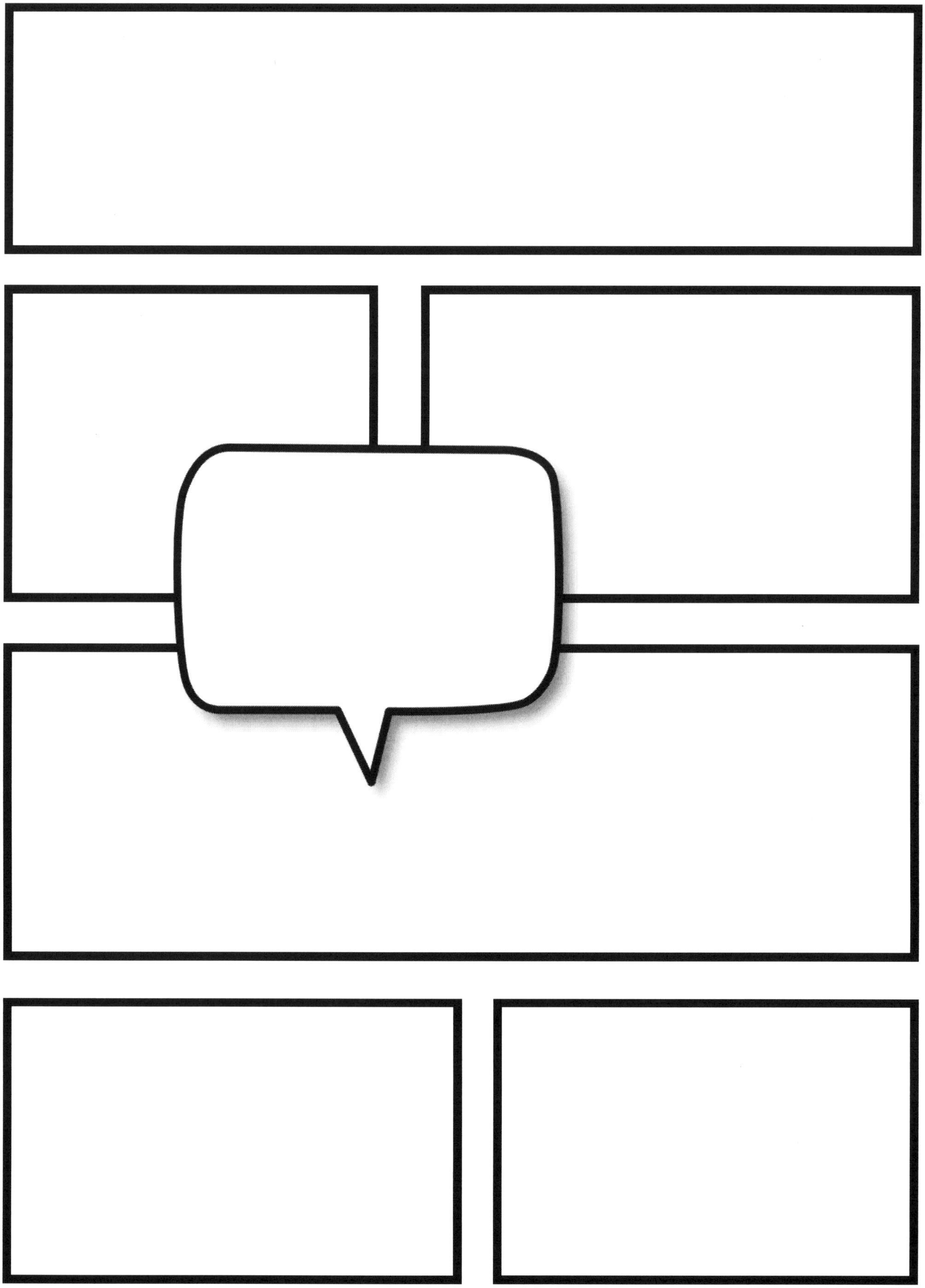

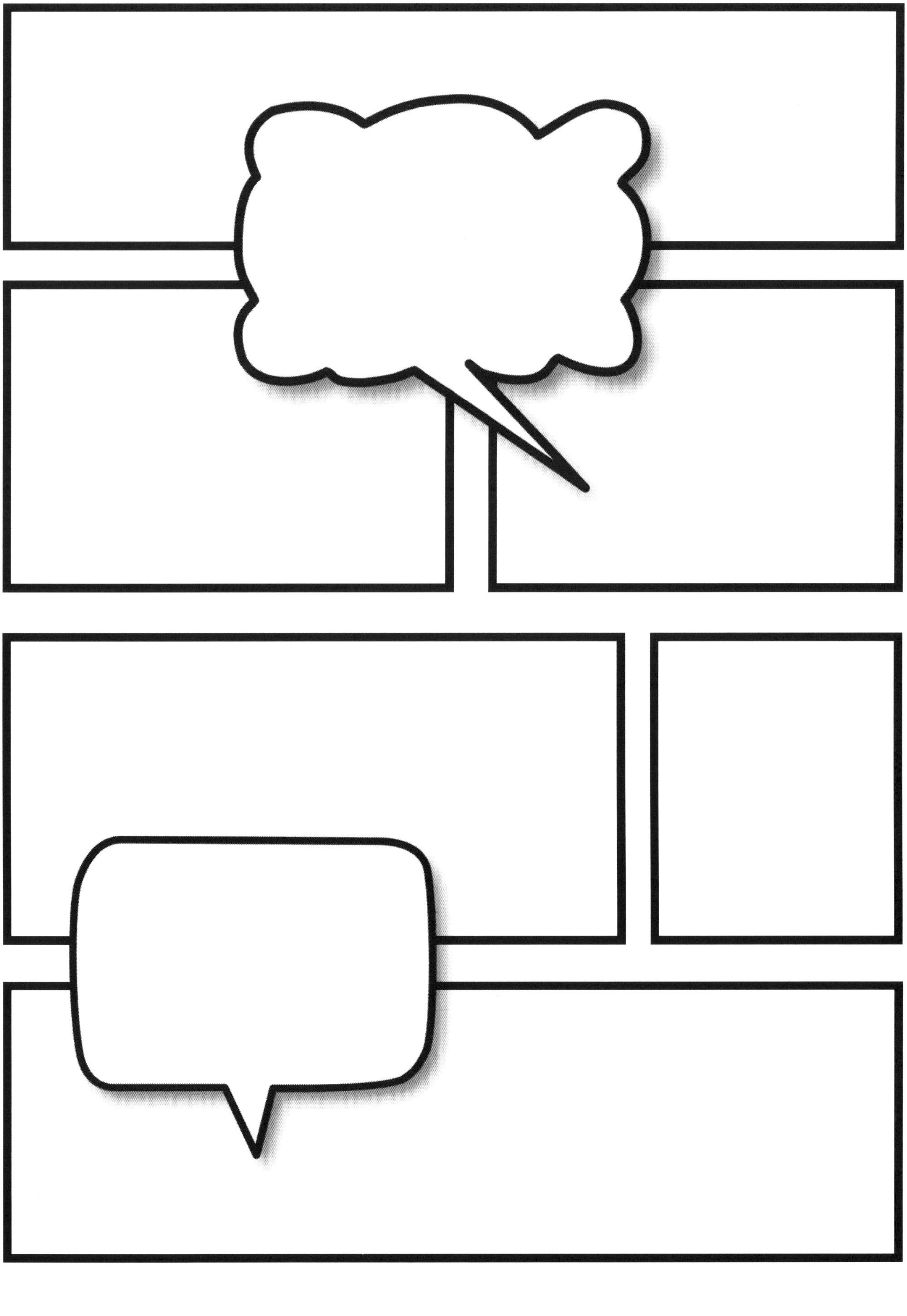

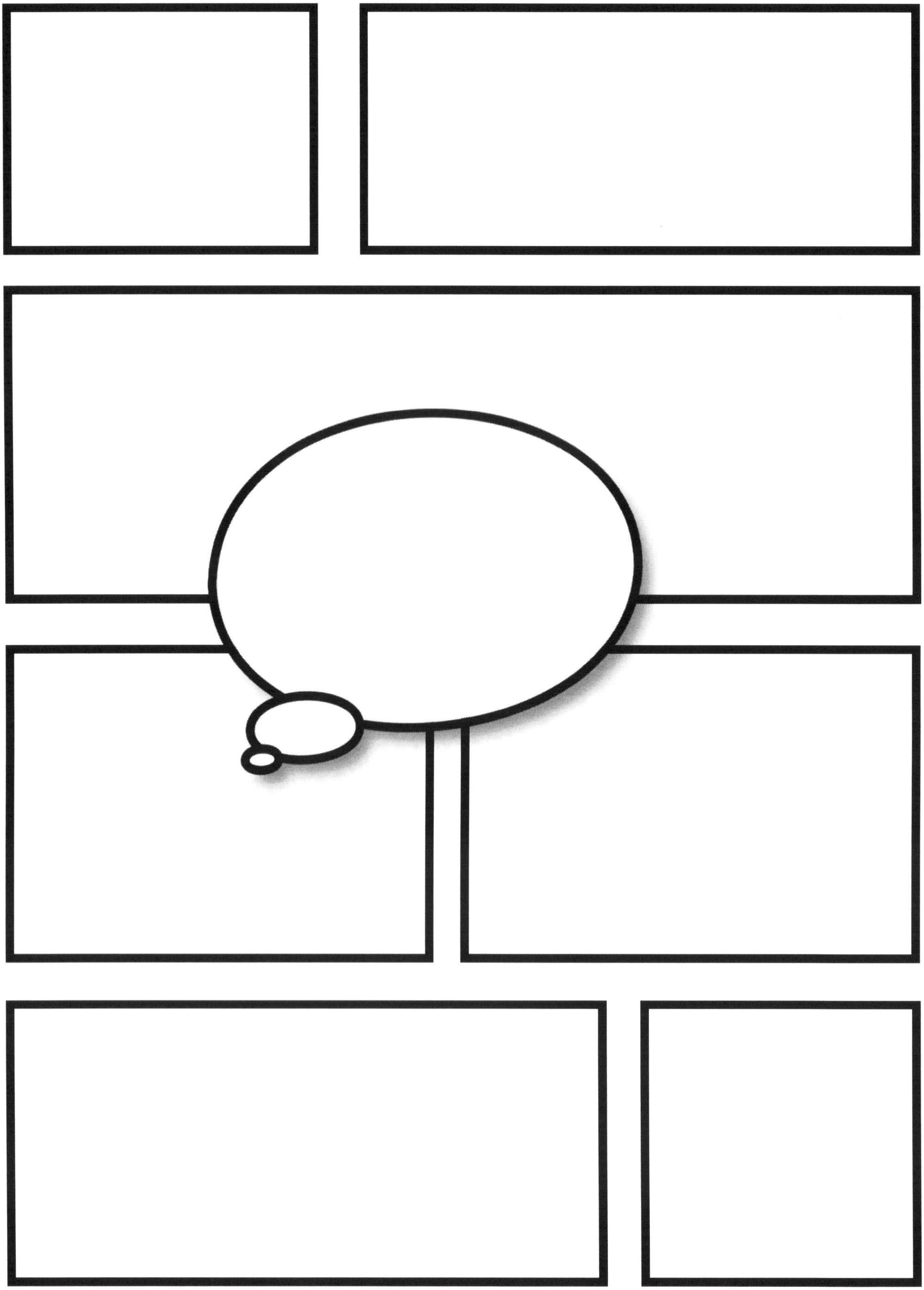

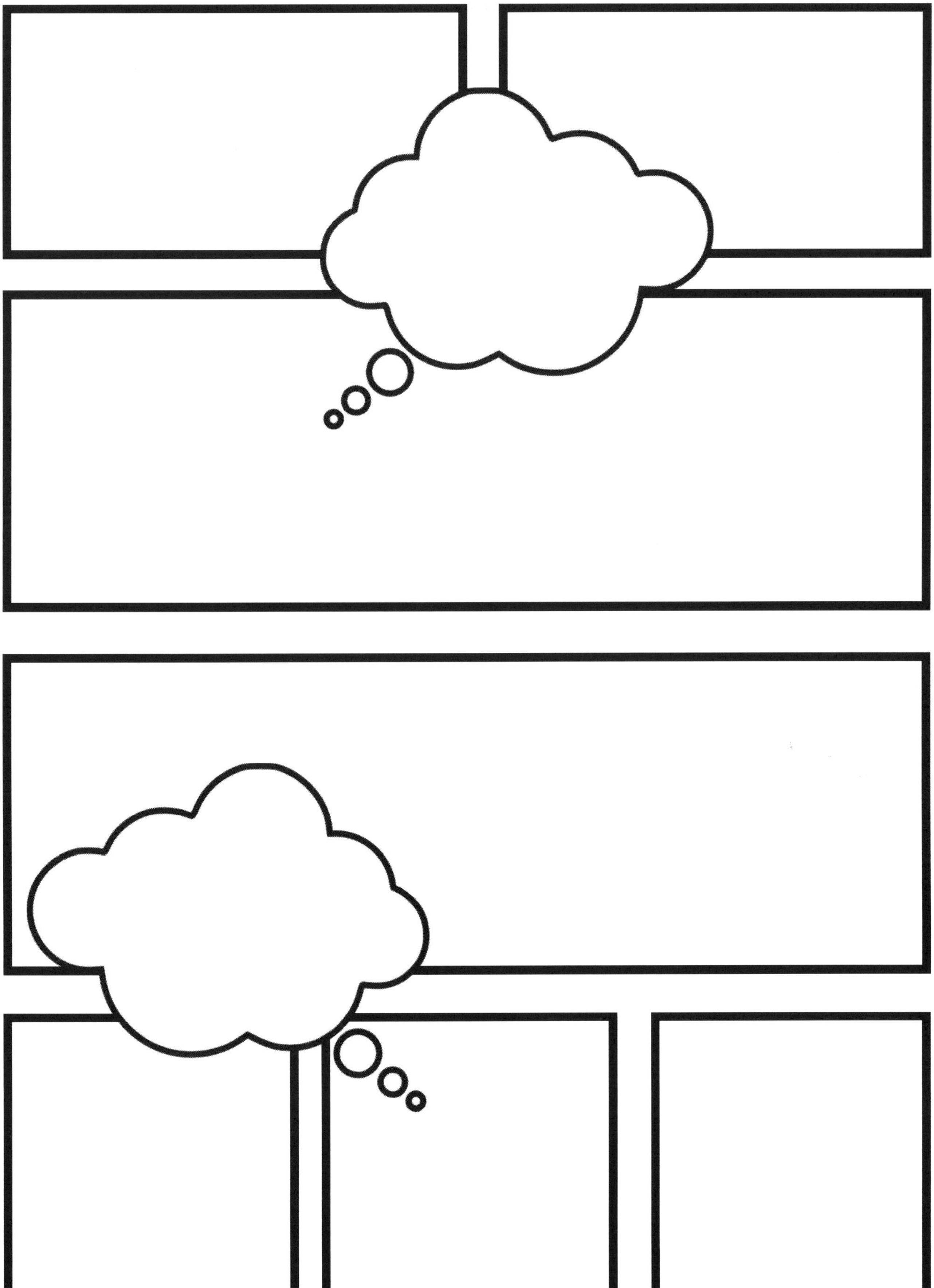

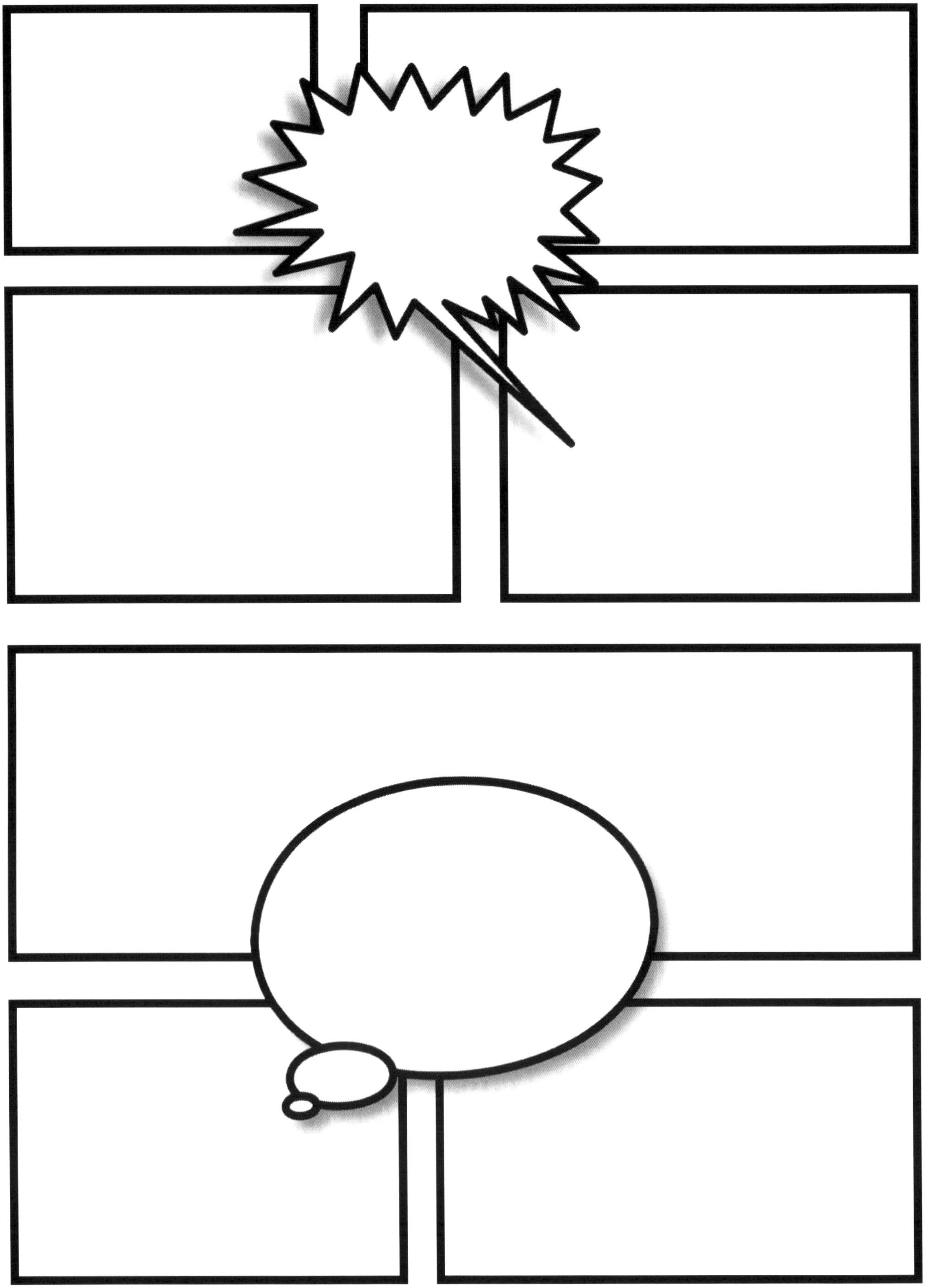

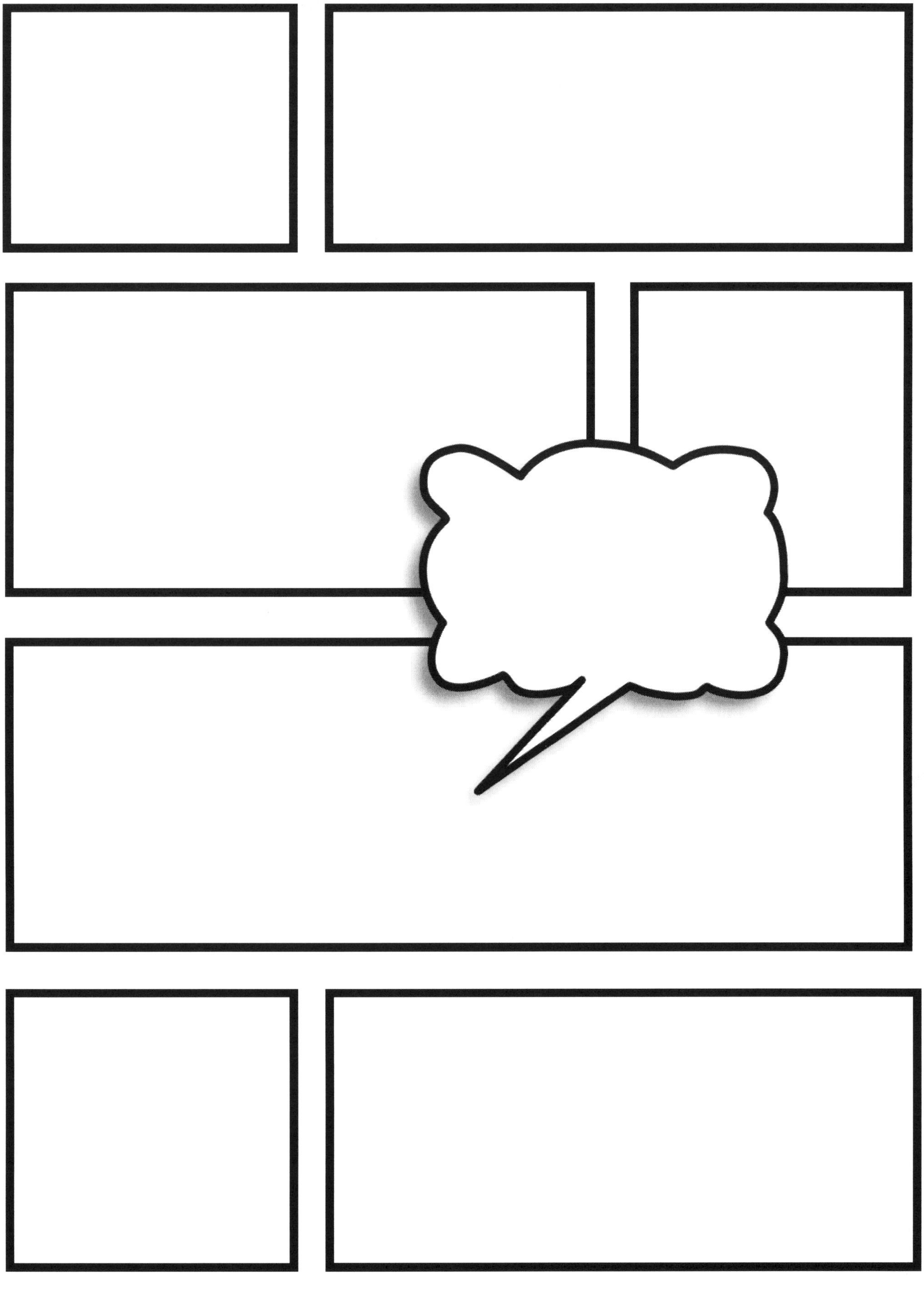

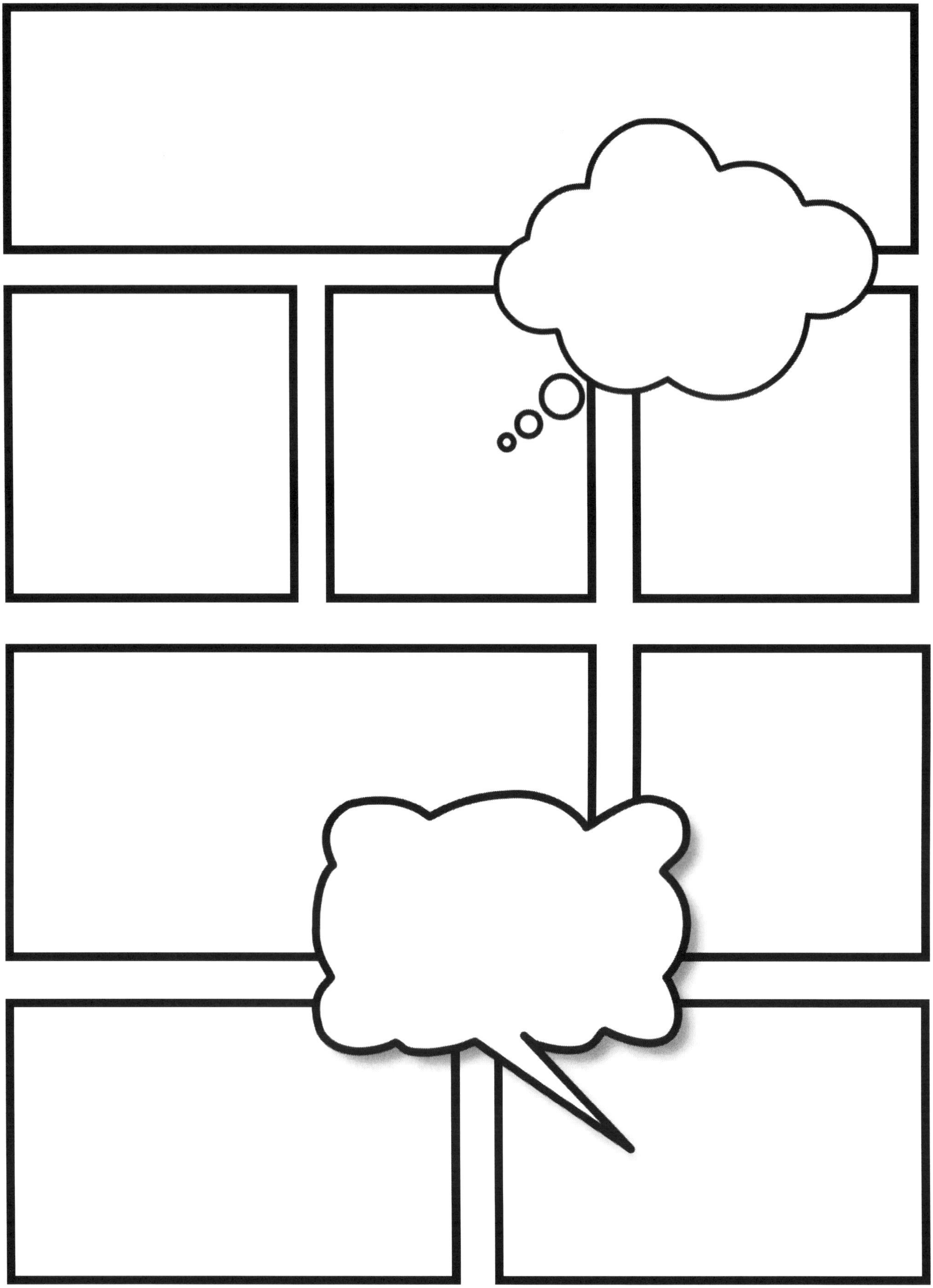

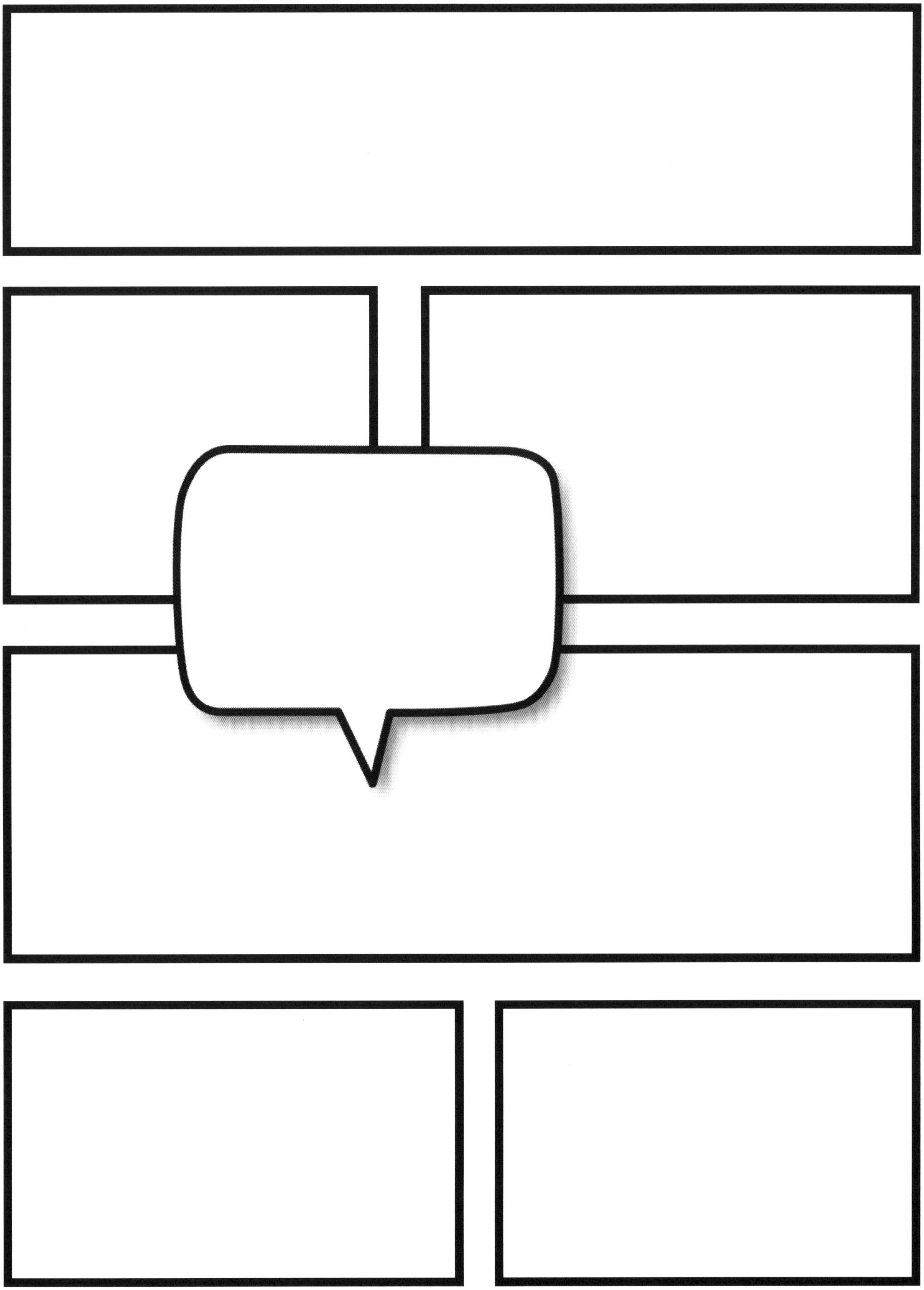

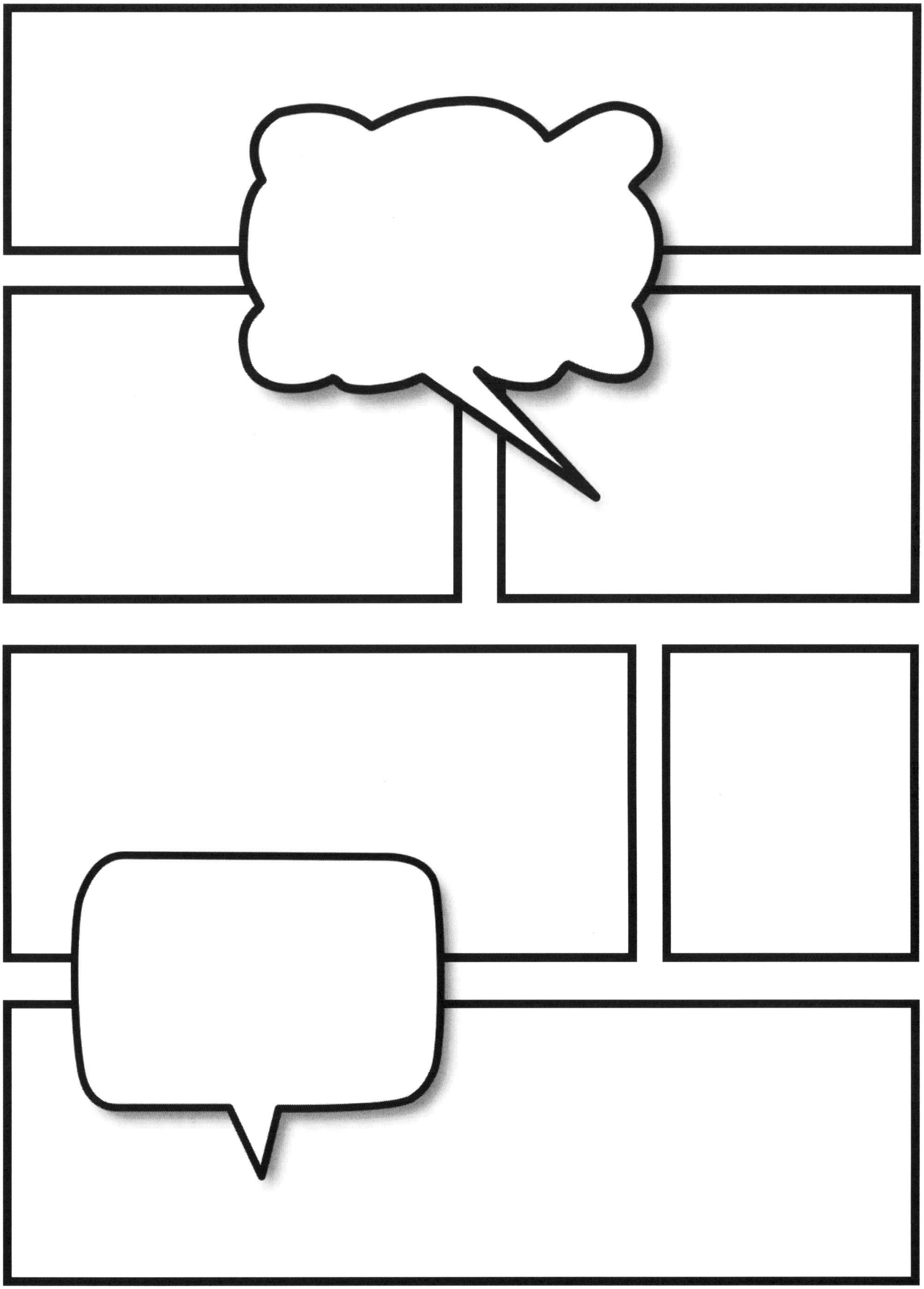

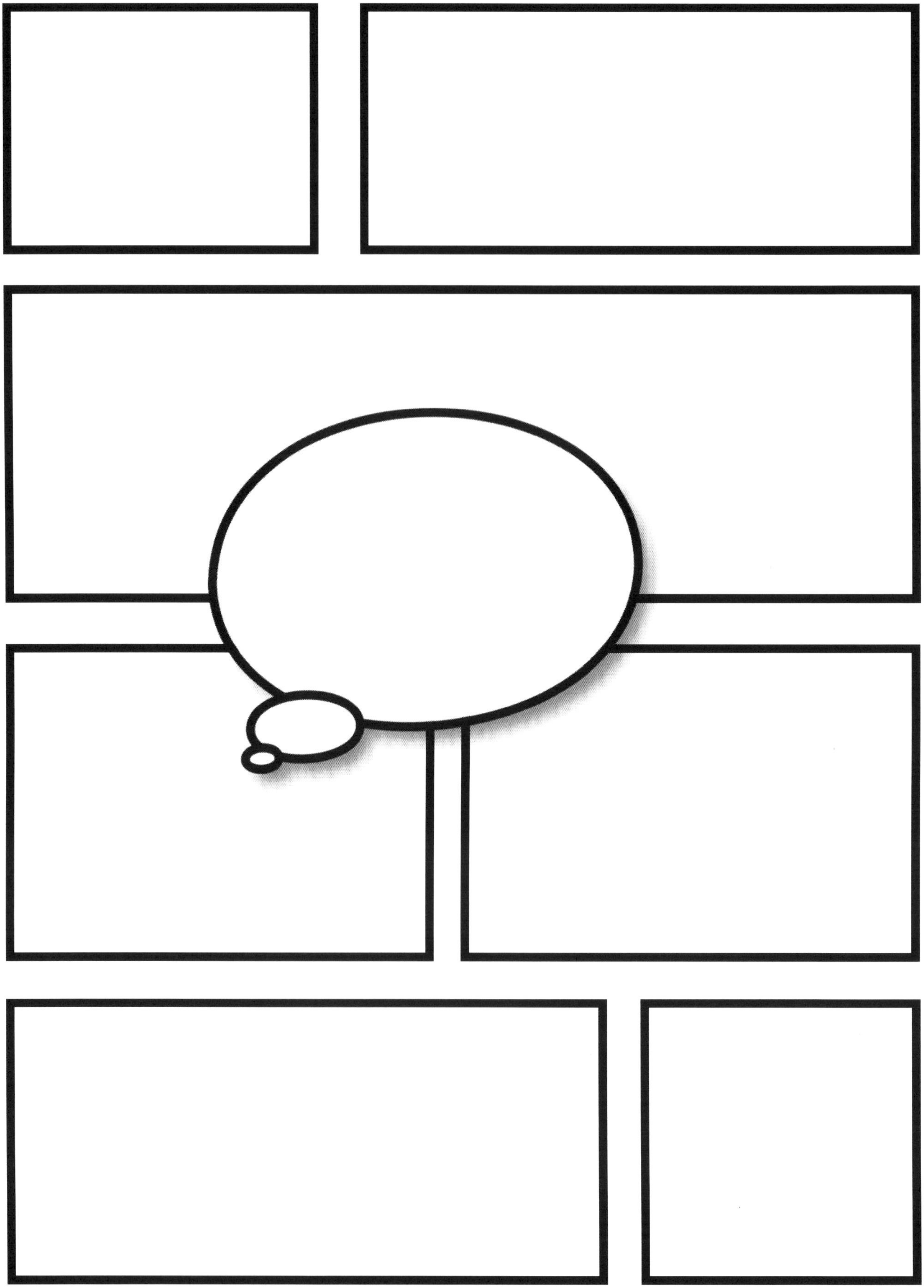

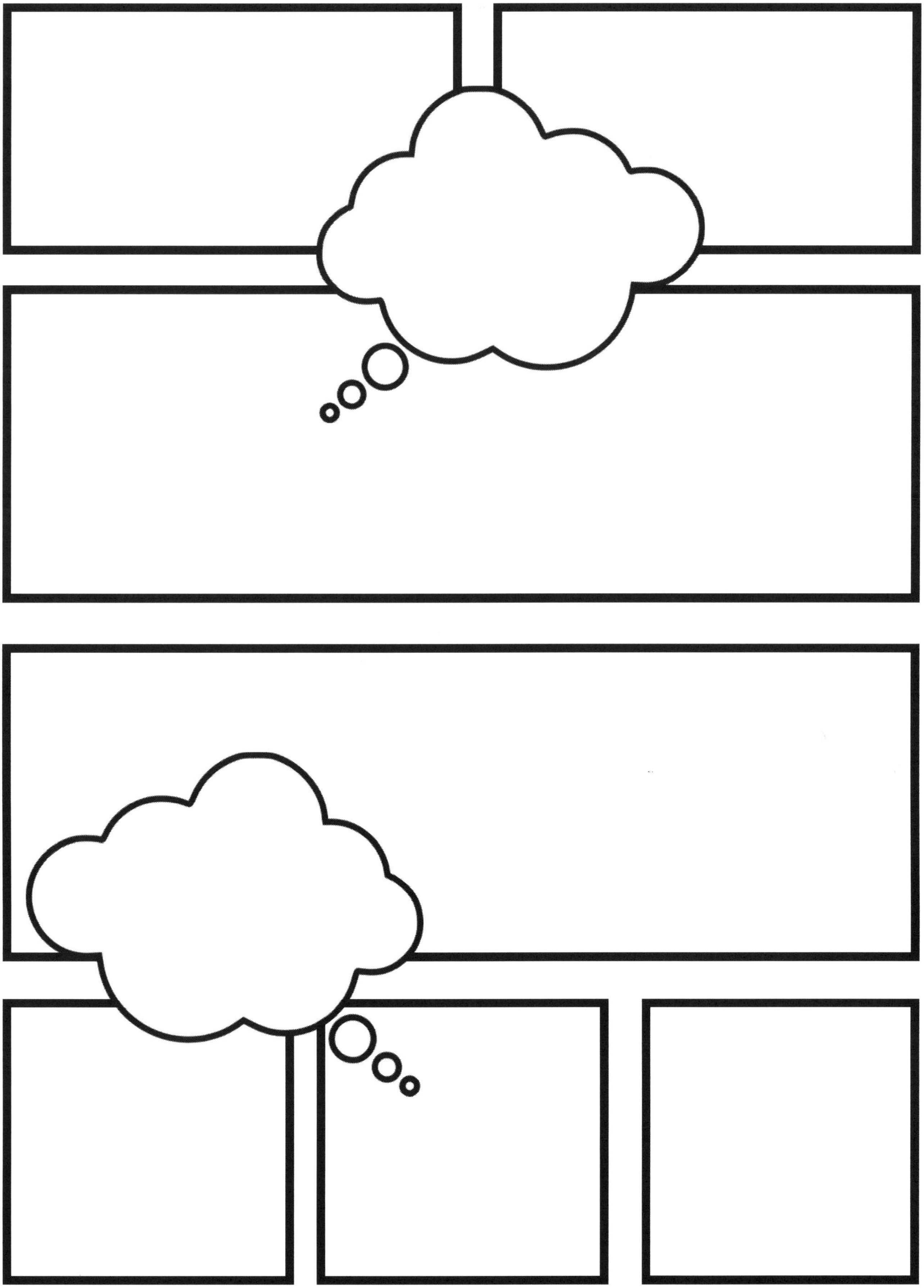

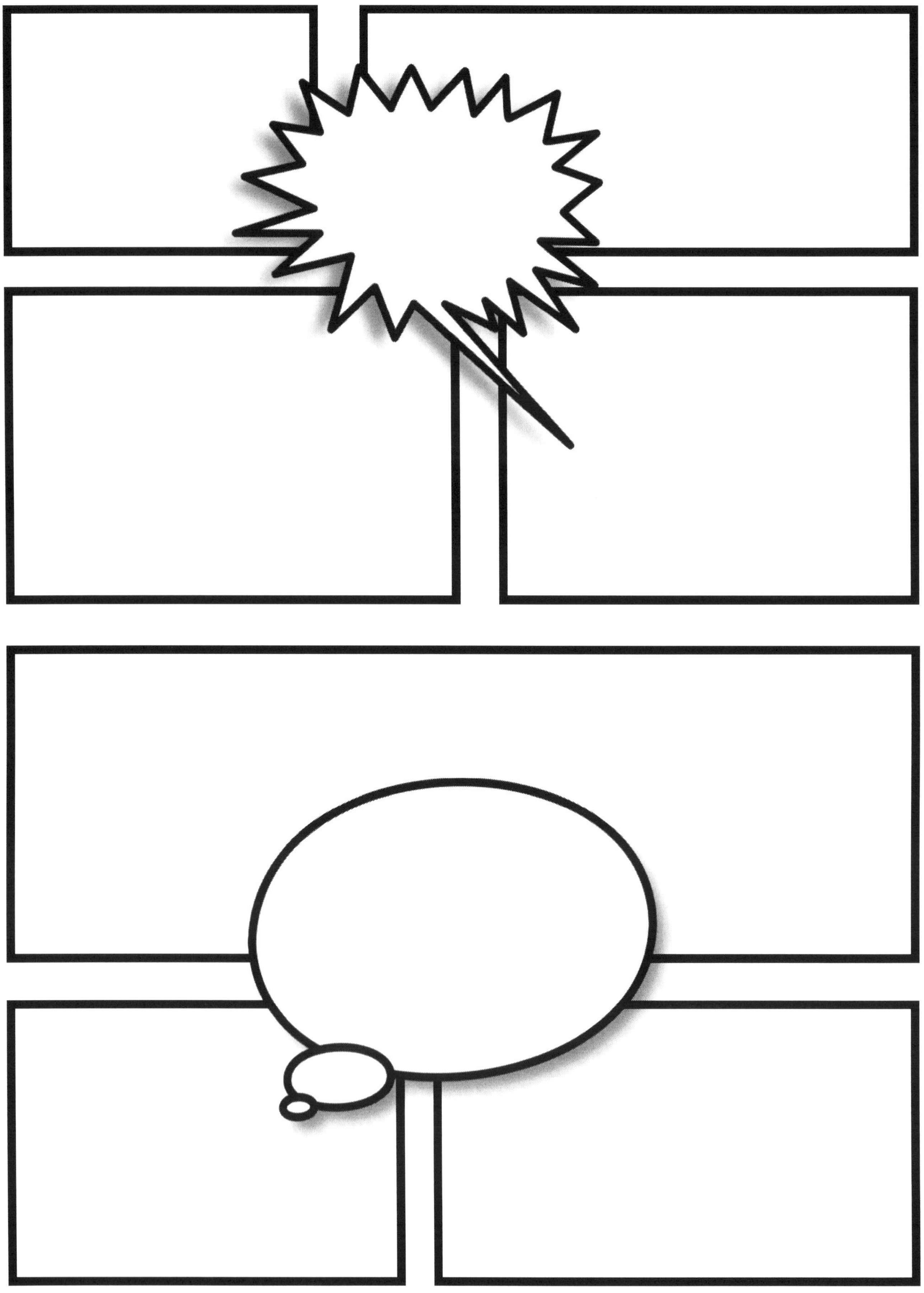

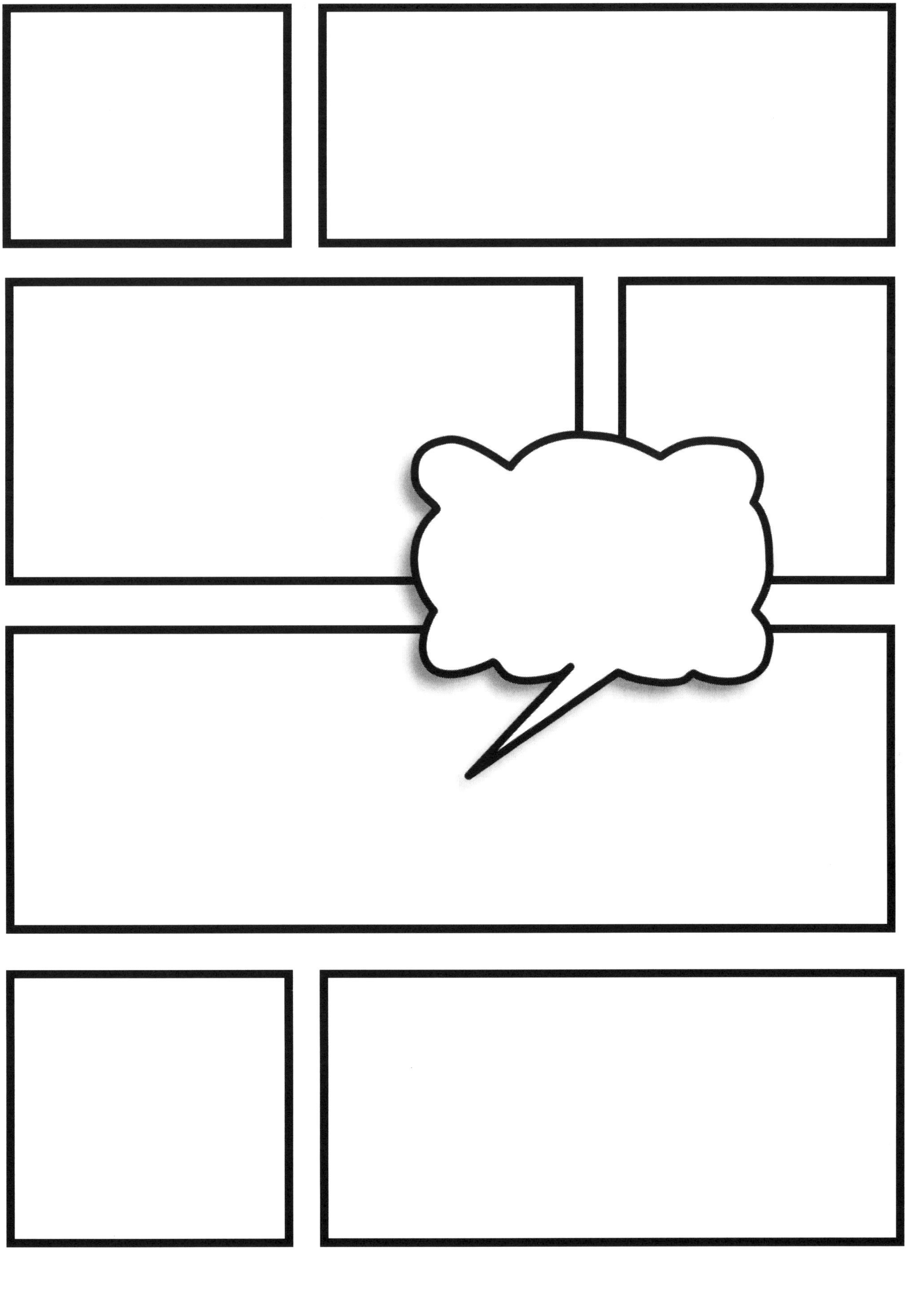

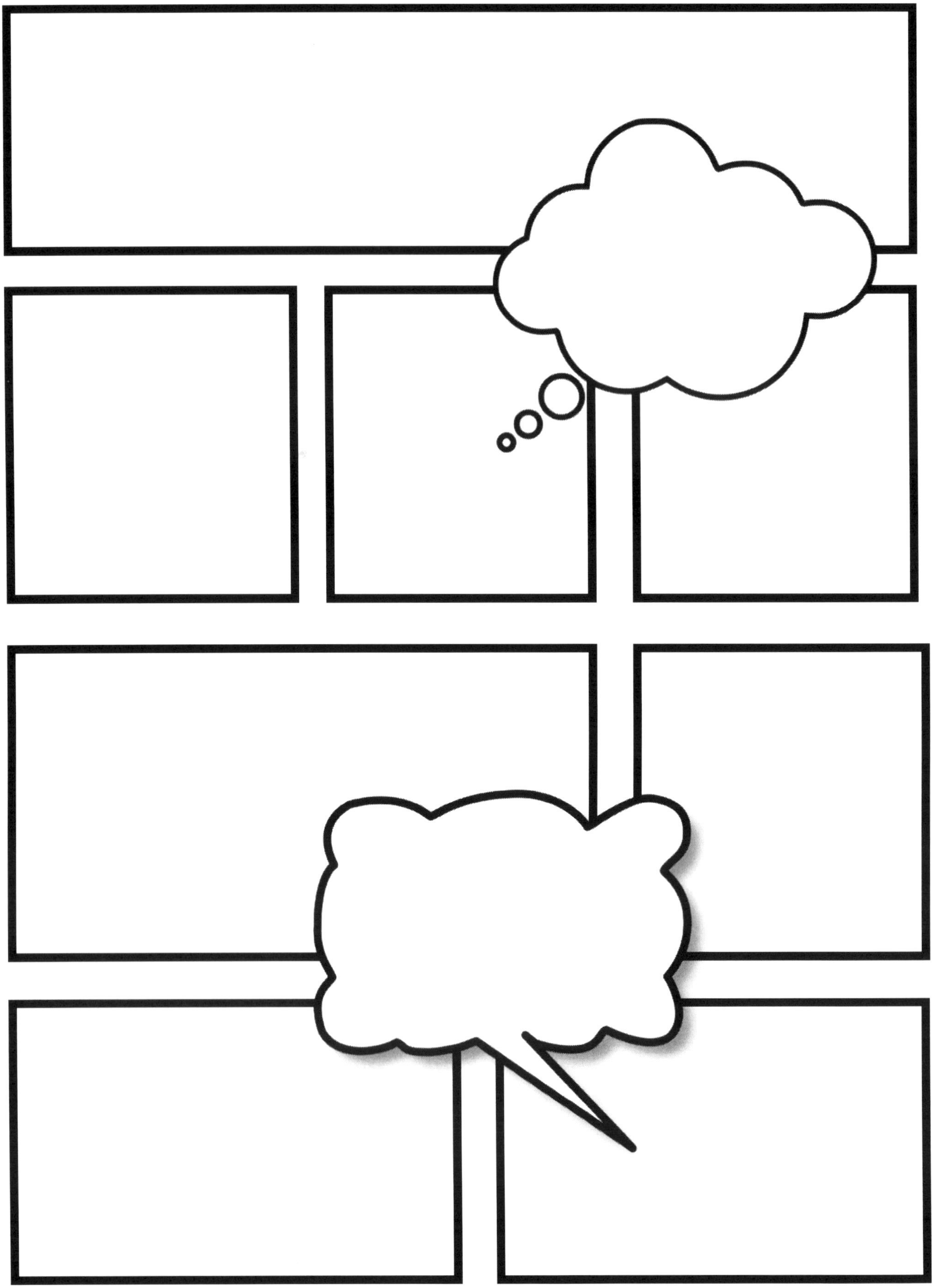

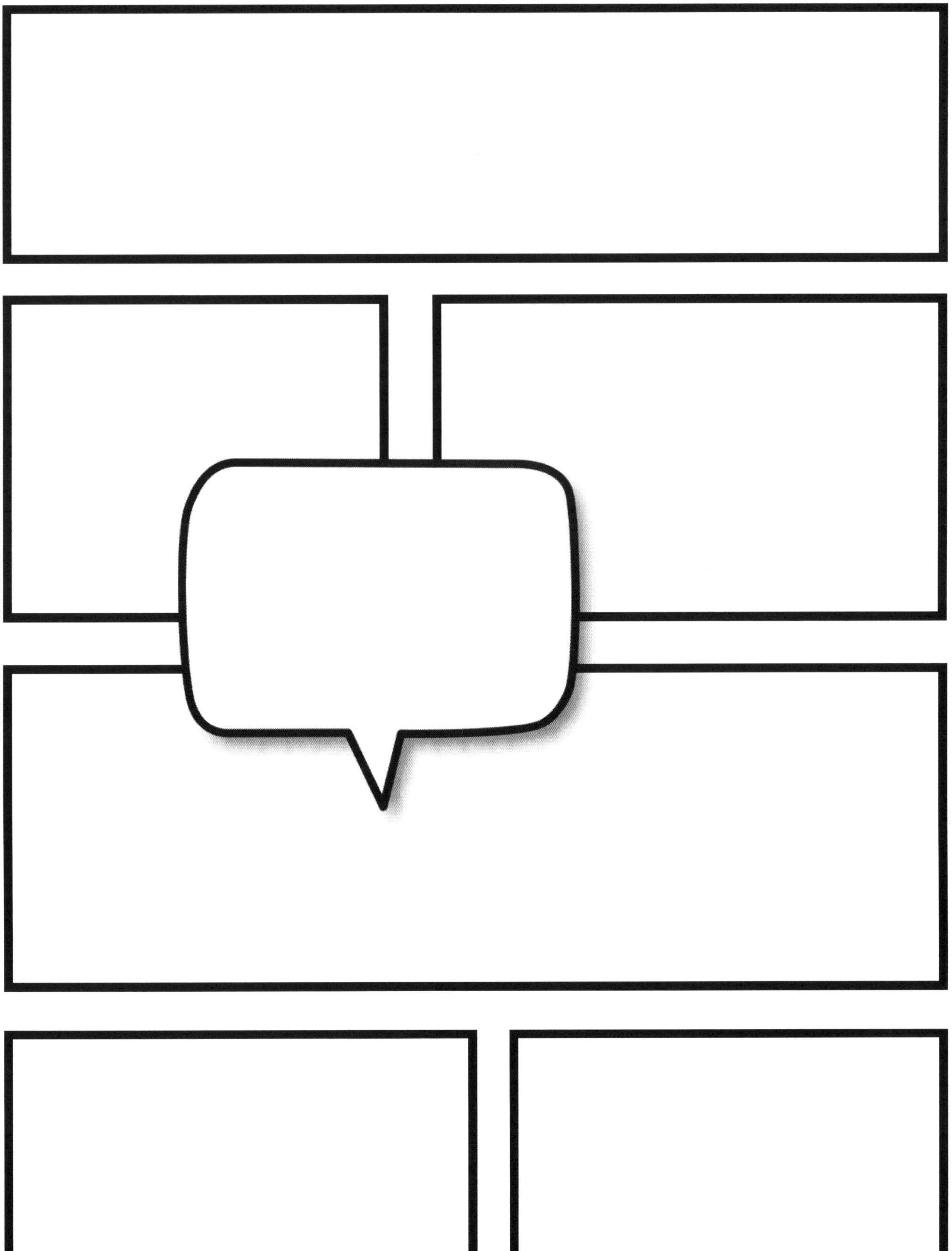

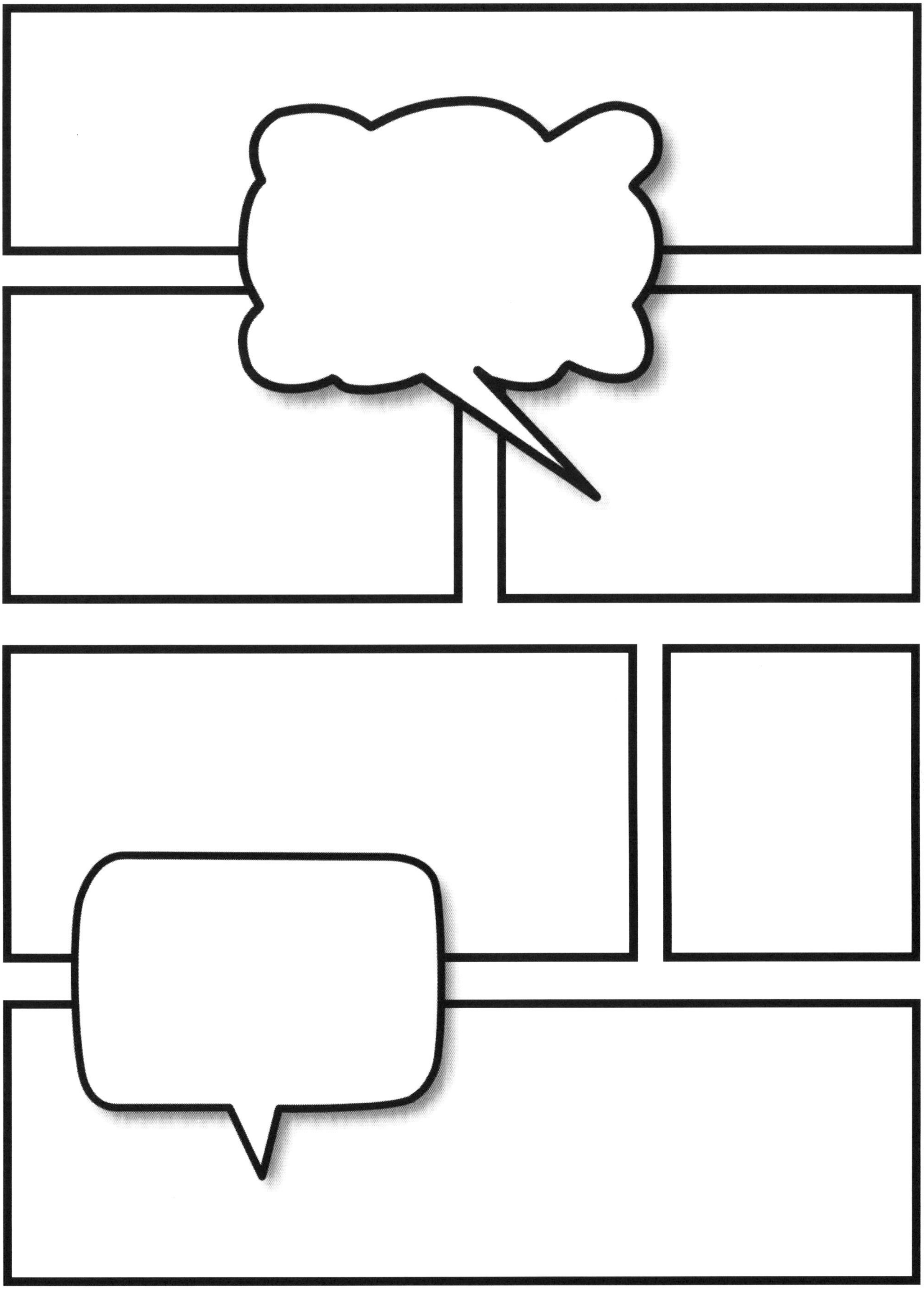

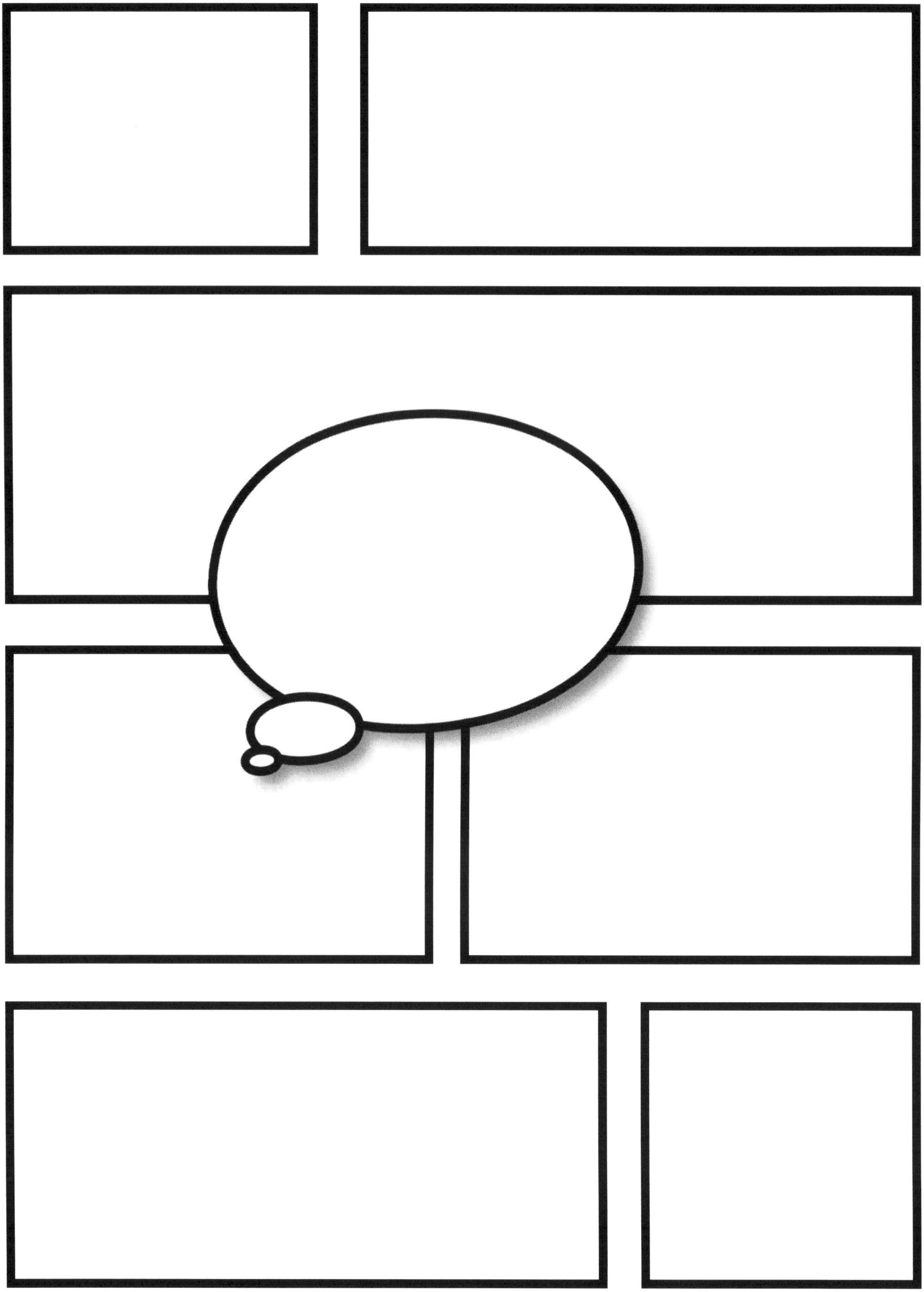

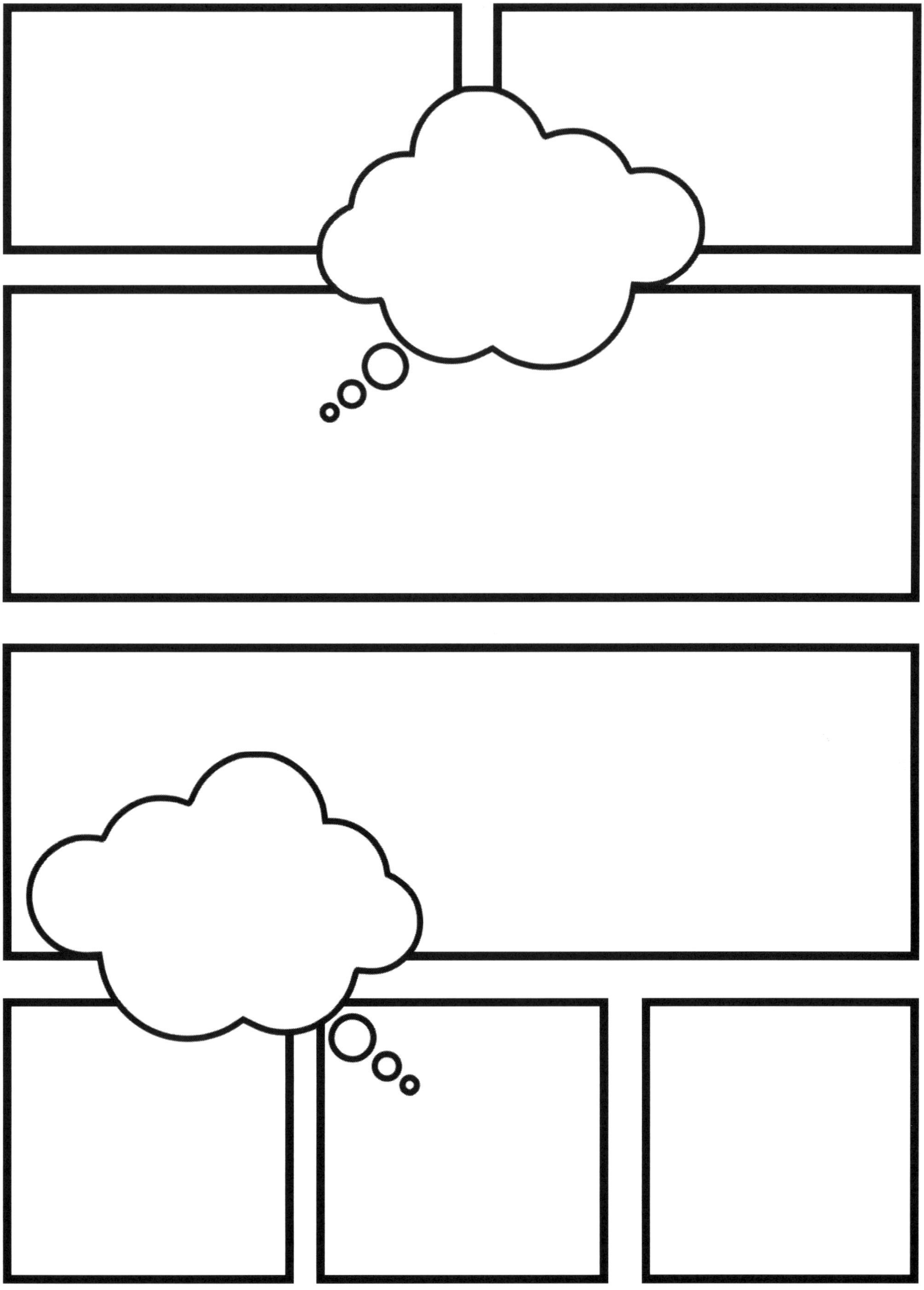

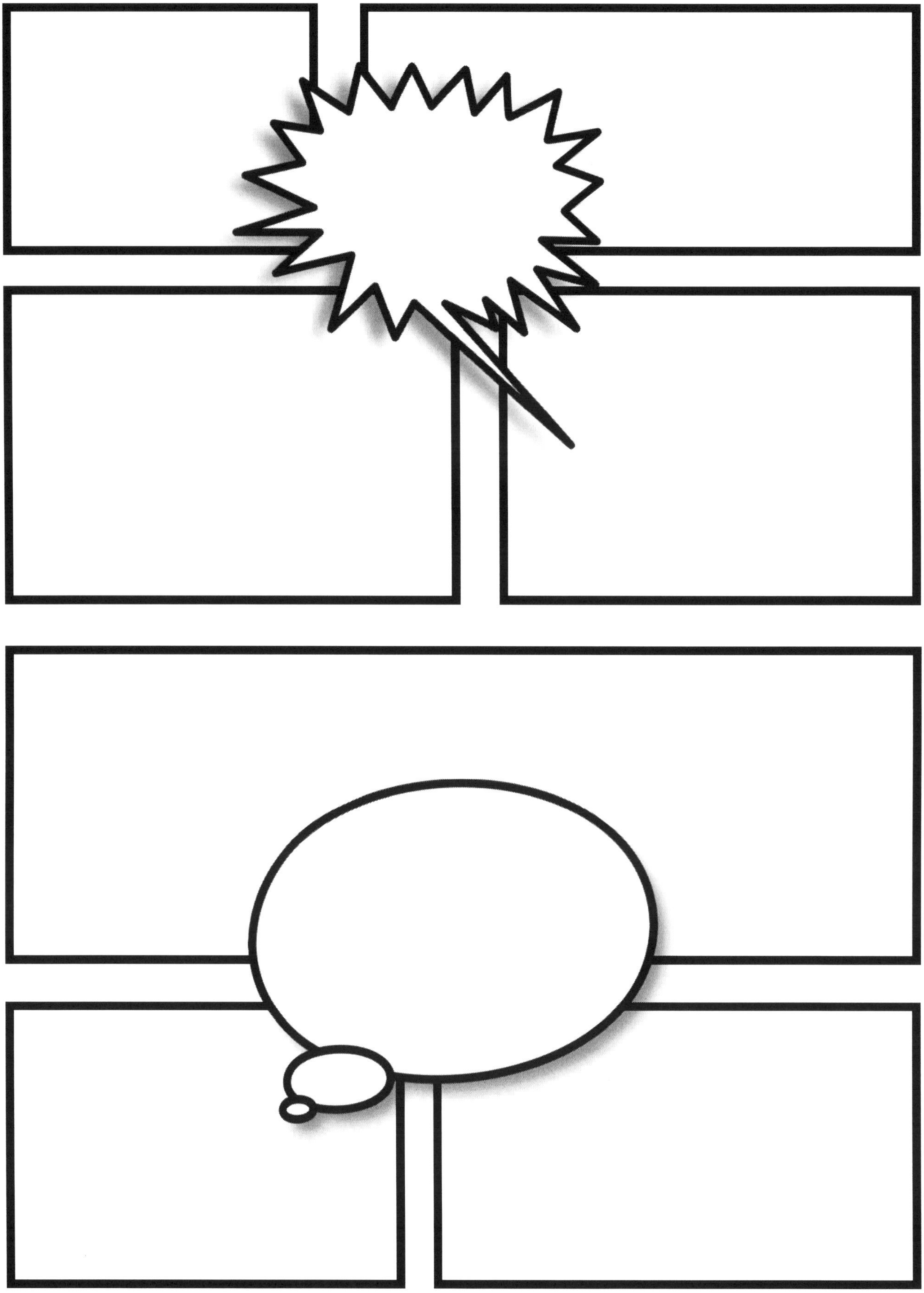

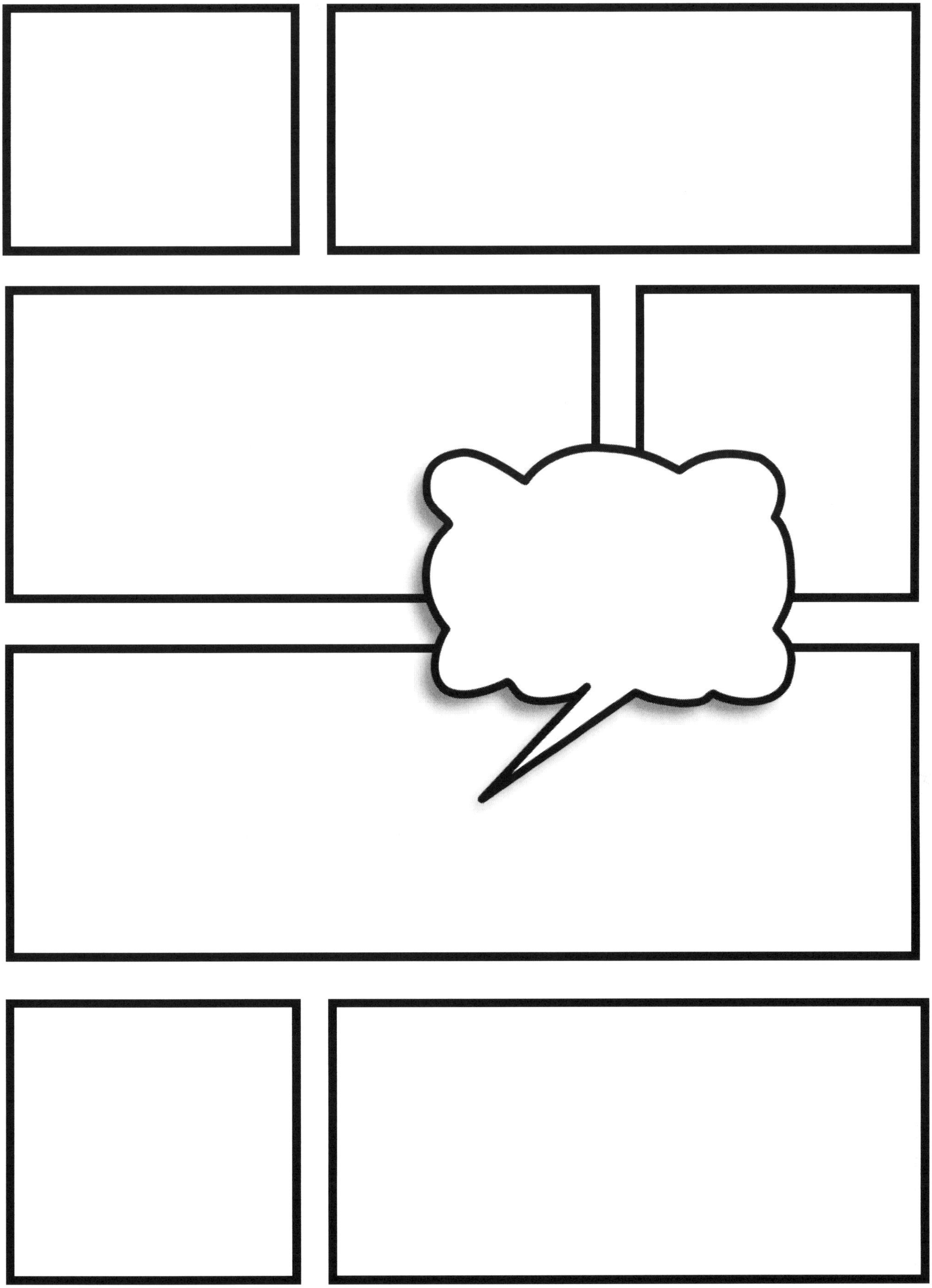

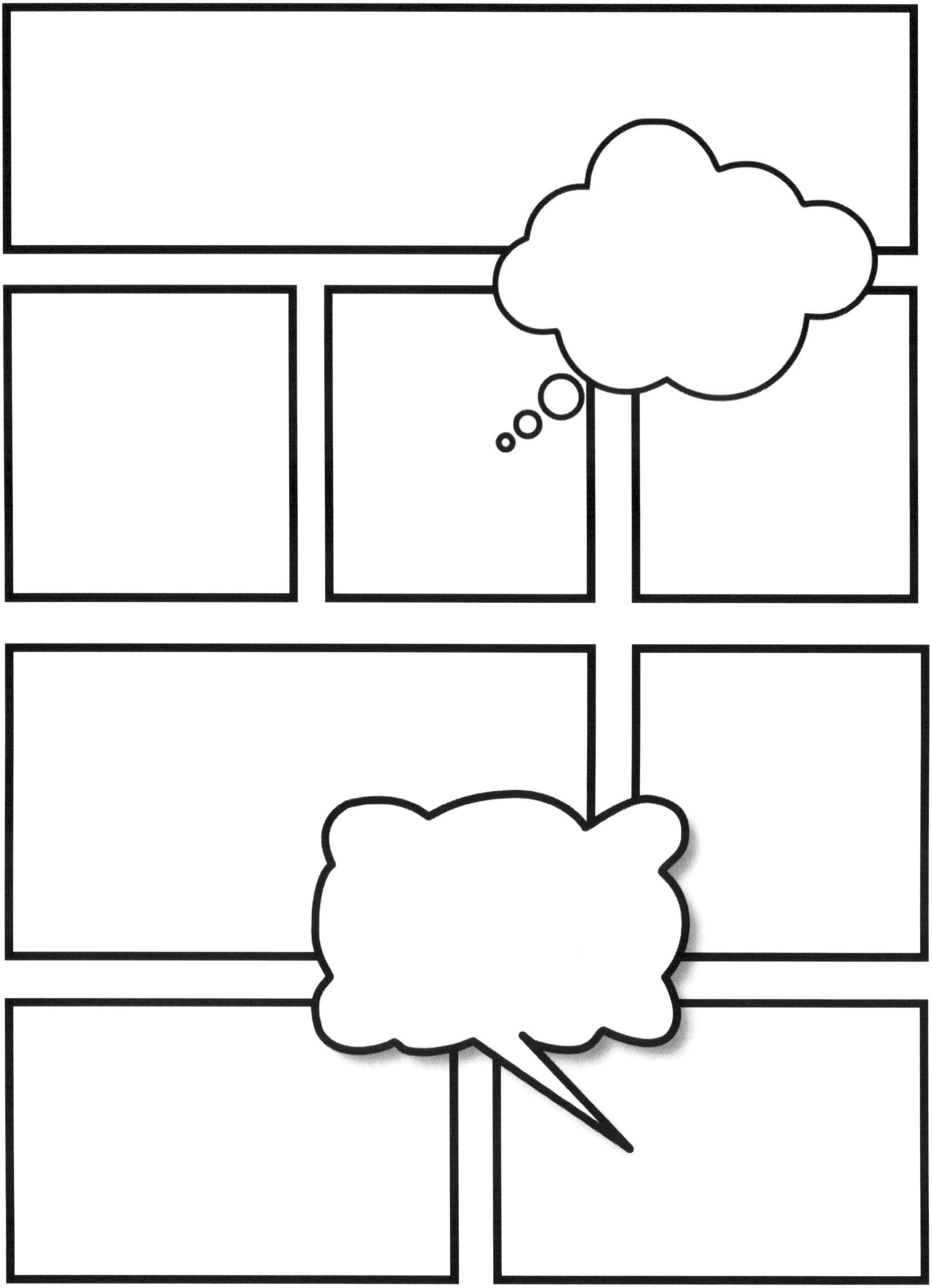

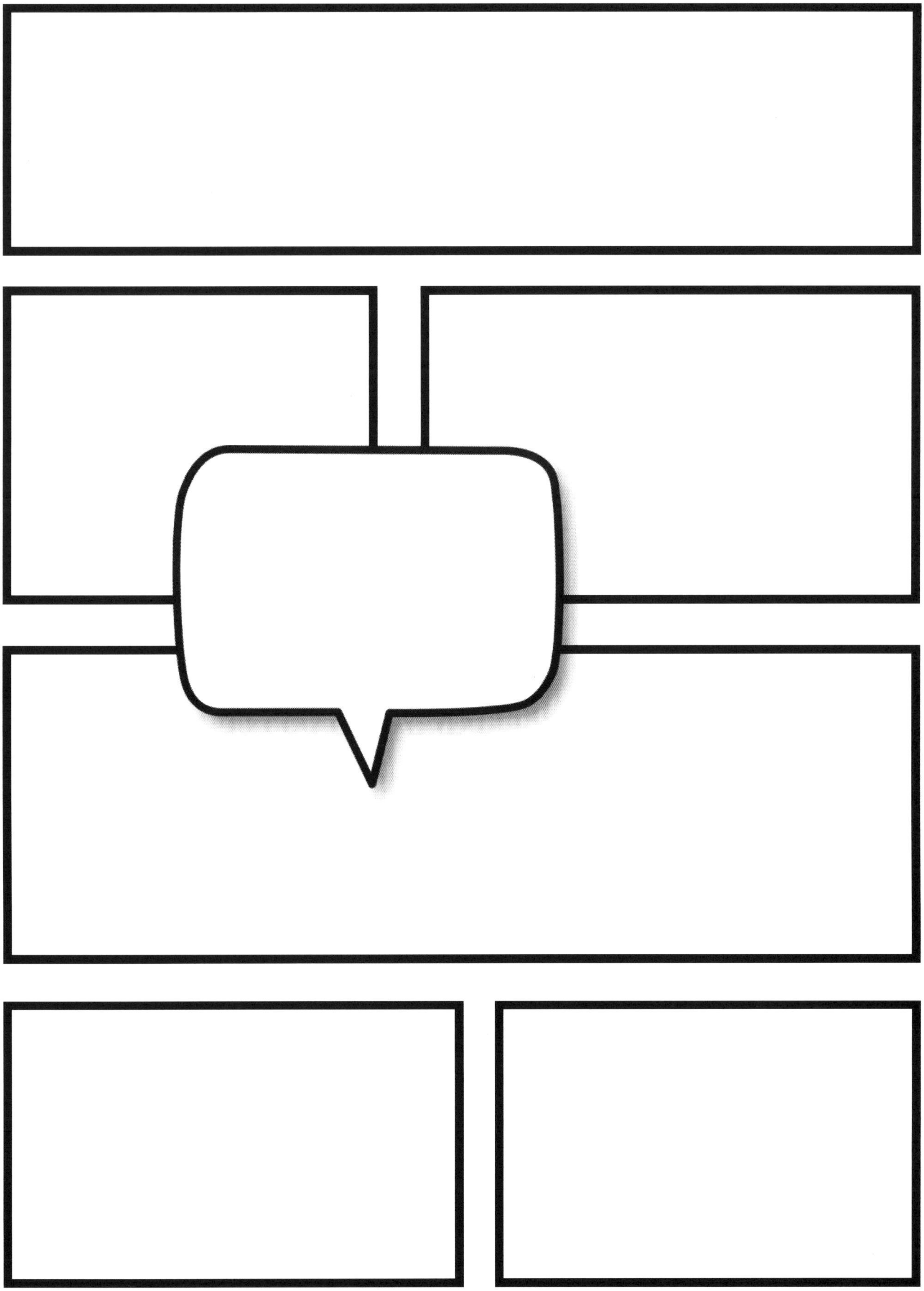

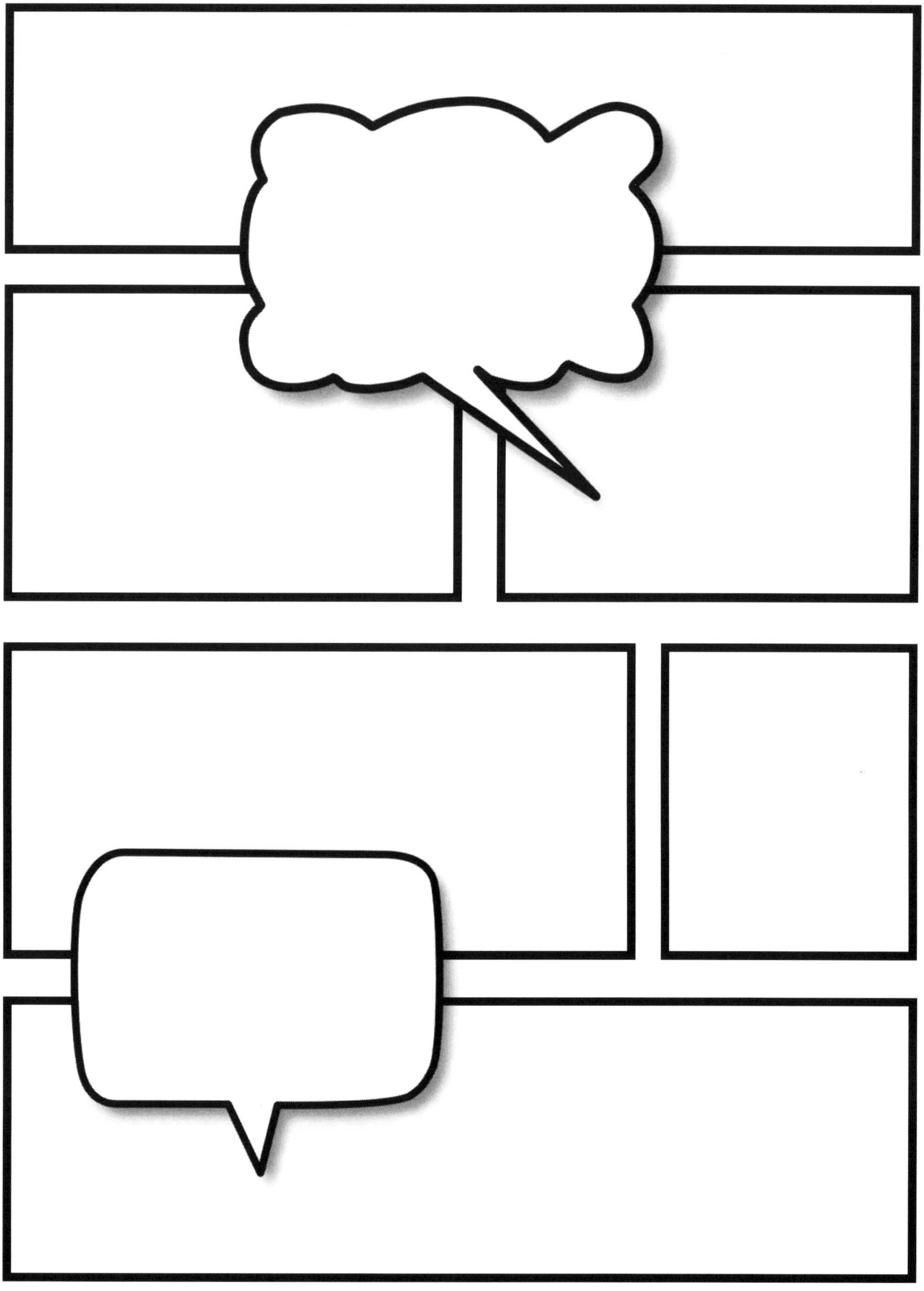

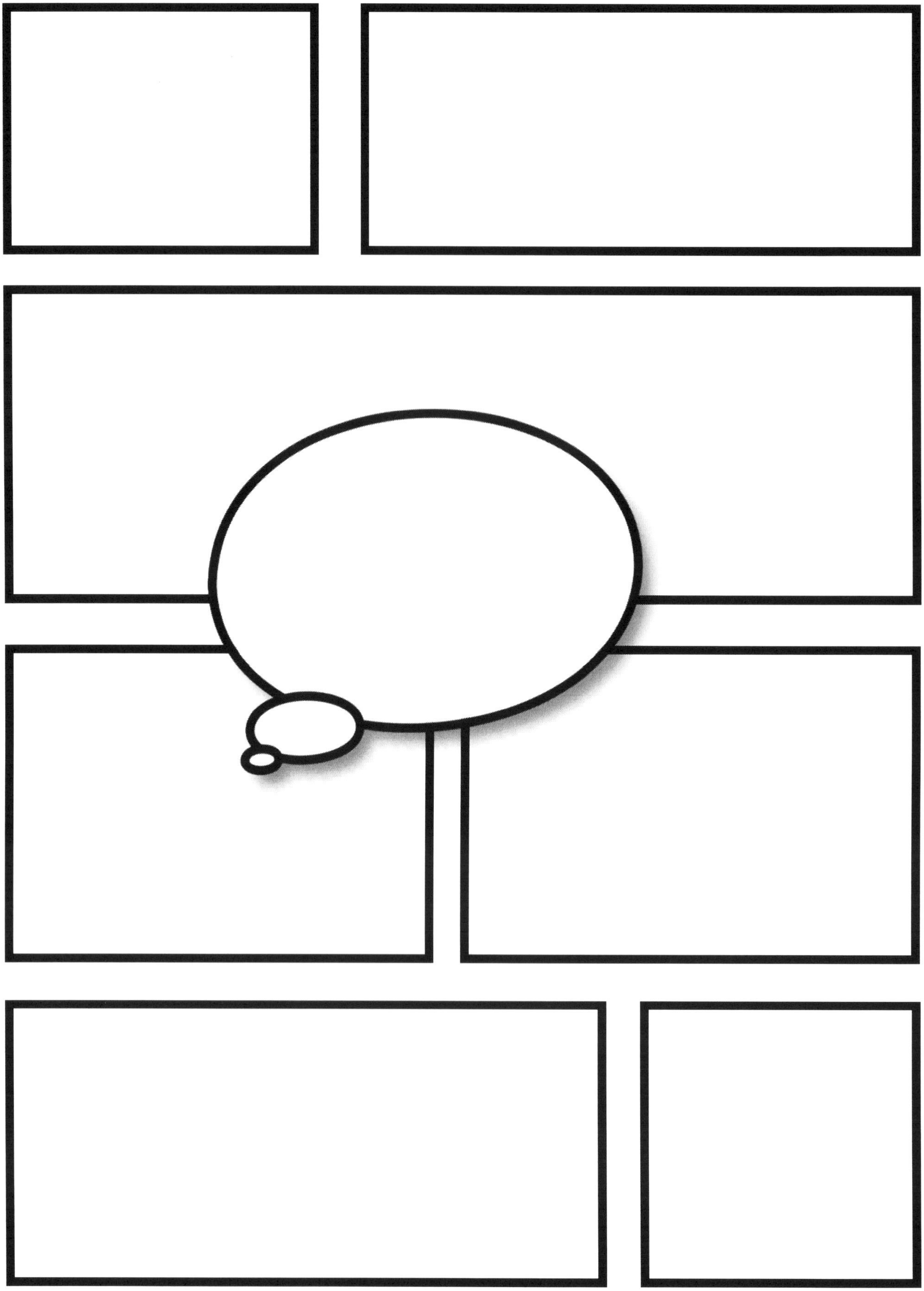

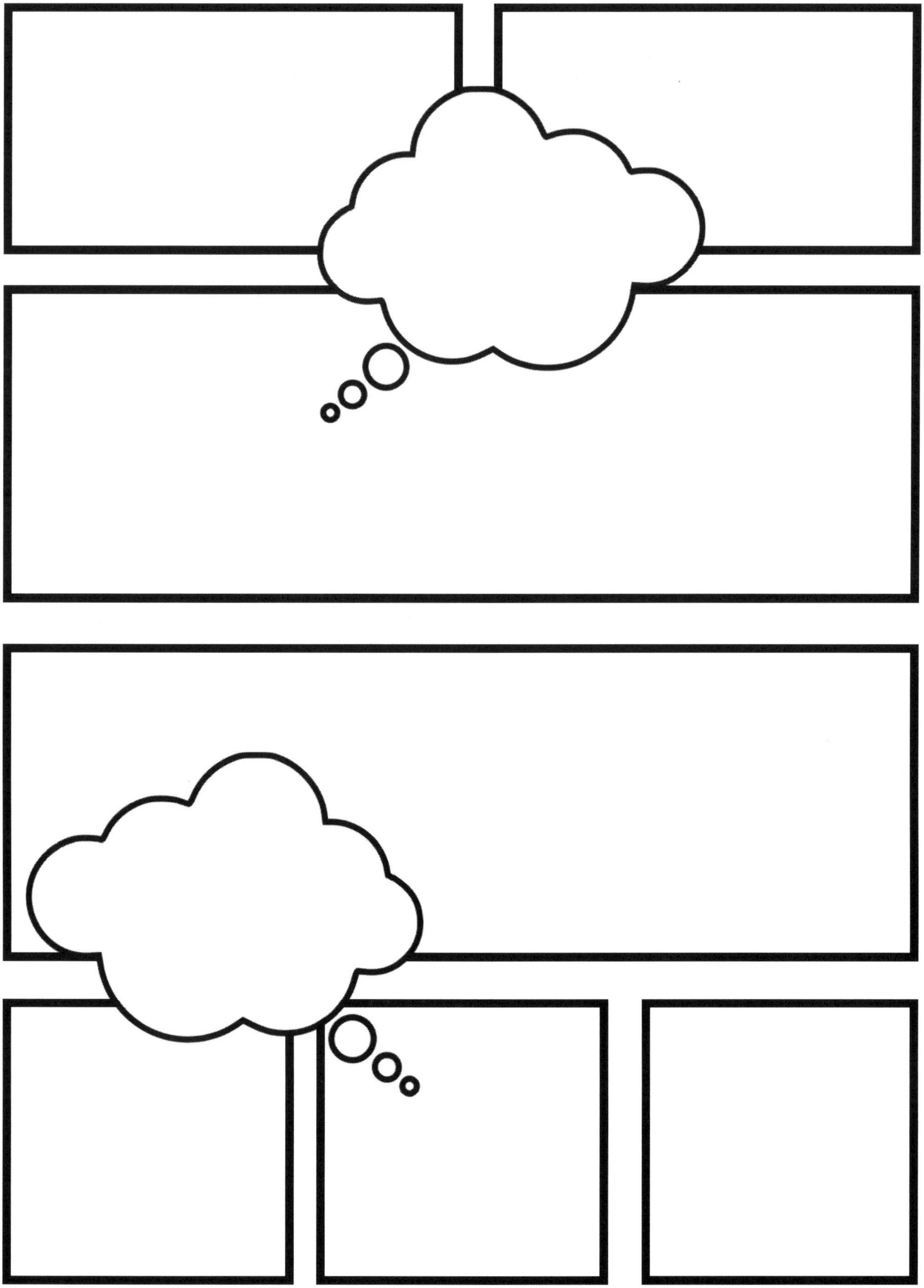

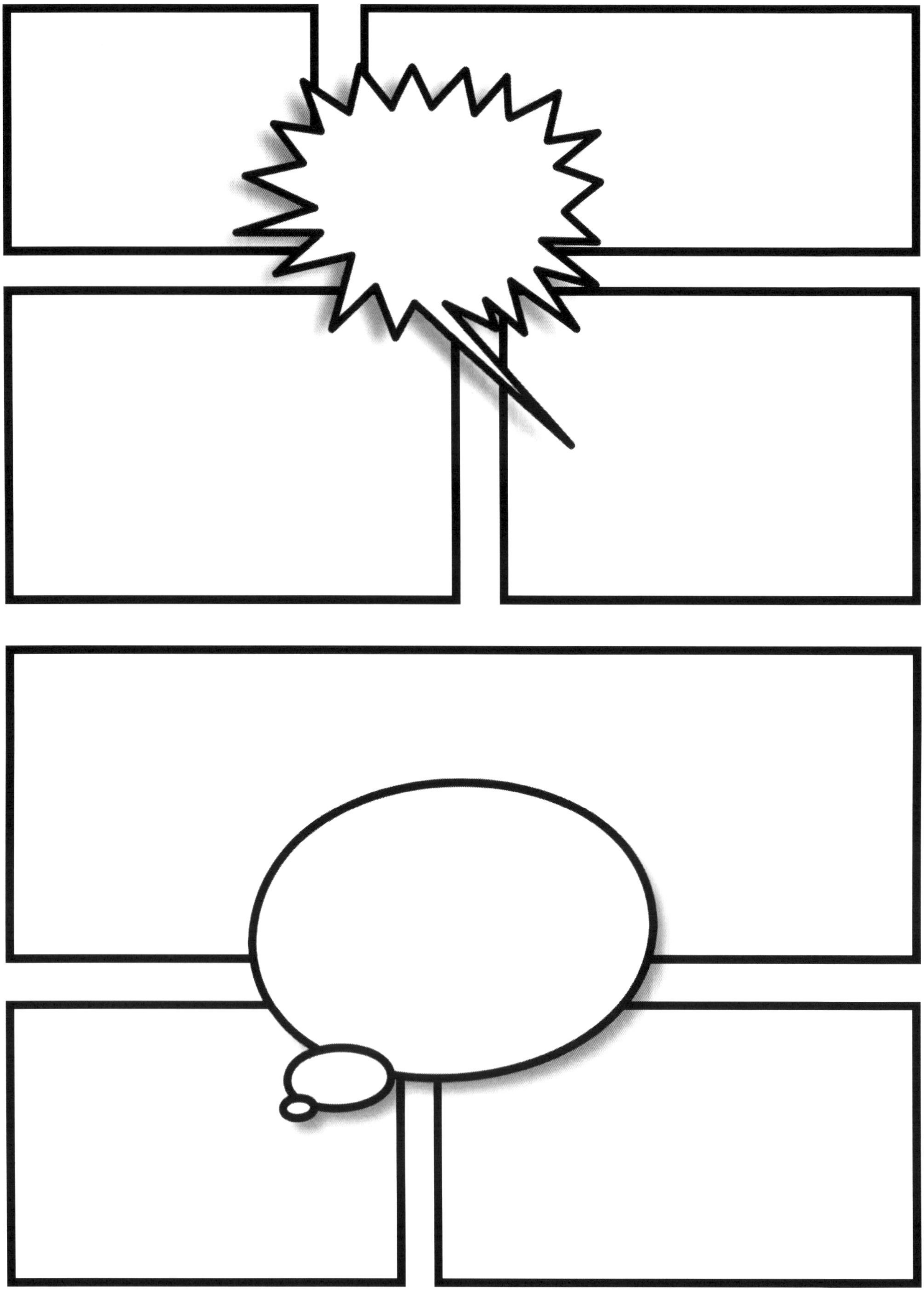

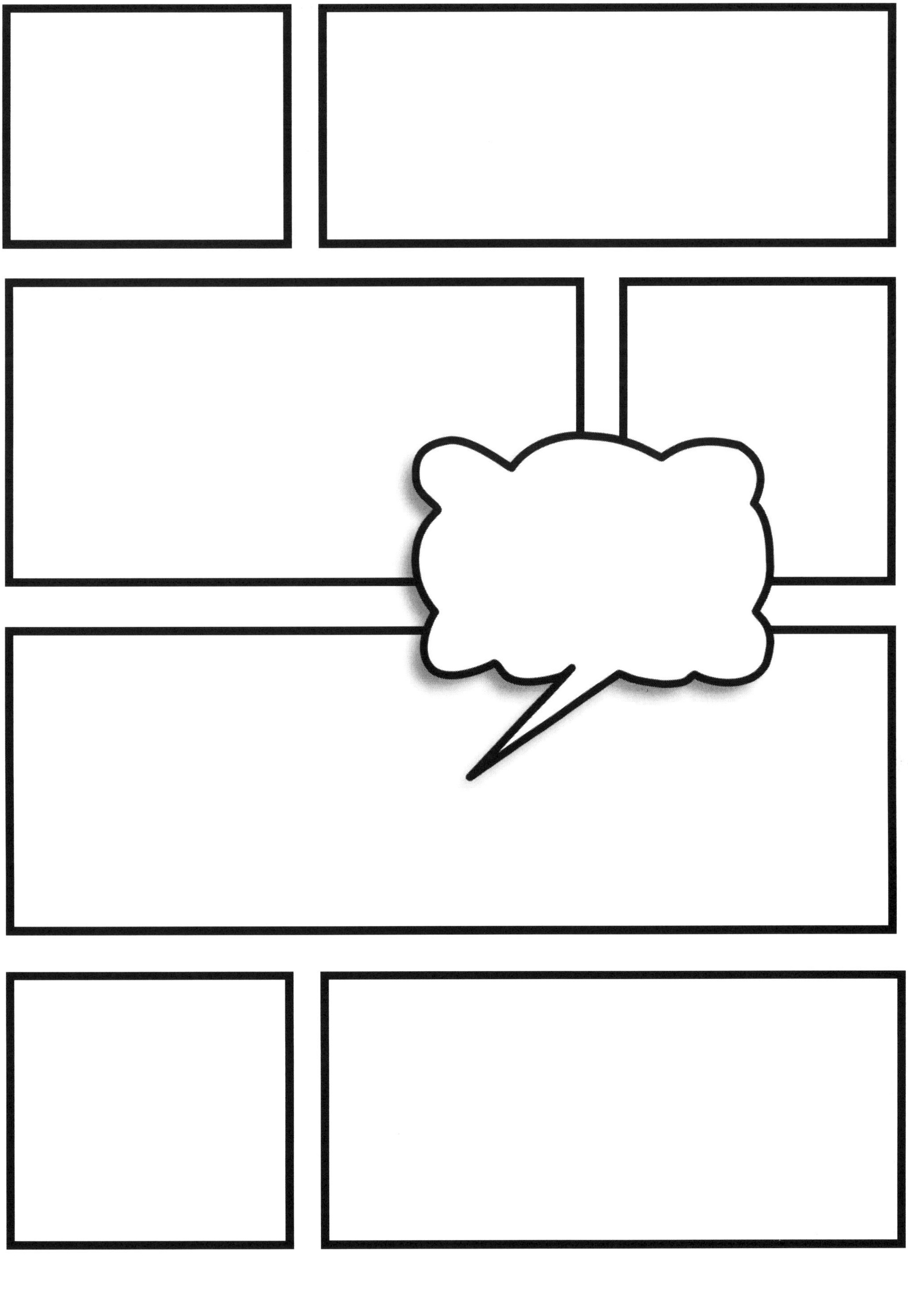

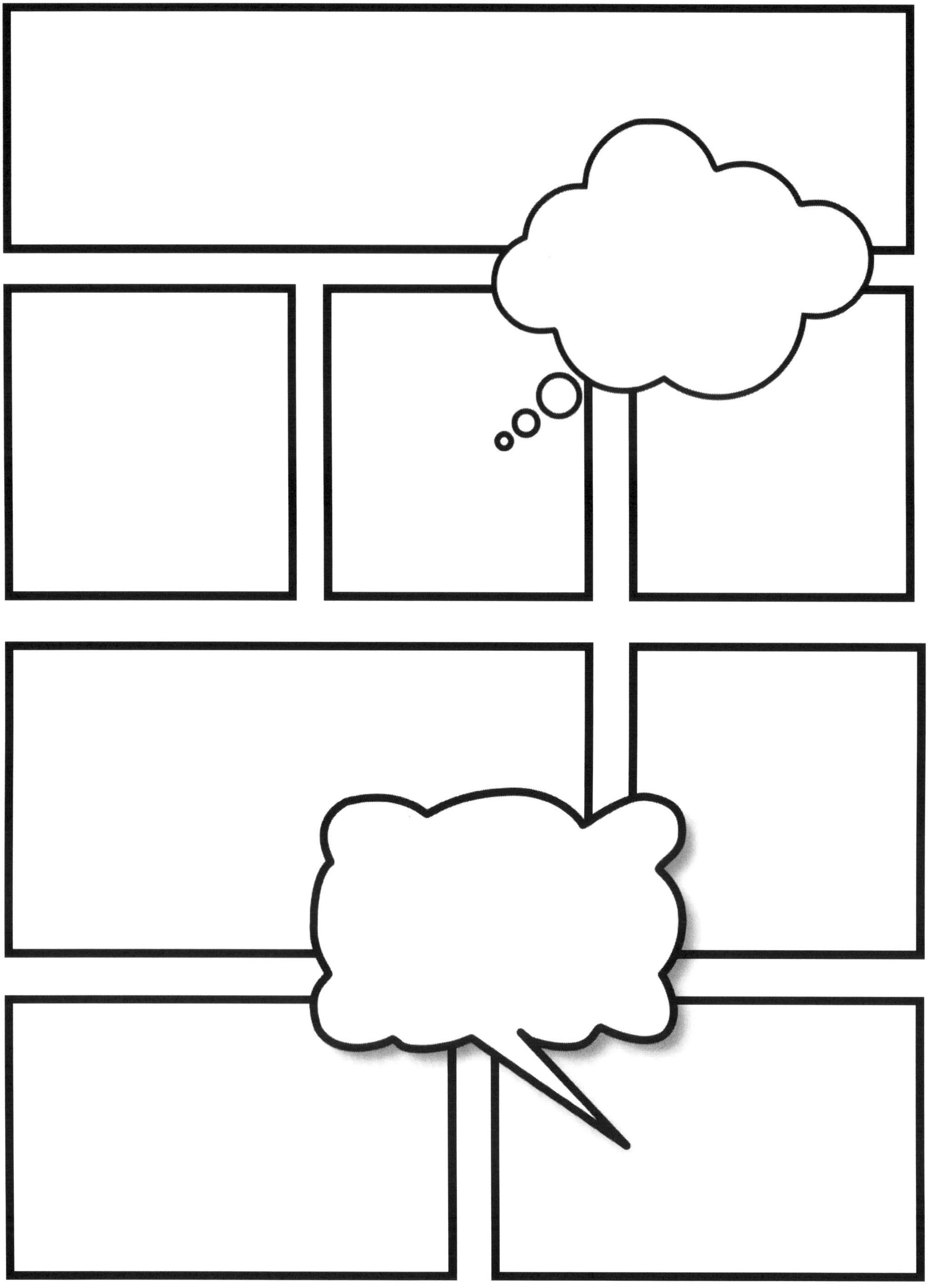

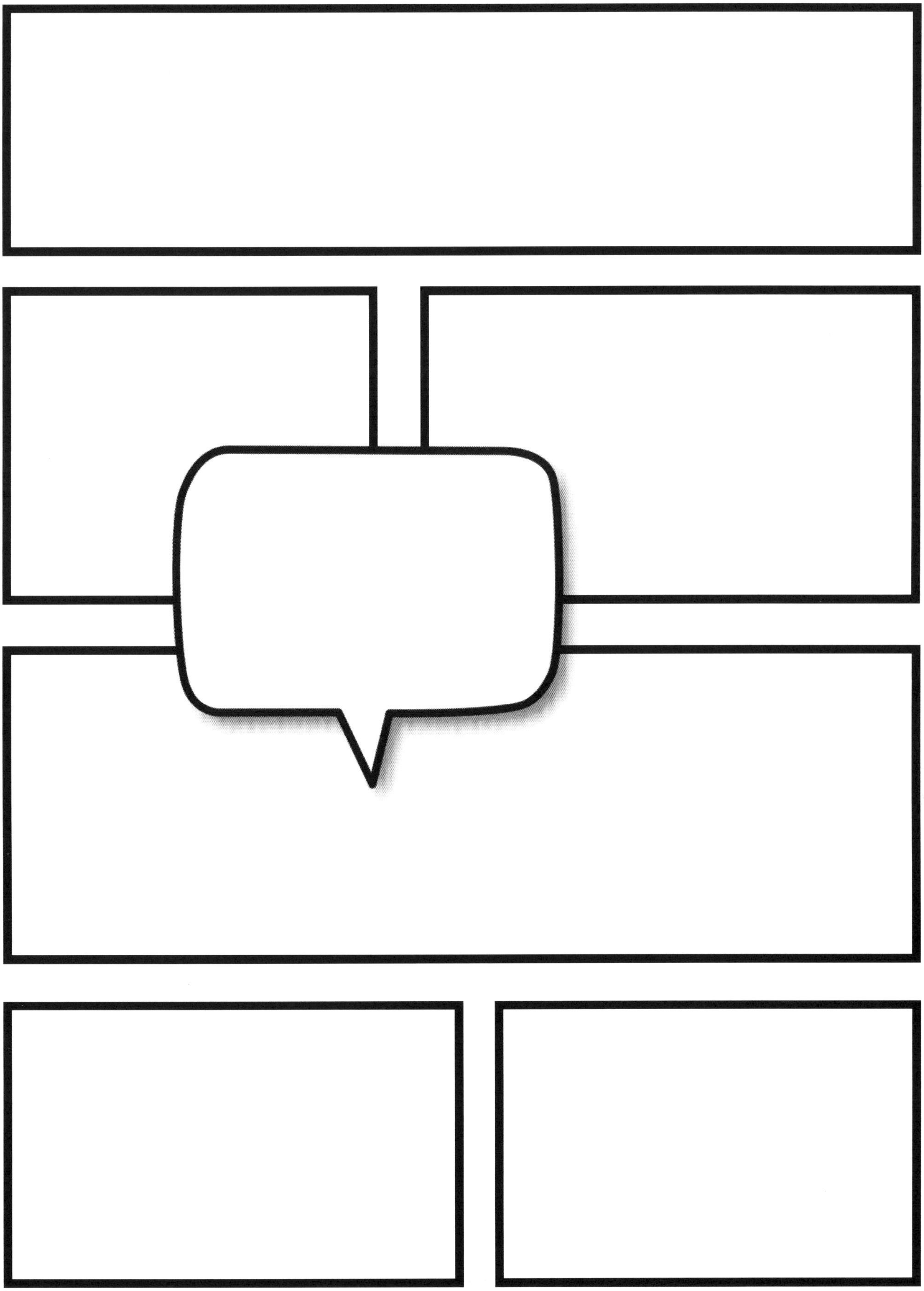

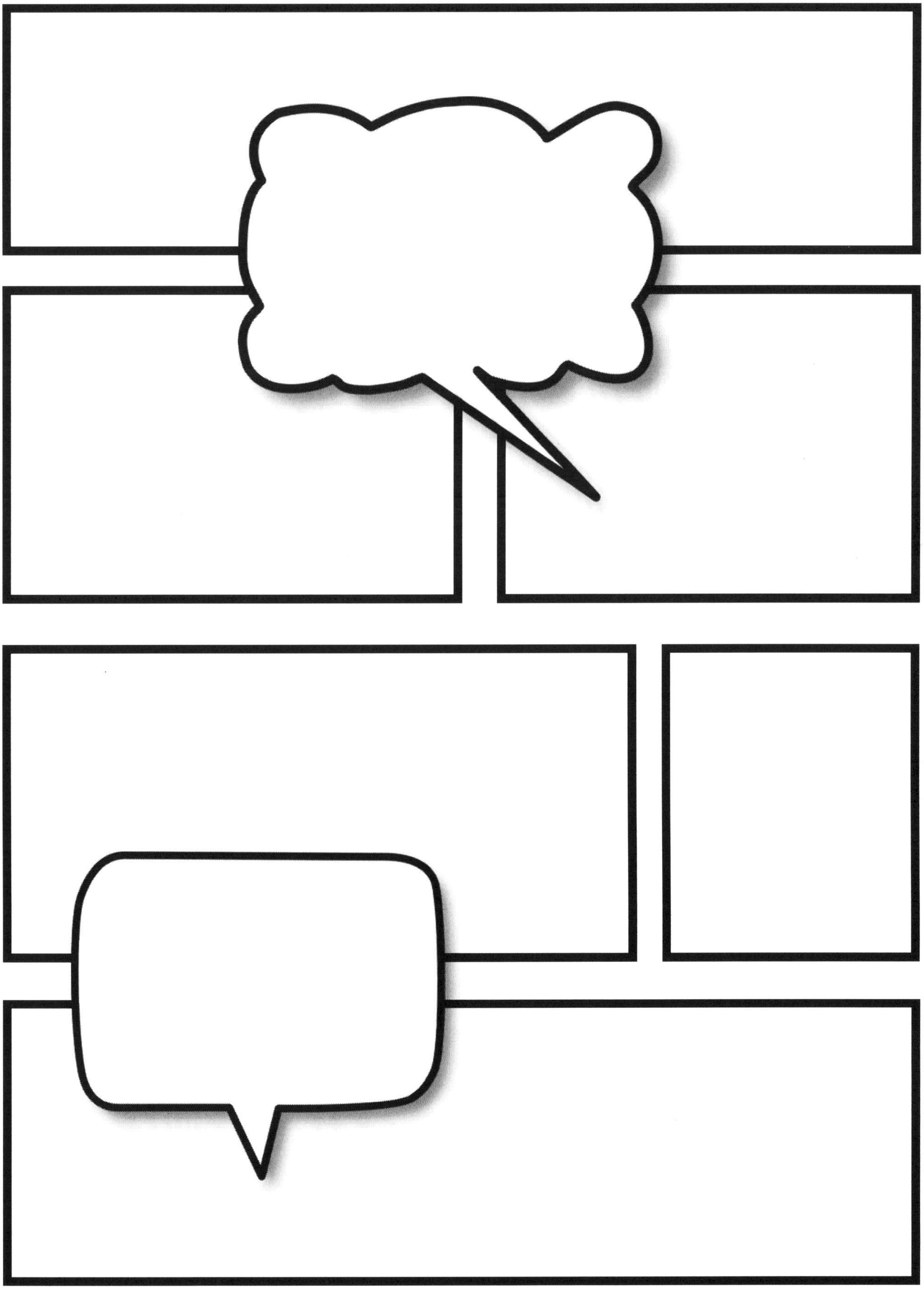

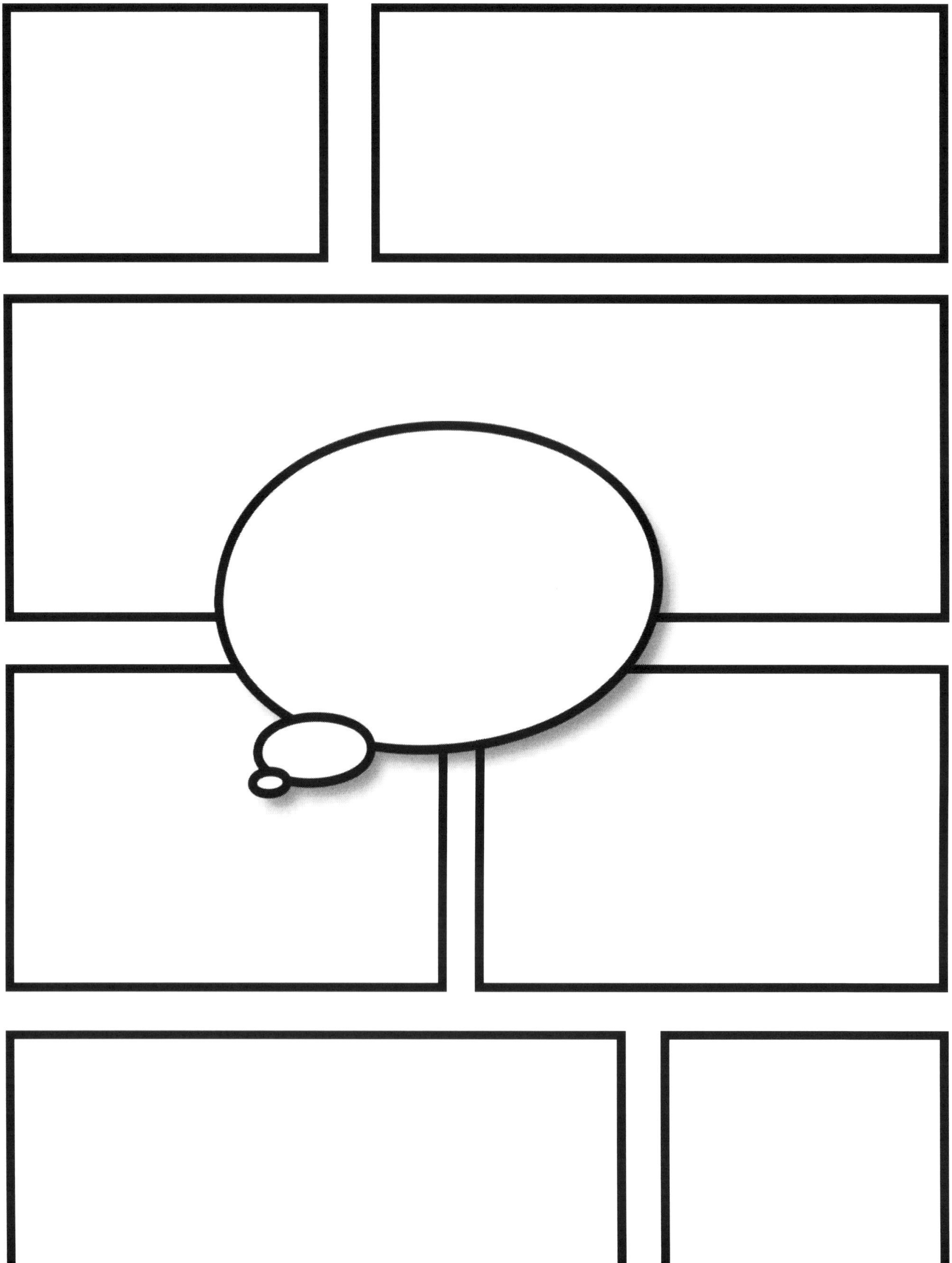

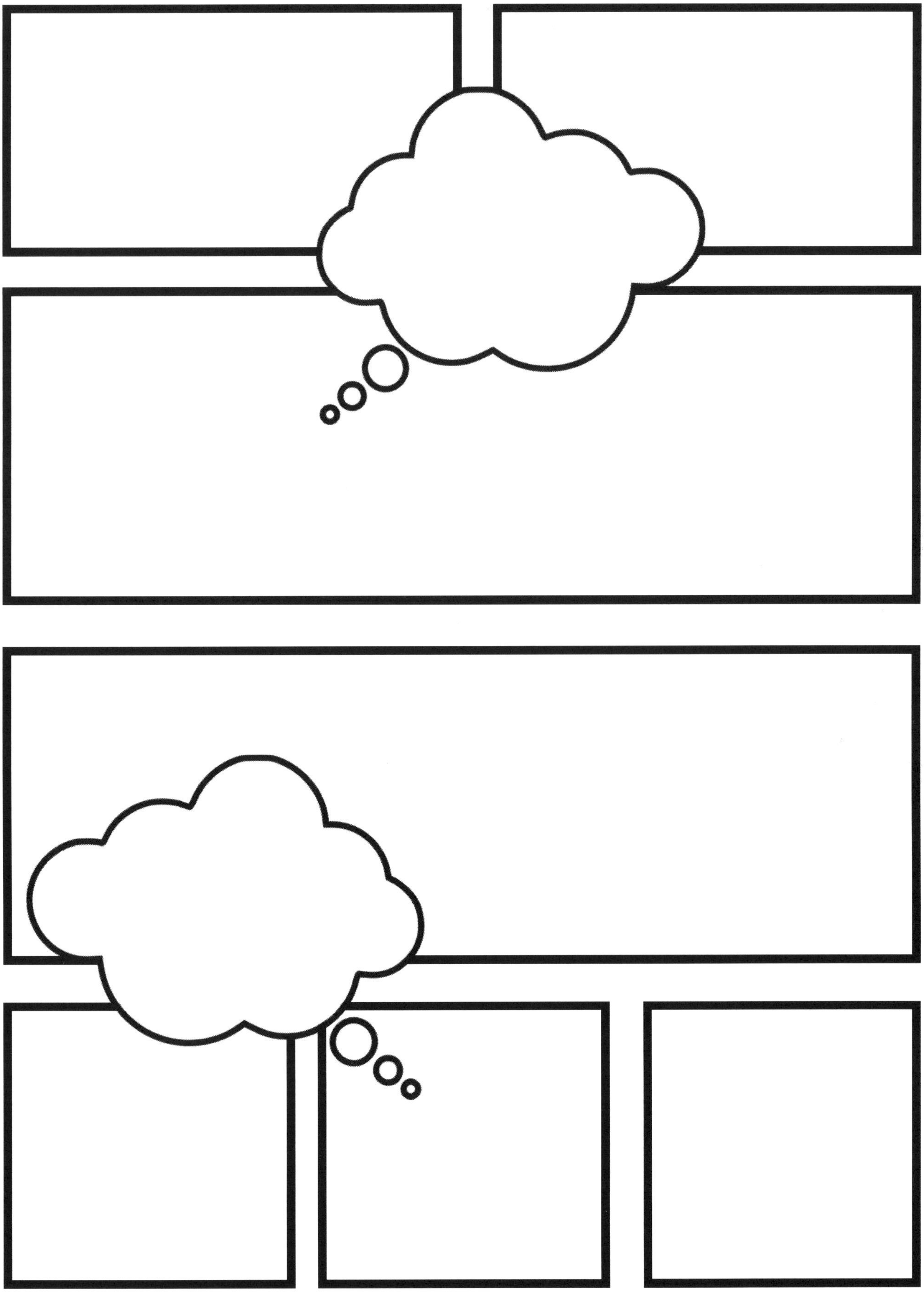

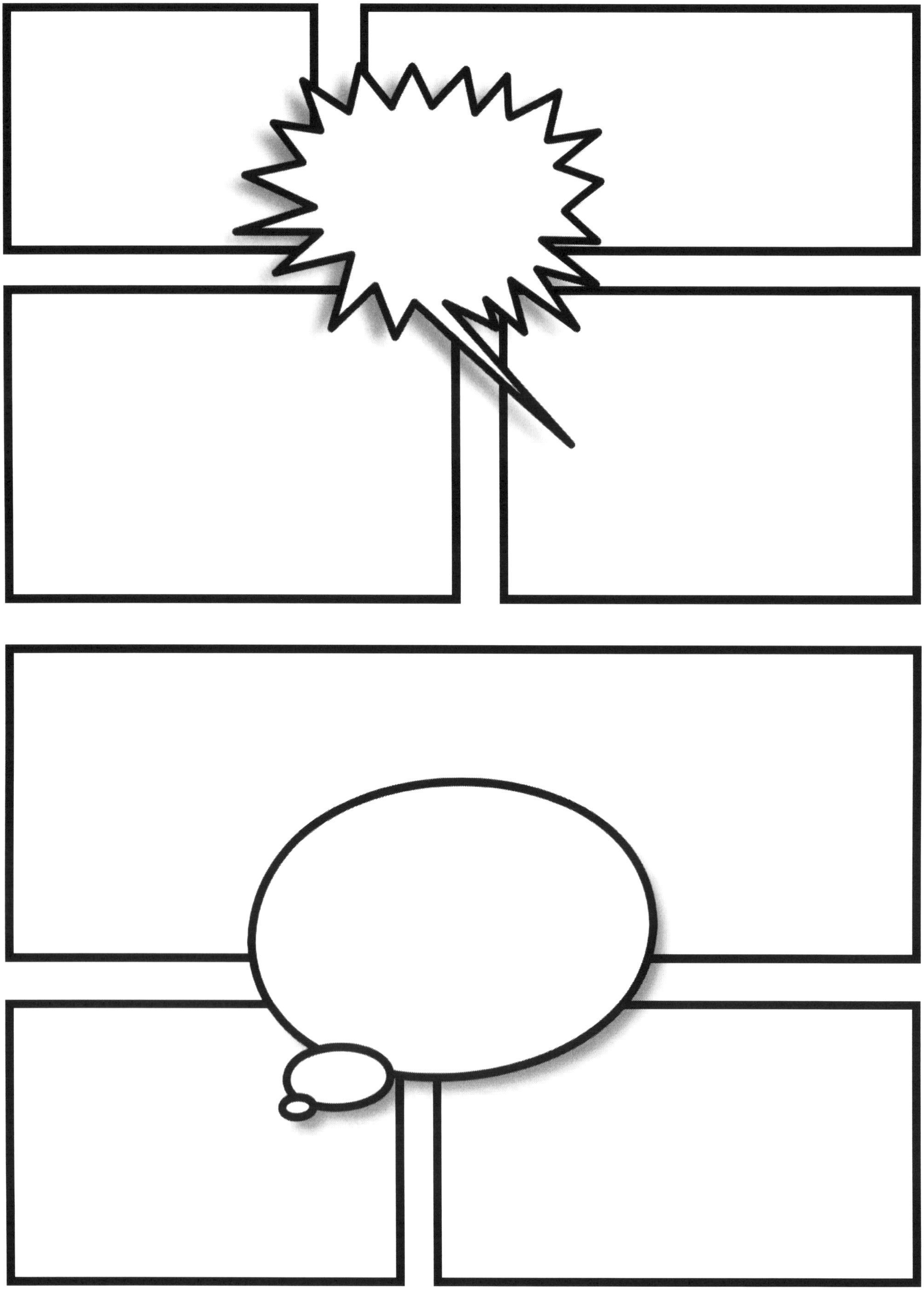

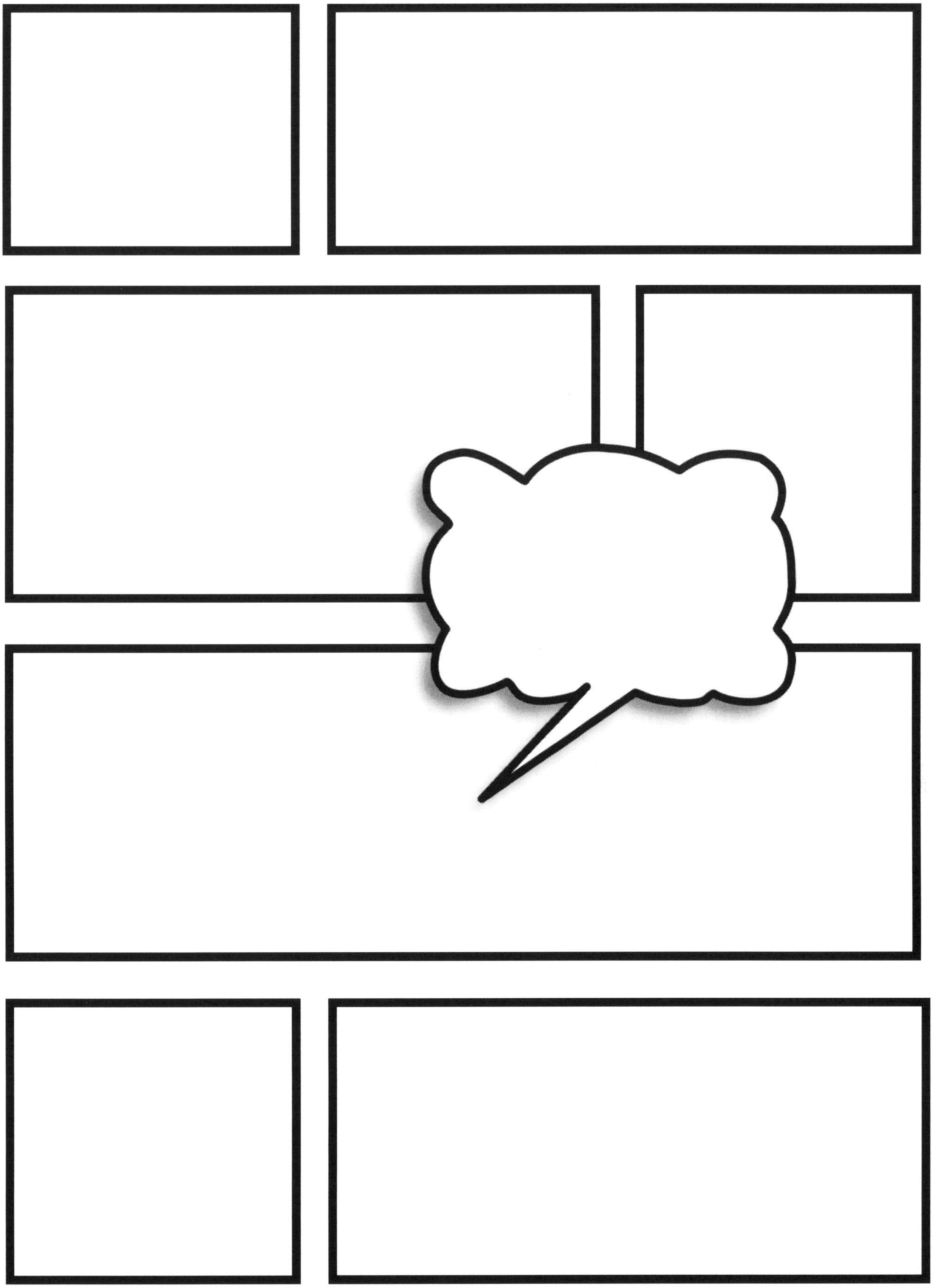

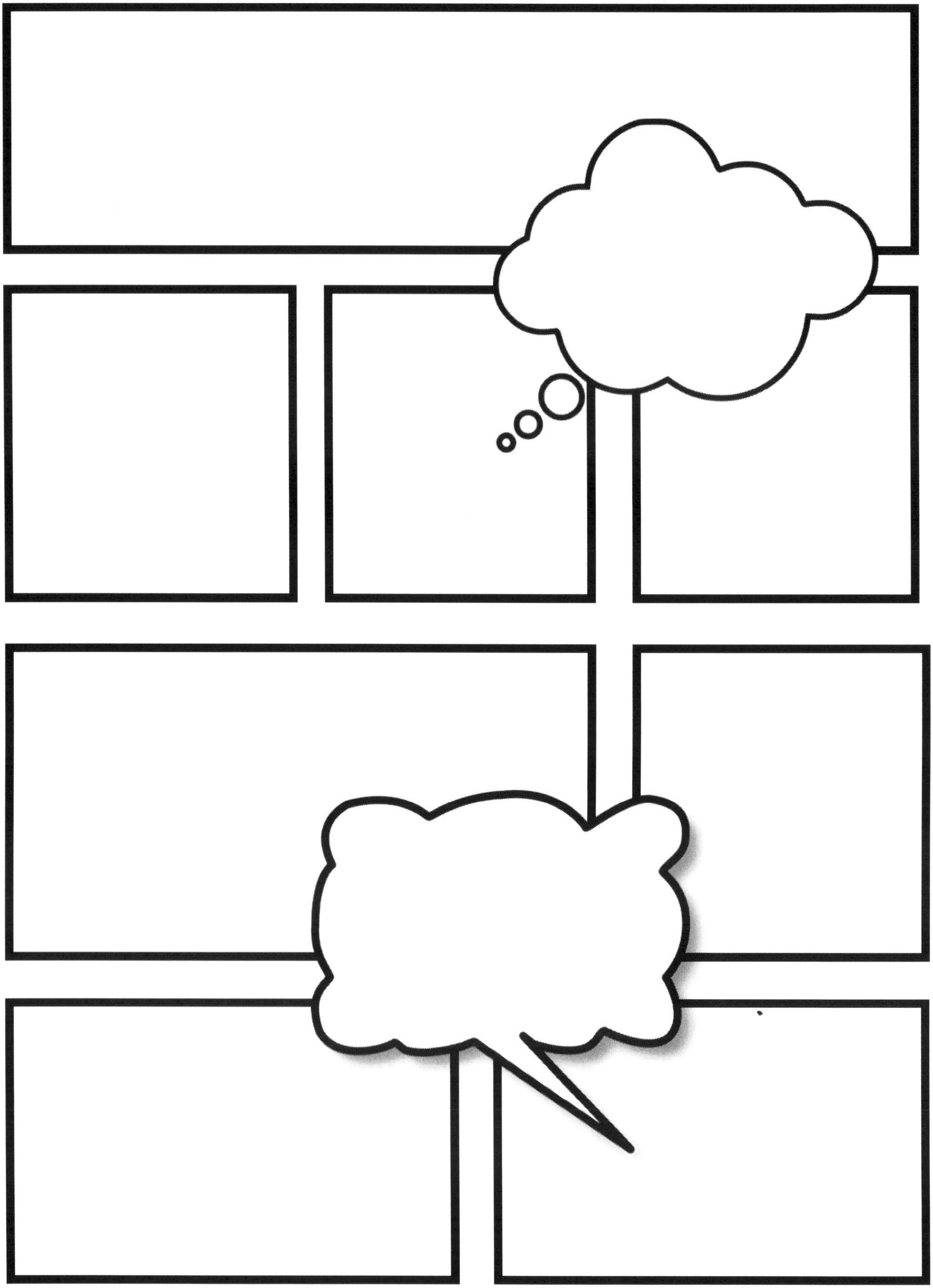

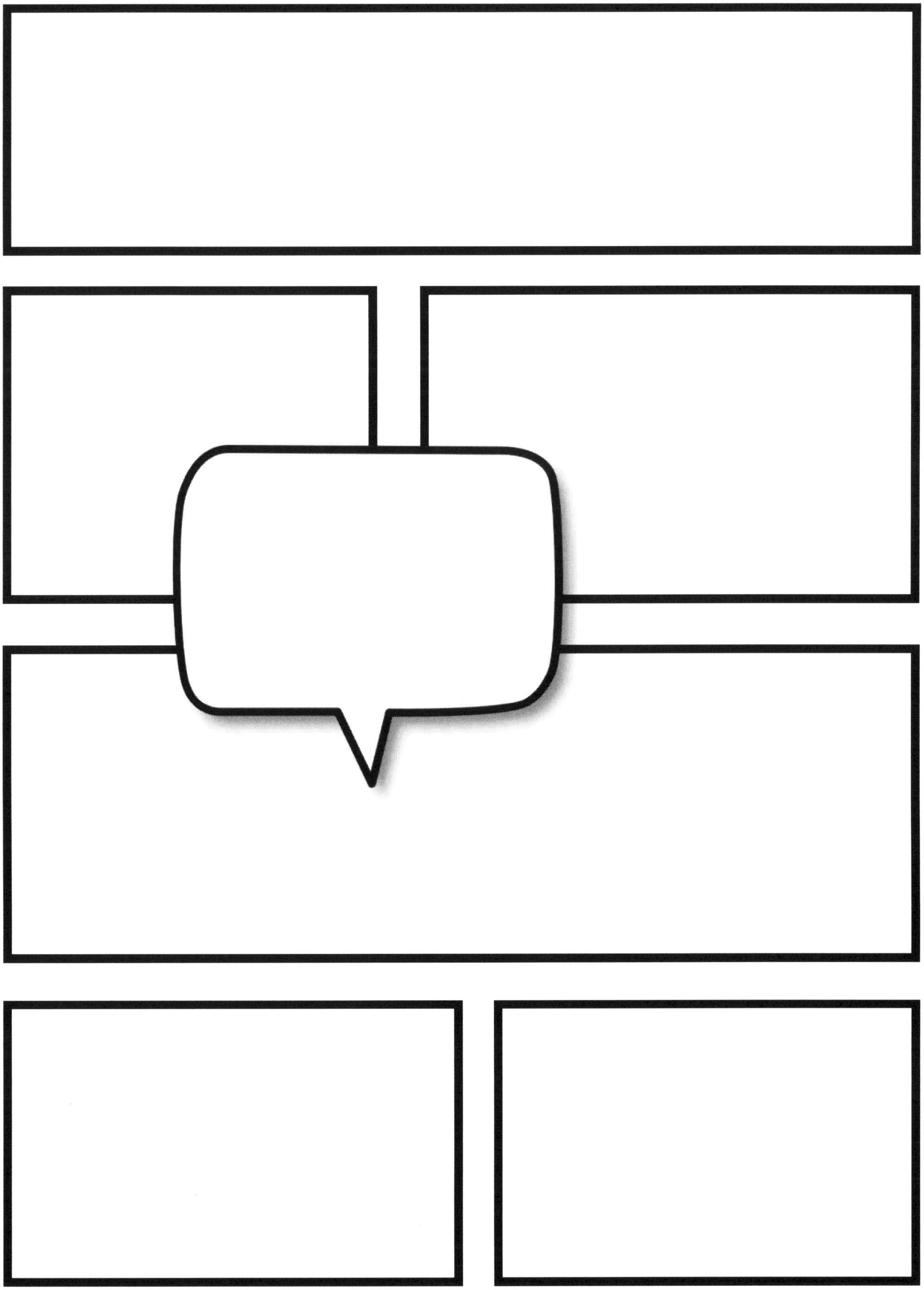

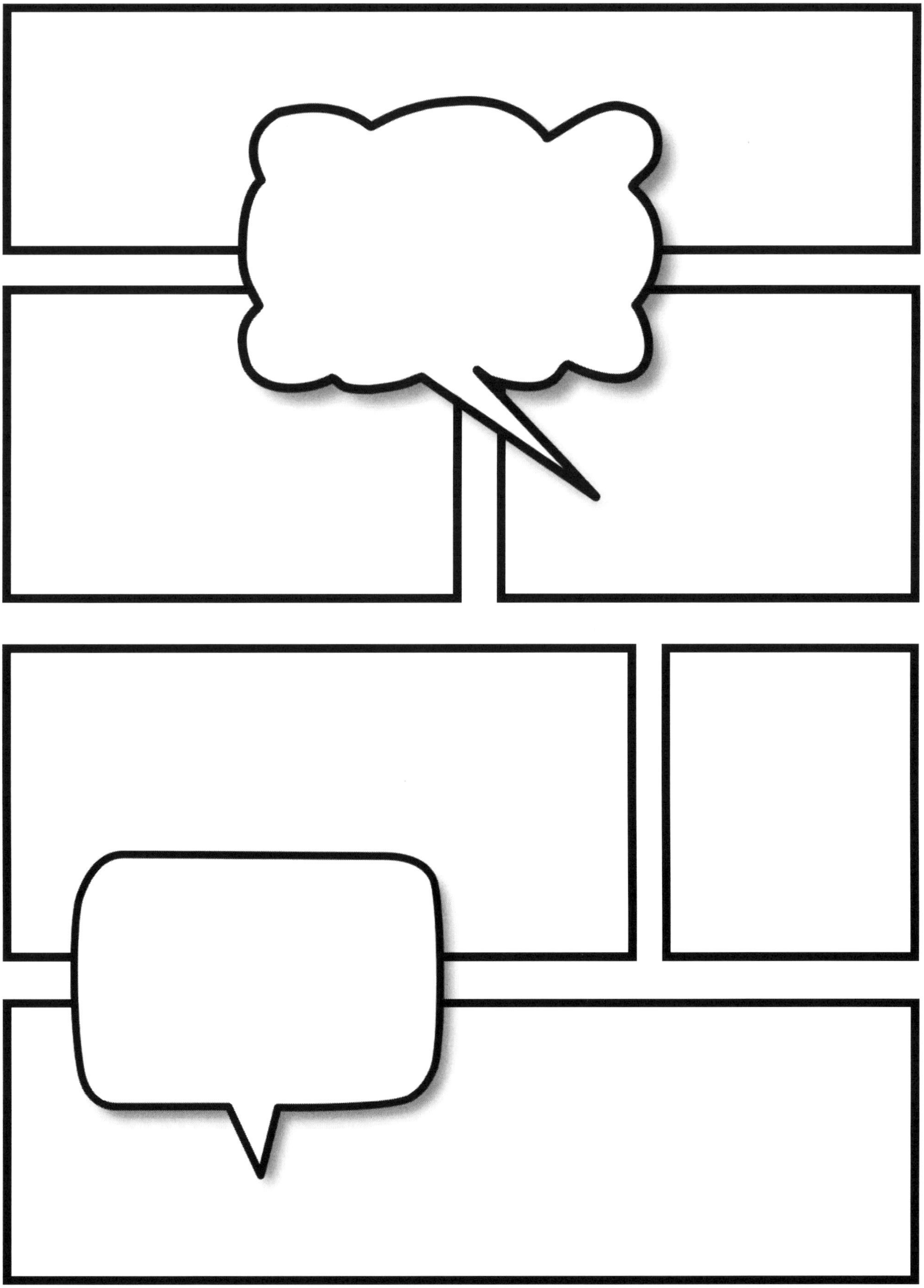

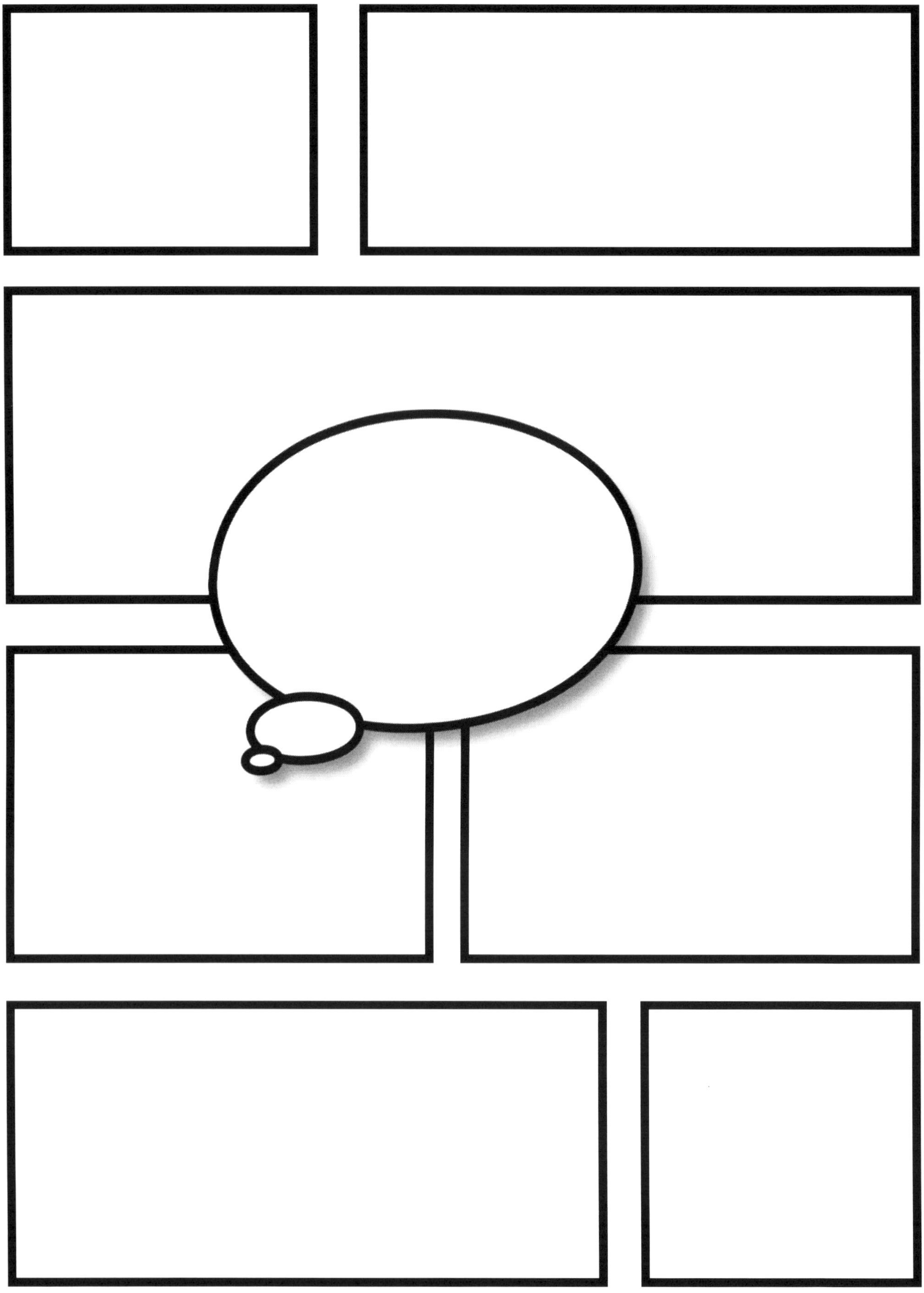

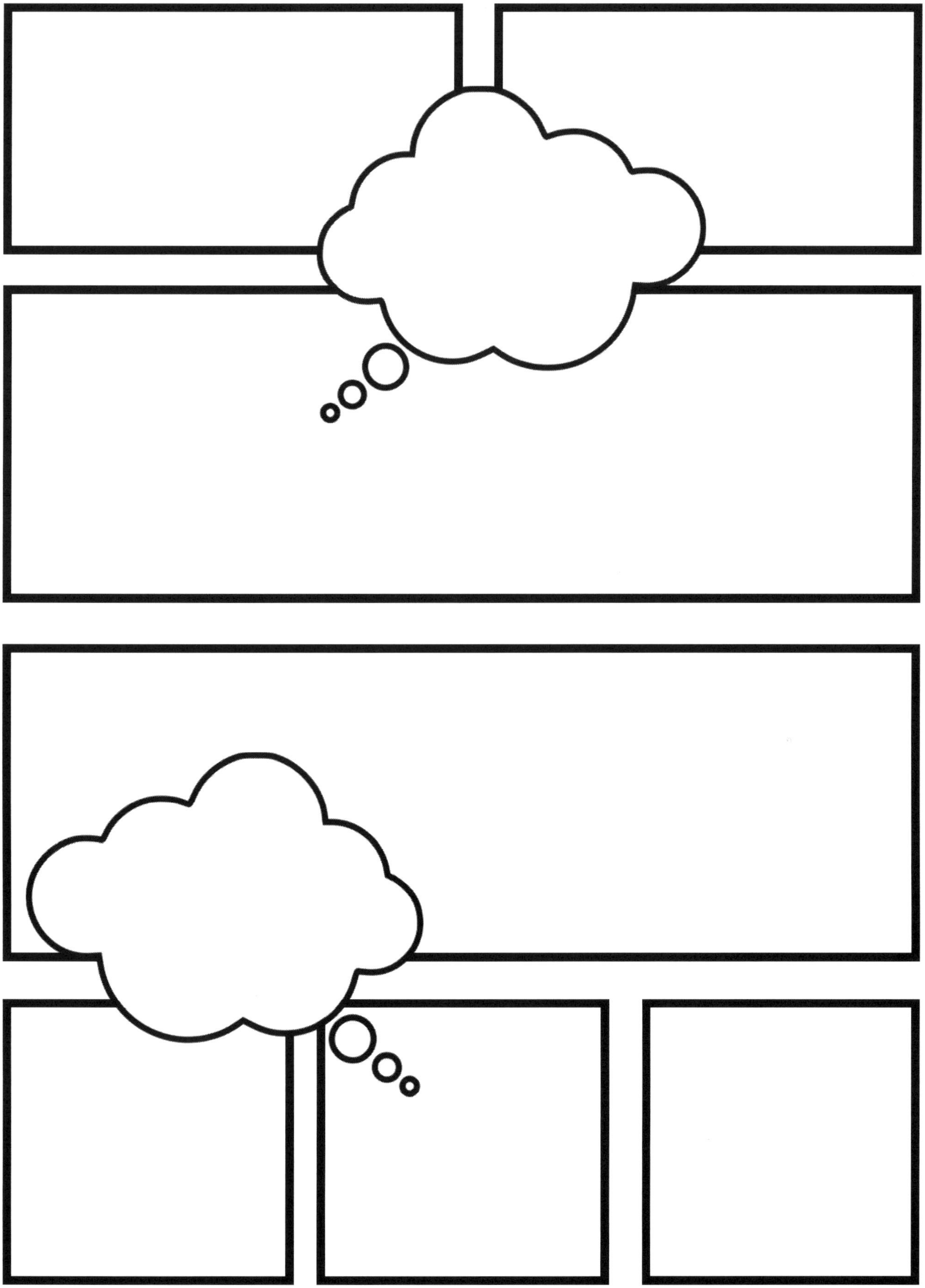

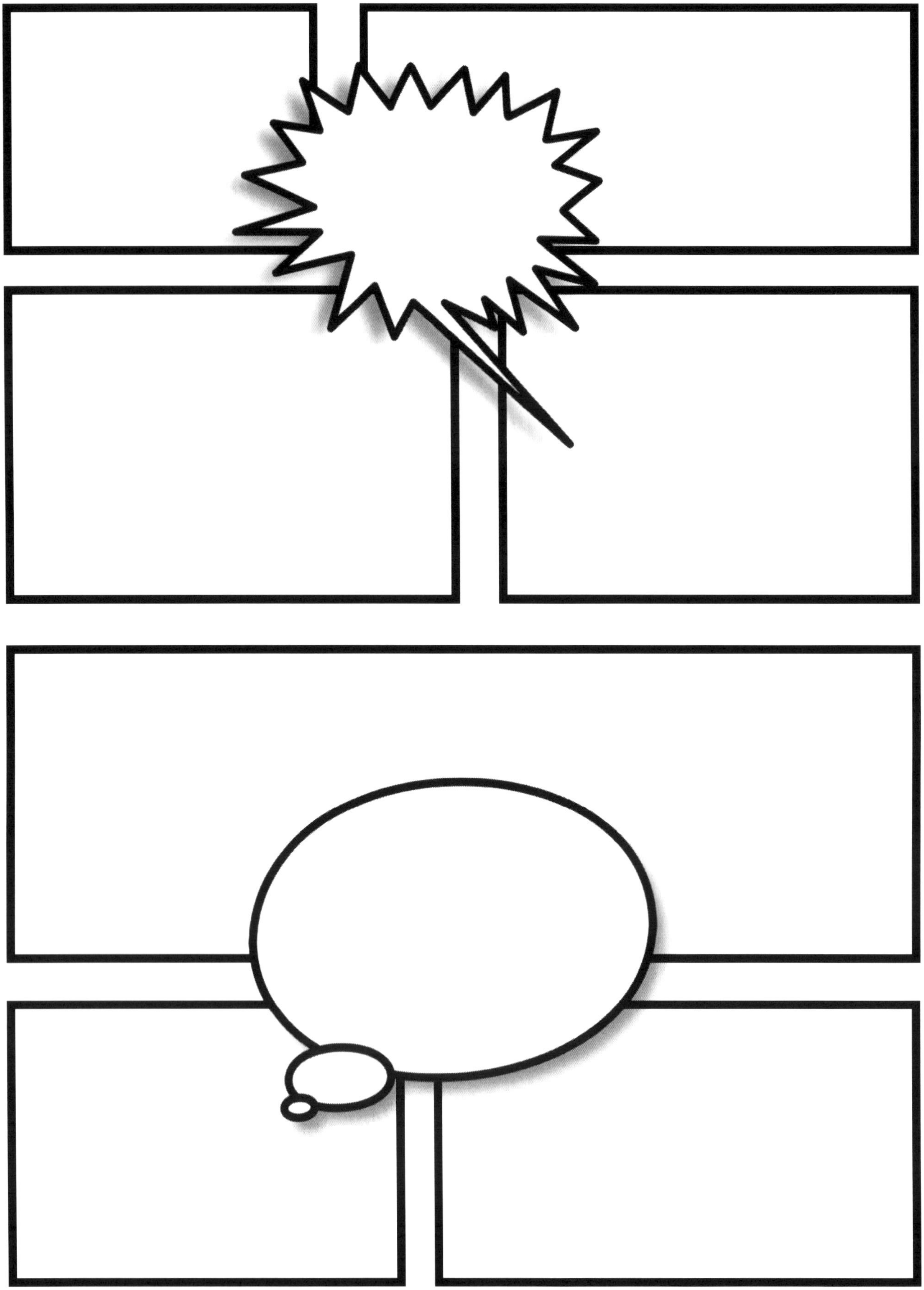

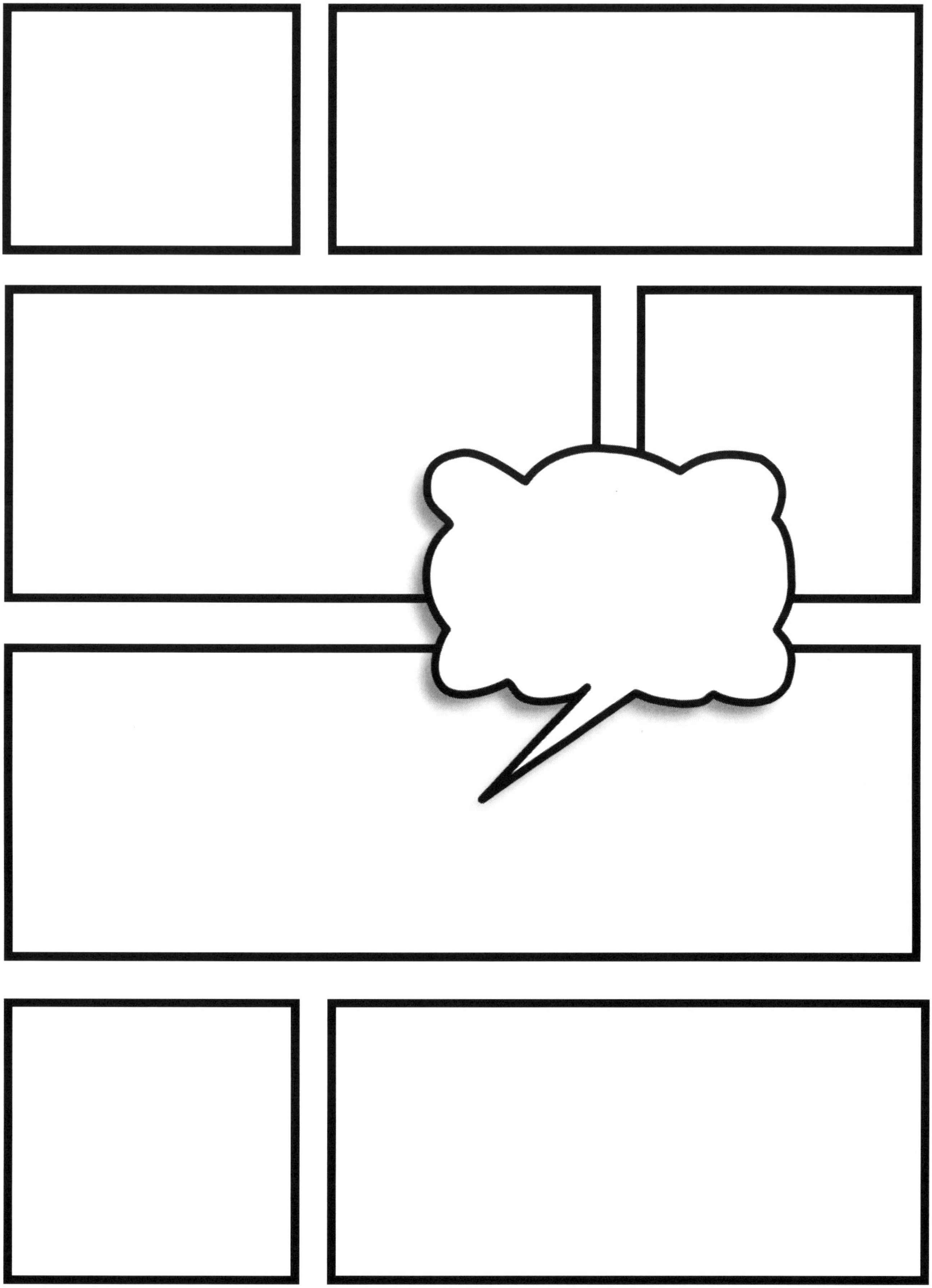

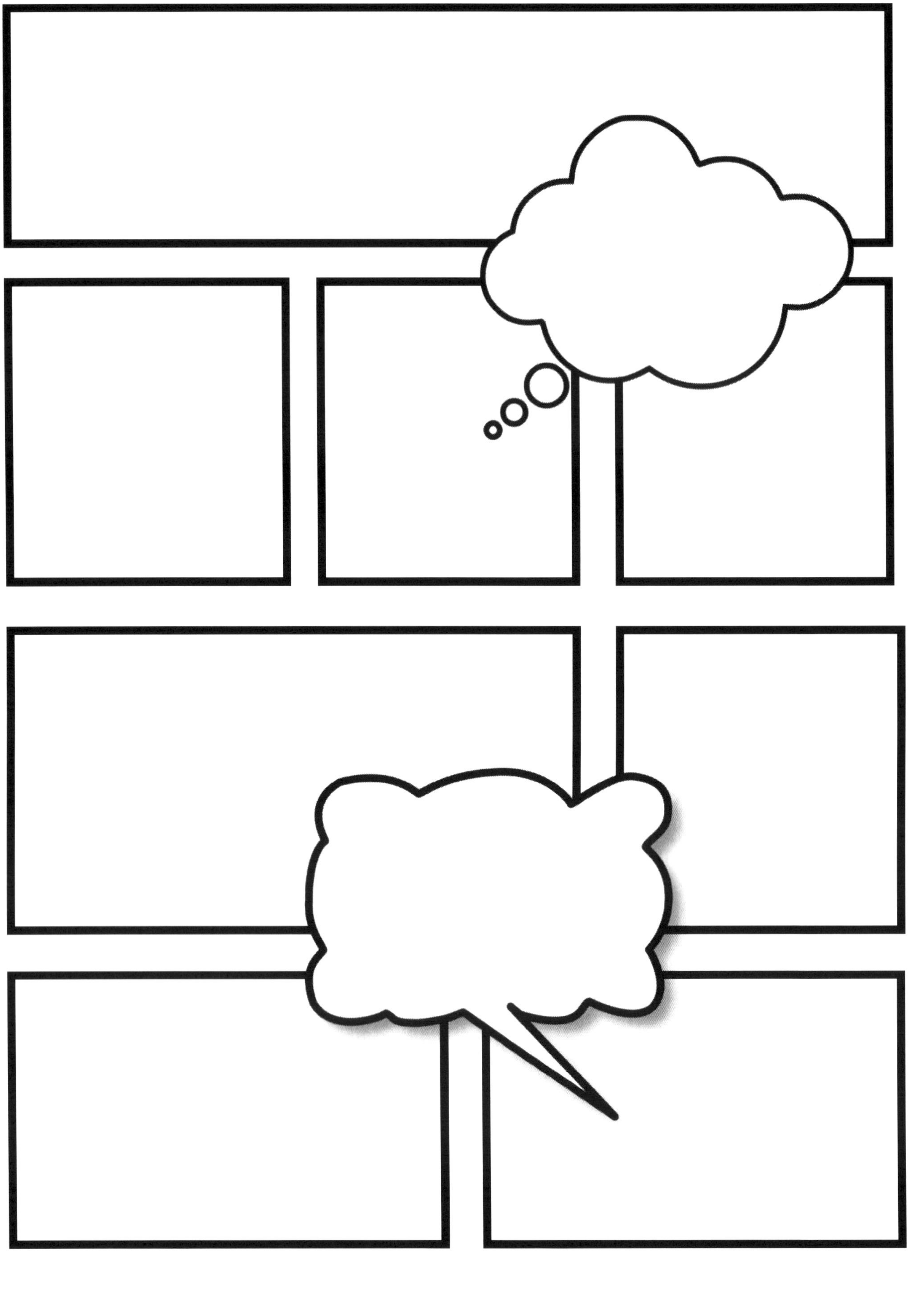

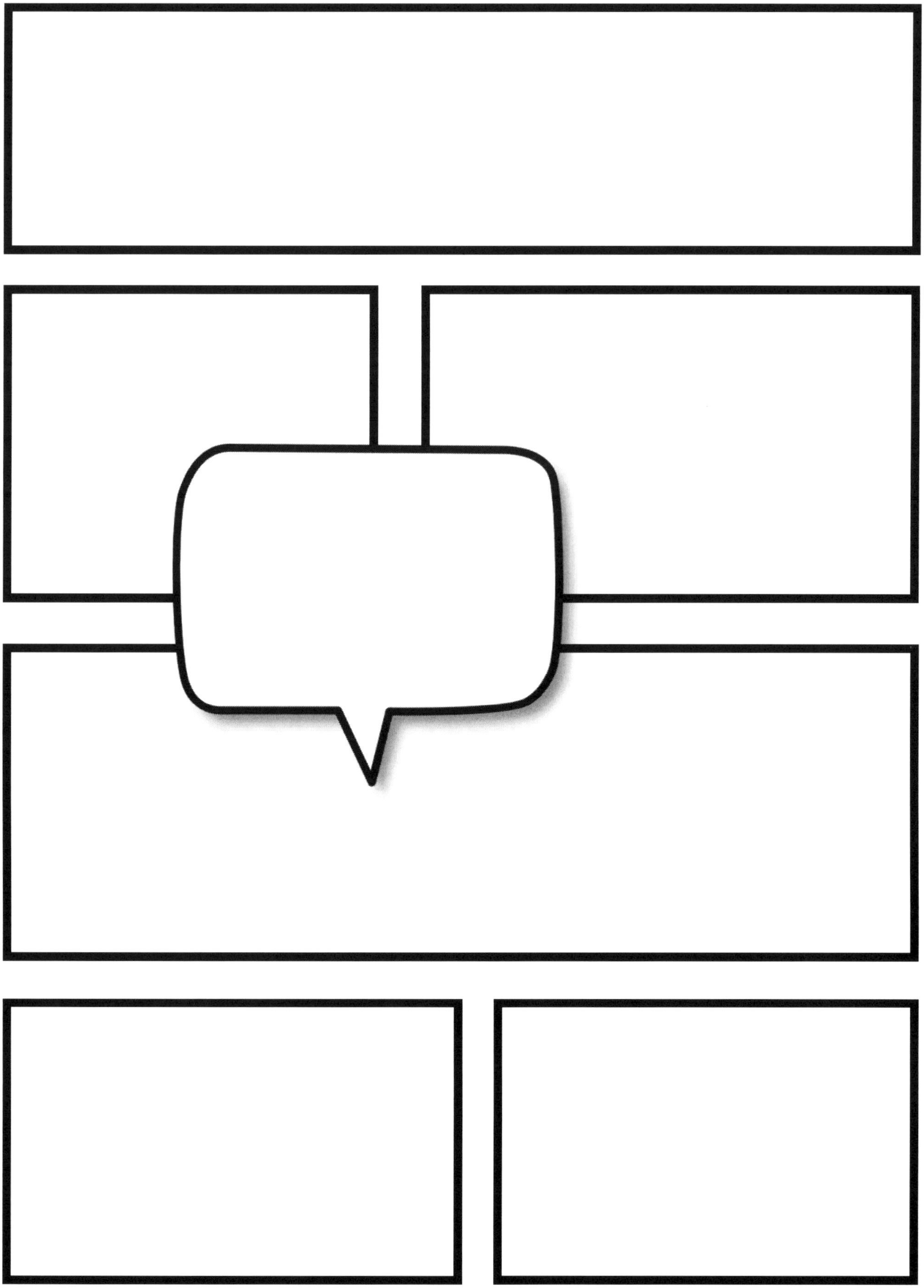

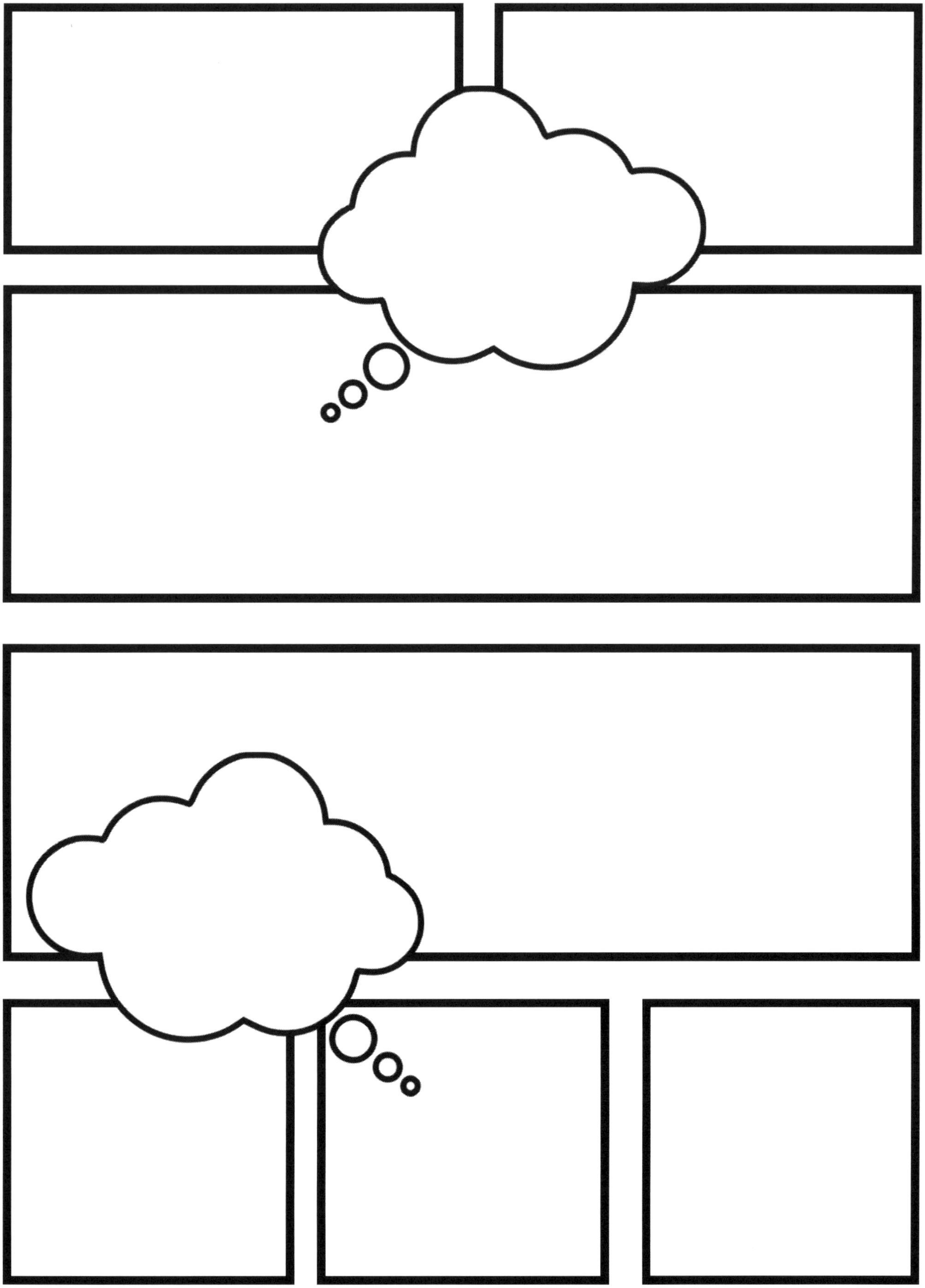

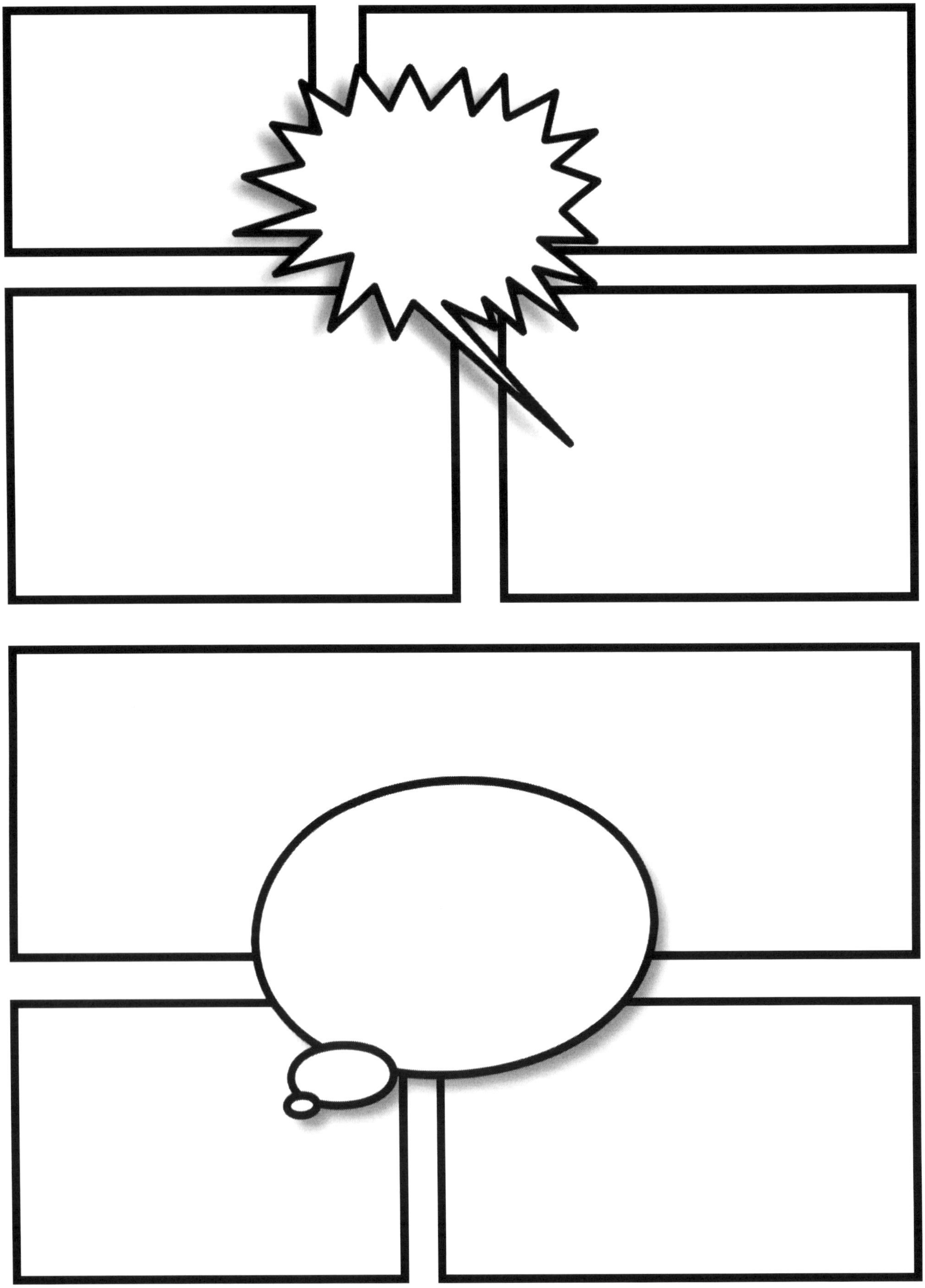

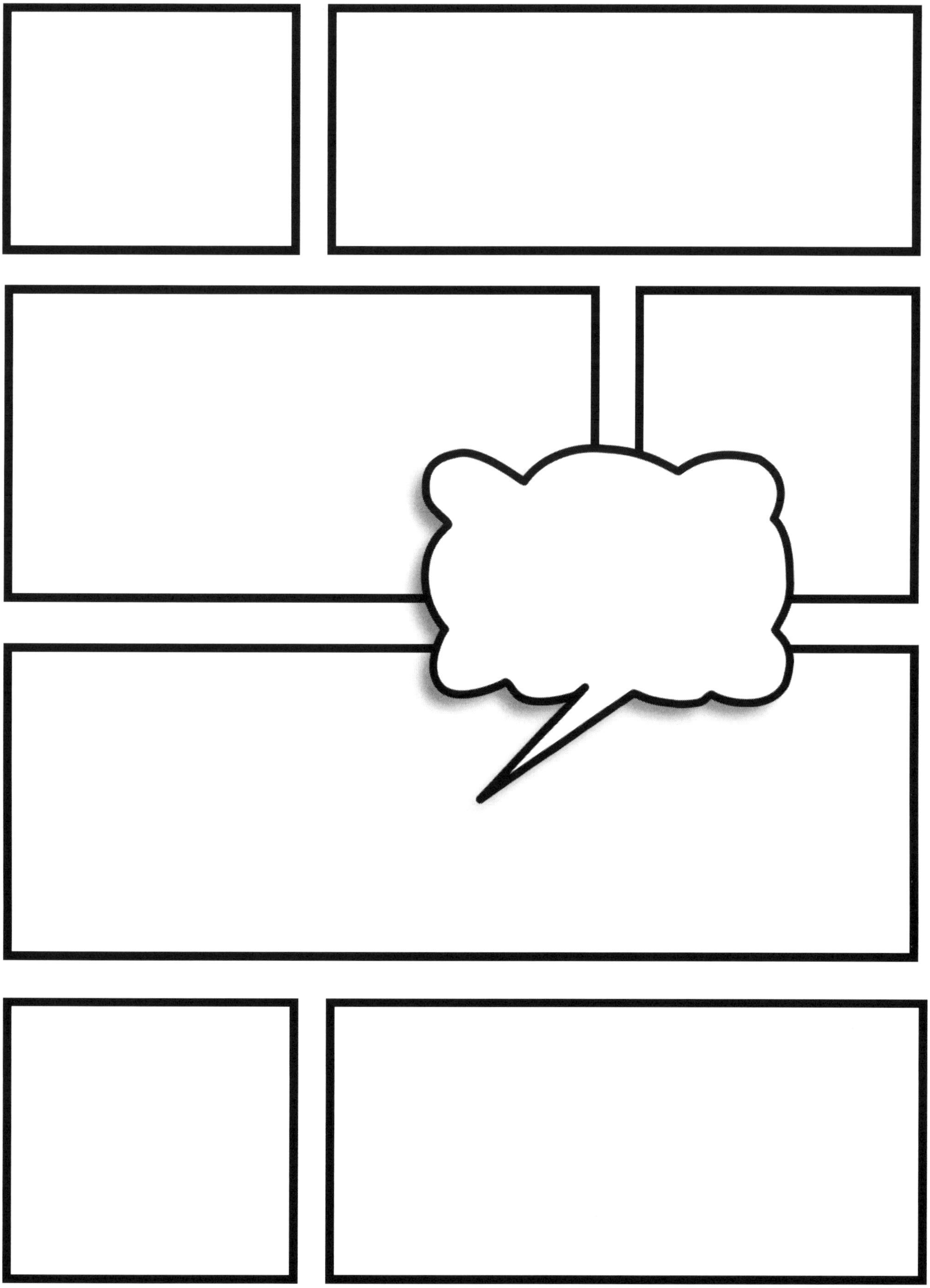

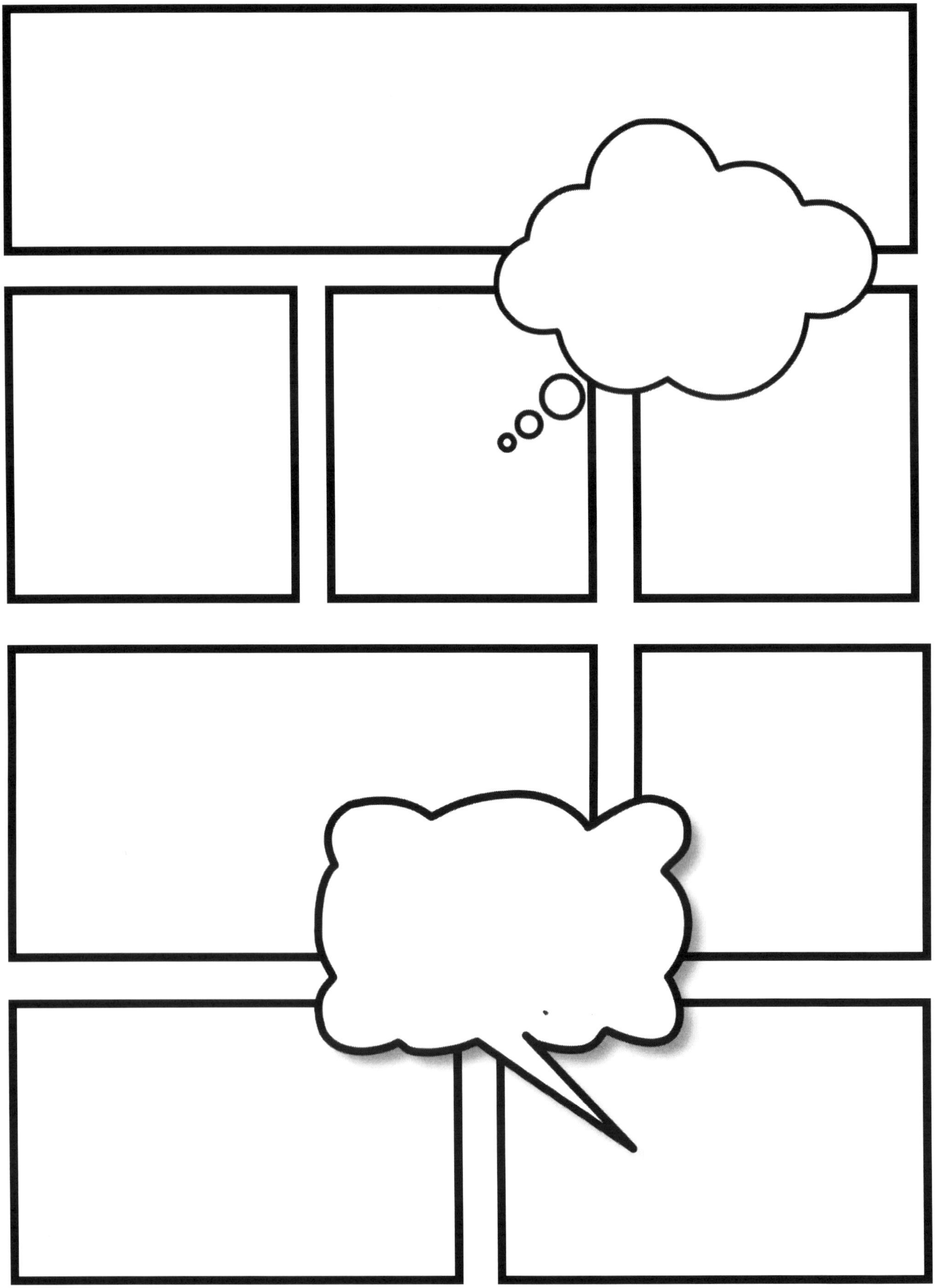

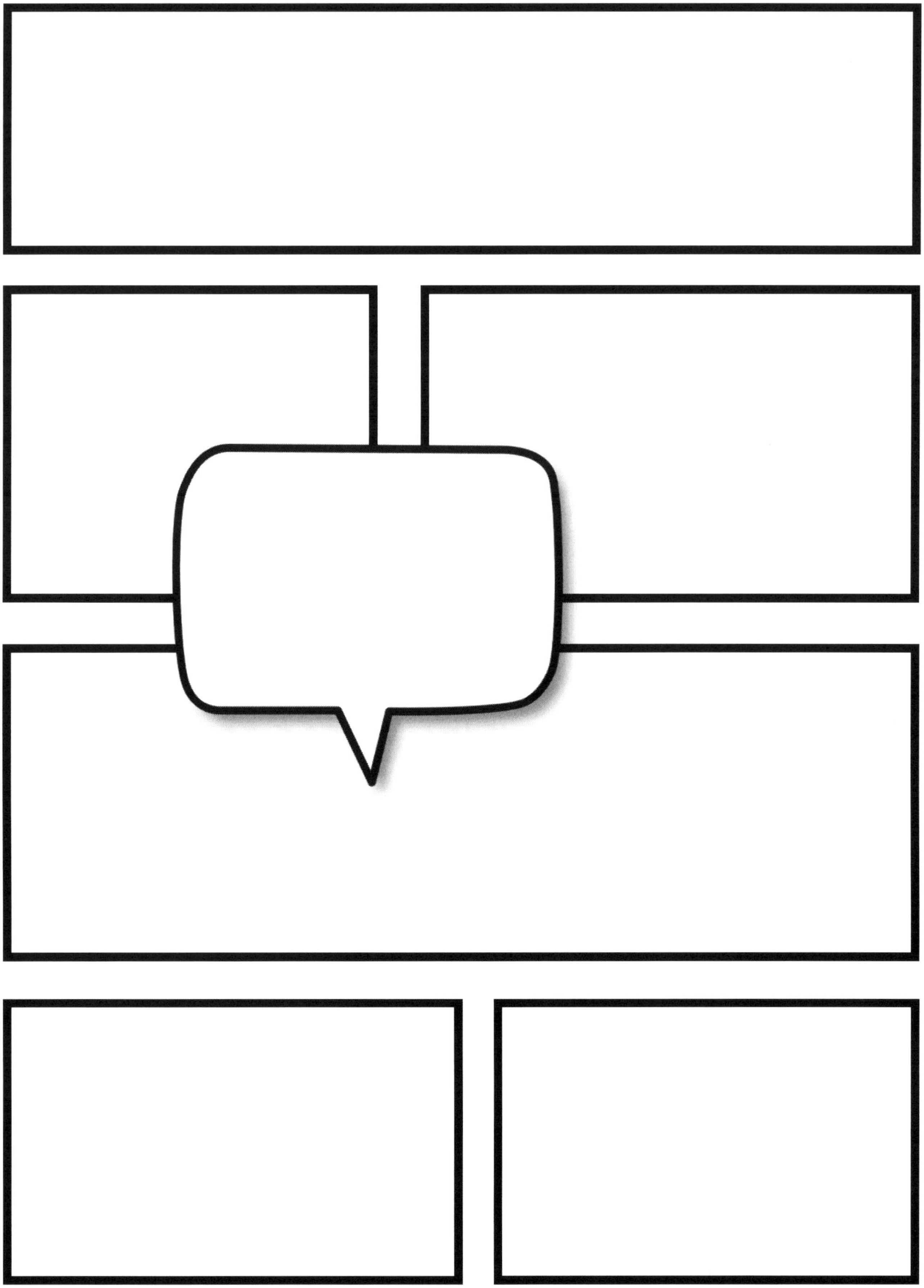

Printed in Great Britain
by Amazon

67674799R00070